Historical Manuscripts Commission
9

CALENDAR OF THE MANUSCRIPTS
OF THE MOST HONOURABLE

THE MARQUESS OF SALISBURY

K.G. P.C. G.C.V.O. C.B. T.D.

PRESERVED AT

HATFIELD HOUSE

HERTFORDSHIRE

Part XXIII
Addenda 1562–1605

Edited by G. Dyfnallt Owen, PH.D.

LONDON
HER MAJESTY'S STATIONERY OFFICE
1973

SBN 11 440042 3★

CONTENTS

INTRODUCTION

This is the first of two volumes intended primarily to furnish Addenda to the material, published in the preceding volumes of the Calendar, covering the years 1603–68. The original intention was to restrict the contents of these volumes of Addenda to those documents which could be placed with any degree of certainty within the limits of this period. But further investigation at Hatfield House revealed that there were a number of items appertaining to the reign of Elizabeth which had not appeared in the relevant volumes of the Calendar, nor in the two volumes of Addenda published in 1915 and 1923. It was decided to include them on the grounds of their historical interest.

A substantial proportion of the documents presented in this volume are petitions, of which some 2500 have survived amongst the papers at Hatfield House. Their very number suggests that a direct approach to the three principal repositories of power in the land—the King, the Privy Council and Sir Robert Cecil, was considered to be the best way of redressing personal grievances or obtaining favours. It was a way open to all classes, and from whatever quarter the petitions emanated they received equal treatment, at least to the extent of being read. The fact that many of those addressed to the King eventually found their way to Hatfield House shows that James 1 passed them on to Cecil, in the belief that his Secretary of State was in a better position to judge the merits of the case and the advisability of further action. So did the Privy Council and some of its members who were personally presented with petitions. Cecil handled them as he did all matters, with a high sense of responsibility and with discretion. But he could also be moved to irritability by specious or fatuous assertions, and would express his opinion of their authors in an acidulous comment at the bottom of the offending petition.

In general terms petitions served to bring complaints or requests to the notice of people who were in a position to do something about them. For this reason, suitors, or those who framed petitions on their behalf, advisedly set the tone of the supplication in such a way as to bring the maximum desirable effect upon the recipient. Petitions to the King were usually based on arguments of legality, since he was expected to enforce due observance of the law, the demands of equity and the suppression of improprieties in judicial proceedings. Another method of approach was to remind him of the traditional practice of monarchs to reward long years of military service, particularly where it could be shown that the petitioner had suffered loss of property or limb in the wars against Spain or the rebels in Ireland. For the Privy Council were reserved complaints of negligence or refractoriness on the part of those in authority in the implementation of previous directives from the Council. This was a point on which the latter was very sensitive, for it was constantly being frustrated and exasperated by the uncooperative attitude of the gentry and town authorities who carried the weight of local government, and upon whom the Privy Council relied for the vigorous application of its decisions. Concerned as it was with the encouragement and protection of the mercantile interests of the nation, the Council was also solicited to intervene in commercial disputes between English and foreign merchants, and to undertake something more than ineffectual protests when English ships and cargoes were pillaged on the high seas by the subjects of neighbouring states. It was commonly accepted that these were matters which could only be successfully prosecuted by the highest executive body in the kingdom.

Because of his position and prestige as principal Secretary of State, Cecil was inevitably singled out for the attention of suitors, and the more his status and influence grew the greater was the inflow of the most diversified petitions. These show that very little was regarded as being beyond the reach of his beneficent mediation, if he could be persuaded to use it. For instance, as Master of the Court of Wards, an institution repugnant to the propertied classes, he was implored on all sides to mitigate the harsh conditions of a system whereby the land of deceased tenants holding by knight's service was leased to the highest bidder whose temporary administration (until the heir came of age) could result in its utter spoliation and ruin. Cecil could not always have found it easy or convenient to do so. There were too many occasions when such lands were deliberately concealed from the Crown, and the King cheated of revenue which was legitimately his. Stringent measures had to be taken from time to time to eradicate these abuses, and appeals could not always be entertained. But there is evidence that Cecil held the view, shared by others, that although exploitation was unavoidable, the system of wardship enabled the Crown to protect its wards by a preliminary inquiry into the circumstances and background of prospective lessees, and the selection of the most suitable and reliable (and possibly humane) amongst them. He himself often granted wardships to people whom he could trust, including some in his private employment, as well as to members of the wards' families who could be counted upon to act in their interests.

Cecil appreciated, of course, that self-interest actuated most of the suitors who submitted petitions to him. Occasionally it could take a crude form. When the Mayor and Aldermen of Hull pressed him to relieve them of having to support a group of townsmen ruined by the action of the King of Denmark in seizing their goods, they not only wrote that " the town can no longer maintain the whole burden of alleviating their misery ", but enclosed the fee due to Cecil as Steward of Hull. There was sometimes the gratuitous information that the late Lord Burghley had favoured the petitioner, as if to imply that Cecil was under a moral obligation to continue his father's benevolence. The discovery of conspiracies could be a trying time for him. The Main and Bye Plots in 1603, in which Lord Cobham, his brother, Ralegh and others were implicated, provoked a rush of creditors who demanded that the debts of the condemned men should be paid out of their goods and lands sequestered by the Crown. Two years or so later the Gunpowder Plot was to produce a group of clamant patriots who differed in their views as to who exactly had killed or captured the plotters, but were united in their opinion that their loyalty should be suitably rewarded.

There were, however, a few petitioners who had little to recommend them except their destitution, and less hope of a sympathetic hearing without calling to their aid Cecil's undoubted feeling of compassion. The case of the " ladies of Desmond " provides one example. They were three of the daughters of Gerald FitzGerald, 14th Earl of Desmond, who had rebelled against the English Government and had been killed in 1583 while still under attainder. At the close of Elizabeth's reign they were in London, living in conditions of extreme want, as Lady Jane FitzGerald informed Cecil. " I need not to your Honour agravate our miserie, who for want ly pawned in our lodginge at Greenewiche, being debarred of the small meanes formerly allowed us, so that we are not able to follow the court to be suitors." Cecil took up their case, and he may have argued that the late Earl's son, James, had amply proved his loyalty to the Crown prior to his recent death, for he succeeded in procuring an adequate pension for the sisters. He showed the same commiseration with Elizabeth Woodrove whose husband had likewise been attainted for treason. She wrote to Cecil that she felt impelled to seek his help, " for the good report of your honorable and pittifull disposition towards the distressed hath perswaded me chiefly to depend upon your Lordship ", and his mediation would " do me more good then if I were dead to restore my life ". She also obtained a pension, and it is conceivable that Cecil, in pleading her cause, may have made good use of the fact that she was the daughter of Thomas Percy, Earl of Northumberland, who had been beheaded in 1572 for his treasonable attachment to Mary, Queen of Scots, the King's mother. Not the least convincing testimony to Cecil's reputation for charitableness and his disposition to support a commendable cause, is the petition submitted by a groom of the King's Privy Chamber, whose son had shown a taste for intellectual studies and was " verie apt and forward in learning to your suppliants great comfort ". This had encouraged the petitioner to request Cecil to obtain a scholarship for his son at Cambridge, " knowing your Lordship to be a lover and favorer of learning and a relever of the poor ", since he was not in a position to pay the expenses of the boy's education.

It cannot be claimed that the petitions are an important primary source of materials for contemporary history; their authors were too concerned with their prospects of gain or advantage to communicate anything more than was strictly relevant to their suits. But neither are they valueless as circumstantial evidence concerning events at home and abroad. They show that recusants were on the whole mildly treated by the authorities before the Gunpowder Plot, and the consequent wave of antipathy towards the Catholics, made life somewhat oppressive to them. John Arundel, of Lanherne, Cornwall, who was under house detention at Highgate, London, saw no reason why he should not write to the Privy Council for leave to move to his own house in Dorsetshire, with an offer to comply with any conditions accompanying that concession. In the same expectation of having his wish gratified, Thomas Bramston, a priest who had defied official banishment and been caught when he returned clandestinely, asked Cecil for permission to leave Newgate prison and proceed to Bath for a health cure, adding that he would provide enough sureties to satisfy the Privy Council that he had no intention of escaping abroad. In the atmosphere of relaxation which followed upon the accession of James I and in view of the diminishing threat of Spanish attack, such petitions could be considered with equanimity, although Cecil, for his part, had to exercise discretion. He could not entirely ignore the many persistent rumours in the country that he was a Catholic at heart and partial to those who professed that religion.

The smooth transfer of the crown to James I guaranteed the continuity and stability of government which, in its turn, gradually overcame whatever repugnance existed towards the idea of a Scottish King on an English throne. But to many tenants and officials on royal manors throughout the kingdom the advantages were less discernible. The uneasy feeling that Crown lands may have been alienated in the process led the tenants on one manor in Lincolnshire to postpone the payment of their rents until they had received assurance that their landlord was still the monarch. What was no less alarming and disagreeable was the replacement of the late Queen's manorial officials by a new set, particularly in the Crown lands allocated to James's wife, Anne of Denmark, as part of her jointure. This change of personnel often led to the disruption of hitherto unchallenged arrangements whereby such offices as the bailiffship had been retained by the same family for generations; and to deliberate attempts to undermine and violate ancient manorial customs. As High Steward of the Queen's lands Cecil had a decisive voice in the nomination of her manorial officials, and not a few of those appointed by him were his own servants whom he wished to reward for their services.

The only event of national consequence published in this volume is Cecil's embassy to France in 1598 which, although it was accounted a diplomatic failure, revealed his shrewdness and percipience when sparring with a King, Henry IV, whose maxim was " Qui a le profit a l'honneur ", but whose honour was the least definable of his many excellent attributes both as a person and monarch.

There were positive indications in late 1597 that the military alliance between England, France and the United Provinces against Spain was weighing heavily on Henry, and that the possibility of negotiating a peace with Philip II was a matter in which he was seriously engaged. One important factor in his calculations was the precarious health of the Spanish King who, it was known, was filled with trepidation at the thought of leaving his inexperienced son to continue the war against a redoubtable soldier like Henry. Another was the likelihood of being able, with one stroke, to oblige the Spaniards to restore the towns taken by them in Picardy as well as certain places occupied by their troops in Brittany, and thus establish his rule over a reintegrated and united France. A third consideration, which he was not inclined to minimize, was the desperate need of his kingdom for a peace after years of bitter and destructive fighting between the Catholic League and the Huguenots.

Elizabeth and her councillors were aware that Henry meant business in the preliminary talks which were already proceeding with the Cardinal Albert, Governor of the Low Countries, who was acting on behalf of Philip II. French interests were in the charge of Villeroy, whose adroitness was to move even Cecil to admiration, although he could hardly regard him with affection. And Villeroy was probably more dedicated to peace than any other statesman in France at that moment with the exception of Sully.[1]

The Queen, with her ineradicable distrust of Philip, could only bring herself with great difficulty to contemplate a peace with Spain. It seemed to her an inopportune moment to do so, so soon after the successful expedition against Cadiz, and the Islands' voyage in the following year (1597), had demonstrated the superiority of English naval power, much to the benefit of English commerce. Henry's engagement of the main Spanish army had also relieved the pressure on two fronts in the land struggle against the domination of Spain. The Dutch garrisons and allied forces along the sagging frontier of the United Provinces were able to go over to the offensive and take a string of towns and a large slice of territory without interference. In Ireland, where the Earl of Tyrone was leading a dangerous revolt against the English Government, the decisive aid which Philip had promised him had to be curtailed and partly postponed because of the King's commitments in his war against France. As far as Elizabeth was concerned this satisfactory state of affairs could have continued indefinitely, and she felt her position to be so secure that not even the fall of Calais into Spanish hands caused

---

[1] J. Nouaillac, *Villeroy, Secrétaire d'État et Ministre*, pp. 366–78.

her excessive anxiety. Henry's withdrawal from the alliance, however, would remove its cornerstone, and permit Philip to redirect his still considerable military resources towards crushing England and the Dutch. What is more, France's defection would throw the responsibility and burden of continuing the war on Elizabeth, a prospect which she hardly relished when she considered its past and current expenses. The dangers and consequences of such a contingency were alive to her when she wrote to Henry : " Quand le fagot bien lié se separe il devient proye au plus fort et debile en soy. Vous estez trop sage pour ne boucher l'oreille à si séduisantes Syrènes."[1]

But Henry had decided that if he had to turn a deaf ear in any direction, it would be towards Elizabeth. The retaking of Amiens by troops under his personal command in September, 1597, had revived his confidence and induced the Spaniards to be more tractable in the peace talks. However, the situation was still fluid enough to require a further reminder to Philip that France was not irrevocably committed to peace, and that he might have to pay a higher price to detach her from the anti-Spanish axis. Some kind of show of allied solidarity was needed for this purpose, and in January, 1598, Hurault de Maisse was despatched from Paris to engineer such an exhibition.

Maisse's mission to London was soon accomplished, for all he was instructed to do was to explain to Elizabeth, without too much diplomatic verbiage, that his master was discussing peace with Spain and was desirous of including England and the United Provinces in the final settlement. To this extent Henry was conforming to the terms of the alliance which stipulated that none of the three signatories should unilaterally engage in peace nego-tiations without informing the other two. Maisse was to be explicit on one point. If France's allies were reluctant to make peace or, alternatively, were disinclined to prosecute the war with appreciably more energy than they had shown recently, then the French King would consider himself discharged from all obliga-tions towards them and, more important, from the undertaking not to negotiate without them.[2]

It was clear to Elizabeth, and not less so to Cecil, that a down-right refusal to enter into discussions would be exploited by Henry to justify his self-help peace policy. Brooding over the situation Cecil detected one disagreeable development. The French King had shown no enthusiasm for wresting Calais from Spanish hands as he had done in the case of Amiens. There was a hint here that the town might be surrendered by Spain as a condition of a peace treaty. If so, Elizabeth would be deprived of any chance of acquiring the town as she had hoped to do, even by handing over the Brill and Flushing—her security for the repayment of Dutch debts to her—to Spain in exchange for it.

---

[1] PRO, State Papers, France (S.P. 78), Vol. 41, p. 11. Elizabeth to Henry IV, January 4, 1598.

[2] P. Laffleure de Kermaingant, *Mission de Jean de Thumery, Sieur de Boissise.* p. 143.

The fact had to be registered that Henry was not particularly mindful of English interests.

The French King had proposed through Maisse that an embassy should be sent to confer with him, and this was accepted. To find out what exactly he had in mind required consummate skill in the dissection of motives, and Elizabeth chose Cecil as the man best qualified to do so. Moreover, he could certainly be relied upon not to commit the Queen to any foreign entanglements, not even those conducive to peace, unless they were productive of some advantage to her. The news that the Dutch had decided to dispatch a similar embassy to Henry was reassuring, for it was known that the States General was adamant against peace with Spain.

Bad weather hindered Cecil and his colleagues, with their numerous gentlemen in attendance and servants, from crossing the Channel, but he was in no haste to meet the French King. He assumed, too readily perhaps, that by taking his time he would assist in delaying the peace talks, although the fact that two eminent French statesmen, Bellièvre and Sillery, had been sent to Vervins, where the talks were taking place, should have warned him that Henry would not allow tactics of this sort to interfere with his purpose. So too should the fact that Henry was not in a desperate hurry to meet him. He was not at Rouen to welcome the English embassy, as had been expected, but preparing to reduce Brittany and the Duke of Mercœur, the last of the Catholic Leaguers, to submission by a mixture of force and bribery. To break the last link between Philip II and his former confederates in France was of infinitely more importance to the French King than a confrontation with Cecil. With Mercœur's recognition of him as the rightful King of France, the hold of the Spaniards on Blavet, their main stronghold in Brittany, would become untenable and place Henry in a correspondingly better position to demand their retirement from that place as well as the Picardy towns.

Elizabeth, mainly for reasons of prestige, disliked the idea of her Secretary of State running after Henry, but she had tied his hands by her firm insistence that Cecil should ignore or avoid the pacifist ministers of the French King and deal personally with Henry. This suited Cecil's plan, and the embassy travelled first to Paris and then, by way of Orléans, to Angers, where they caught up with Henry and arrived in time to witness the capitulation of Mercœur and the marriage of his daughter to the King's natural son, César. The exchange of opinions between the English envoys, reduced to two by the illness and death of Sir Thomas Wilkes at Rouen, and the French King and his Council made two things abundantly clear : the uncompromising desire of his councillors to make peace, and the inclination of Henry to follow their advice, despite his own feelings as a soldier and King that he owed much of his success to the military and financial aid of England and the United Provinces. It was here too that Cecil discovered, to his disappointment, that even the Huguenots of

France were resigned to the prospect of a peace with Spain. Before leaving England he had written to the Earl of Essex that if the French King was not amenable to argument, matters might be arranged that, " according to the rules of discretion the party of Religion may be sounded, provided and prepared to diverte him and awaken him if he runne into pacts with Spayne and leave out England ".[1] Conversations with Huguenot leaders soon showed Cecil that cooperation from them was out of the question. " Wee find all them of the religion absolutely of the opinion the King will make peace, and can have no other councell of them but that your Ma^{ty} must offer him great helpe, such are the necessityes of Spaine, such are the greedynes of France and such is the unremoveable resolution of the Estates not to treat any way." But help in concrete terms of men and money was the last thing that Cecil had orders to discuss, and in any case he dared not do so without further reference to the Queen and her Council. If he felt frustrated and exasperated by this rebuff, he took some of his irritation out on the Dutch embassy whom he warned bluntly " to bethinke them how to ease the Queens charge if the Queene must bee kept in warre for them ", and had the satisfaction of reporting that the leader of the embassy, Olden-barneveldt " seemed a little awaknd by this ".

A day or so later it was Cecil's turn to have a rude awakening. A letter from the Queen informed him that correspondence from Cardinal Albert had been intercepted " by God's providence ". Its contents disclosed only too plainly that the French pleni-potentaries at Vervins had accepted the Spanish terms, and that there was no provision made for a commission to treat with England. Whether Henry was privy to this or not, Elizabeth chose to suspect his honesty and wrote to Cecil : " Yow shall fynd evident cause for yow to chaunge your course of negotiating with that King, with whome yow shall see wee have more cause to deale openly and roundly then wee thought wee shold have had ".[2] Copies of the incriminating correspondence were attached for Cecil to study and act upon.

Henry was in bed when Cecil and Herbert confronted him, and by the time they had " openly and roundly " expressed their sentiments, Monsieur Le Grand (Bellegard, Master of the Horse to the French King) " was faine to fetche drink for him ". Henry vigorously denied any duplicity on the part of the French nego-tiators at Vervins, and the audience passed off without too much unpleasantness, although the King wrote to Elizabeth that Cecil, " s'est plaint a moy avec plus de vehemence et passion de vostre part et de la sienne que la confiance que vous devez avoir en moy ne merite ".[3] A second audience proved more explosive. Henry went to Nantes to attend to his Breton affairs, leaving Cecil the choice of following him if he wished to pursue the matter any further. Cecil was not averse to doing so, but this time the King

---

[1] S.P. France, *op, cit*, p. 135. Cecil to Essex, February 14, 1598.
[2] *Ibid.*, Elizabeth's Instructions to Cecil, March 17, 1598.
[3] *Ibid.*, p. 364. Henry IV to Elizabeth, March 30/April 9, 1598.

turned on him and Herbert. There was an angry exchange of opinions interspersed with recriminations, during which Henry declared categorically that the behaviour of his allies left him no alternative but to seek peace, and the English envoys pointedly asked for their passports to return home

A final conference of French councillors and English and Dutch emissaries, with Henry in the chair, failed to swing the King round to the point of view of the allies, despite their offers to provide him with a sufficiency of troops and money to continue hostilities against Spain. "Ils avoient d'ailleurs des offres à faire, bien plus capables de séduire un Prince dont on connoissait le penchant pour la guerre," Sully wrote later in his *Mémoires*. "Heureusement le Roi évita ce piege et la considération de l'état présent de son royaume l'emporta sur toutes les autres."[1]

Henry's last word on the subject was convincing enough. His kingdom had no natural barriers against Spain like England and the United Provinces ; its towns were unfortified and lacked munition ; its navy was weak, and its provinces devastated by the late civil war. It was imperative that his authority as King should be universally recognized in France, and his government made strong enough to establish internal order and restore cohesion and harmony to a divided nation. The King could not resist the temptation to make a last dig by contrasting the deplorable state of France with the commercial gains and benefits reaped by England and the Dutch from the war. Such was the effect of his arguments on the allied envoys, so Sully would have the world believe, that they "ne trouvant rien à repliquer se regardoient l'un l'autre avec le dernier étonnement ". But their astonishment may have been caused not so much by Henry's explanatory statement, which could not possibly have surprised them, but by his frank avowal that he needed a breathing space before embarking on the scheme he had in mind to curb the power and pretensions of the Houses of Spain and Austria.

Cecil's embassy was not entirely a diplomatic failure after all. At least he was able to form some idea of what Henry proposed to do eventually, and which the King might well have achieved if an assassin's knife had not cut short his life twelve years later.

---

[1] *Mémoires de Sully*, Vol. II, p. 380.

CALENDAR OF THE

CECIL MANUSCRIPTS

PRESERVED AT
HATFIELD HOUSE, HERTFORDSHIRE

SCHEME FOR A FUNERAL MONUMENT.

[1562].—Drawing of a sepulchral monument in the event of the death of Sir William Cecil and that of his wife, Lady Mildred. The date on the drawing is 1562, and the figures are those of Sir William, Lady Mildred, Thomas Cecil (later 1st Earl of Exeter) and Anne Cecil (later the wife of Edward de Vere, 17th Earl of Oxford). Certain inscriptions at the base of the monument commemorate the death of three younger Cecil children.

1 *sheet* (CPM **11.** 14.)

HERTFORDSHIRE.

[*c.* 1570].—Map of land between Hoddesdon and Cheshunt, co. Herts. Some of the entries are in Lord Burghley's hand. The map shows certain property at Waltham in the possession of Robert Huycke (? *d.* 1581). Huycke or Huicke was physician to Henry VIII, Edward VI and Elizabeth, and purchased land at Waltham in 1570. (See CP. Deeds 227/7.)—*Undated.*

Endorsed : " Hoddesdon, Cheshunt, Waltham." 1 *sheet.* (CPM *supplementary* 20.)

LAWRENCE SMITH to QUEEN ELIZABETH.

[*c.* 1576].—In consideration of many years of service he asks for a lease of all the lands forfeited to the Crown by the conviction for robbery of Richard Cole, of Northway, co. Gloucester, in 1576. He is ready to pay £60 annually as rent, but requests that Cole's life be granted him " in respect that the sayd landes of Coles ys supposed for to bee intayled, whereby your Matie nor any other by your Highnes graunte cannot receave any longer benefytt of the sayde landes then duringe the lyef of the sayde Richard Cole ".—*Undated.*

½ p. (P. 820.)

[See *Acts of the Privy Council,* 1575–77, p. 186.]

JOHN and WILLIAM GOODWIN.

[1576 or after].—A particular of the estate of John Goodwin,
of Muswell Hill, co. Middlesex, who died on December 26, 1575.
The property was inherited by his son William, who was 26 years
old at the time of his father's death. At the *Inquisition post
mortem*, held on May 22, 1576, "apud le castle in St Johns Strete"
in Middlesex, the estate was said to have included Muswell Farm,
Muswell Chapel, and cottages and lands held of the manor of
East Greenwich, with a total annual value of £9.—*Undated.*
Signed : William Tooke, auditor. 1½ pp. (P. 2170.)

MIDDLESEX.

[*c.* 1581–82].—Plan of land between Enfield and Tottenham,
containing notes in the hand of Lord Burghley. The properties
named include Pymmes and Pleasantries acquired by him in
1582 and 1588 respectively. Another named Prior's Grove was
leased to him on February 28, 1581–2, by Gabriel Grymston.
(*See* CP. Deeds 238/14.) The map has also a drawing of the
Minchendon Oak.—*Undated.*
Endorsed : "Lands adjacent to Enfield." 1 *sheet.* (CPM
supplementary 27.)

F. PARKER to RICHARD PERCEVAL.

[1583]. December 2. "I have appoynted a frend of
myne, one Mr Locksmith, to proceed with the offices after the
death of Edward Humberston* and Edward Eyre this vacasion.
[*Marginal note :* Hartford] If any inquier of them (for that I
will not be seene in yt) I beseech you to directe them to the
peticoner and to him ; he is soliciter to Mr Swynnerton, farmer
of thimposts in Aldermanburye. Therefore I praie you, make a
note for a warrante for writts to Mr Hare, and that you would
(if it please Mr Secretarie to graunte the other wards unto my
cozen Warde) certifie me thereof by this bearer, and deliver him
a note for warrants for the writts that I maie fynd the offices
nowe when I am in the country. Also I beseech you, if any
speake in Lucas his warde [*marginal note :* Lincolne] to have a
care in it, and if it prove as I verylie hope to doe, I will geve you
xxᵗⁱᵉ marks."—2 December.
Holograph. Addressed : "To the worthy my very good frend
Mr Richarde Percyvall, Esquier, at his house in the layne leadinge
from Charinge Crosse to St Giles."
⅓ p. (P. 2129.)

WILLIAM CORBETT.

[After December 14, 1584].—A rental of the estate of William
Corbett, of Leigh, Salop, deceased.† The lands include the

---

* Died in 1583. [See *East Herts Archaeological Society Transactions*, Vol. X,
1937–39, p. 28 and n.]
† Died on December 14, 1584. [See *PRO, Wards* 7, 21/177.]

demesne at Leigh, which provide an annuity for his brother Reynold, and tenements situated in Aston Pigot, Asterley, Minsterley, Worthen, Sibdon Carwood, and the manor of Medlicott, in Salop, and Great and Little Hem in Montgomeryshire. The annual value of the estate is £161:4:0½.—*Undated.*

3 pp. (P. 2170.)

HATFIELD.

1588, April 4.—By an Act of Parliament passed in the 18th year of Queen Elizabeth, it was enacted that two Justices of the Peace within or next to a parish in which an illegitimate child had been born, were authorized to take measures for the maintenance of the child and the punishment of the mother and reputed father. " Fforasmuch as Elizabeth Walshe was of late delivered of a childe at Hatfelde in the countie of Hertford, beinge a bastarde, and as she confesseth it was begotten by one Vincente Brandon, then her M^r late dwellinge at Northemyms in the same countie ; and that uppon examination and triall of the circumstances and matters by her declared of that lewid facte it appeareth that the said Brandon is the reputed father of the said bastarde, who for his purgation hath had diverse daies to clere himselfe and faileth therein.   It is therefore orderid and adjudged by us Henrie Coningesbie, knight, and William Tooke, esqr, two Justices of the Peace (and beinge of the Quorum) amongest others assigned within the said countie of Hertford and next to the parishe churche wheare the said childe was borne, that the said Vincente Brandon, the reputed father thereof, shall contribute and paie towards the kepinge of the said childe xii^d everie weeke from the tyme of the birthe duringe the space of seven yeares, and the mother thereof to discharge the reste duringe the said tyme ; and at the ende of the said seven yeares the said Vincente Brandon his executors or assinges to take awaie the said childe from the said parrishe of Hatfelde, so as the said parrishe shall not afterwardes be charged with it.   [*Marginal note :* the money to be paide to the Collectors for the poore within the saide parrishe of Hatfelde for the tyme beinge.]   And for the performaunce hereof we do order that the said Vincente Brandon with sufficient suerties shalbe bounde in the somme of twentie poundes unto William Brockett, gent., Clarke of the peace, William Curll, gent., Edmunde Smythe and Raphe Spier, yeomen, or to the survivors of them.

And furthermore we do order and adjudge that the said Elizabeth Walshe, mother of the said childe, shall on Mondaie the viiith of this moneth of Aprill, sitt in the stockes in the churche yarde of Hatfelde aforesaid from vi of the clock in the morninge of the same daie untill the tyme of the begyninge of devine service, and then to be broughte into the churche there havinge a white rodde in her hande, shall stande before the mynister with her face towards the congregation untill the second lesson shalbe reade; and then she shall publiquelie confesse her fault and aske

M S—B

forgevenes of God and of the congregation, and penitentlie desire
the minister and the congregation to praie for her. And after
devine service ended she shalbe stripped from the waste upwarde
and so to be ledd aboute the streates and circuite of the churche-
yard wall of Hatfelde, and there severelie whipped and so re-
delivered to the stocks againe, there to remaine in the stocks
untill eveninge praier shalbe ended for an example to others."
iiiith of Aprill, 1588.

Note at bottom: to the effect that Brandon gives sureties to
perform the order, the bond being made out to the parishioners.
Signed: Harry Conyngesby, William Tooke." 1 p. (**200,**
185.)

The EARL OF DESMOND.

1588, August 29.—Sessions held at Cork on August 29, 1588,
to deal with the lands of the attainted Earl of Desmond, Gerald
FitzGerald, within the province of Munster.
15 pp. (**366.**)
[See *H.M.C. Salisbury MSS*, Vol. XIII, p. 382.]

LORD BURGHLEY to ROBERT PETRE.

1588, December 13.—"I perceave yow have chested such
mony as Mr Stonly and Taylor had in chardg, but I require yow
not to suffer them to receave any more, but what so ever may
come to be offred to ether of them that yow se it delyvered to
the chardg of the other tellers, for untill they shall gyve better
answer with mony and not in words, I meane not to accept them
for ether tellers or payers. I pray yow observe this and lett the
Chauncellor know the same, and move hym to press them to
mak payment in dede and not to offer words, for nether he nor
I can pacefy the Queens great officer with cold dealyngs in this
so lewd a matter." xiii Dec. 1588.
Holograph. ¾ p. (**213.** 123.)
[See *H.M.C. Salisbury MSS*, Vol. 111, p. 377.]

HENRY ASHLEY to the PRIVY COUNCIL.

[Before September 5, 1589].—He submits three requests: that
the authority by oath be given to Francis Hastings, George
Trenchard, Francis Haly and William Gibbs, or any two of them,
Hastings to be one; that the Lord Marquis personally conduct
the examination of the parties and their witnesses, and report
on the same; and that the case be heard at the Council table.
He also objects to Thomas Hannam, Lawrence Hide and Christopher Anckitell being nominated commissioners on the grounds
that: it is known to some members of the Council that petitioner
and his father have been commissioners against Hannam, and
that as a result relations between them are none too cordial;
Hannam has long been a legal adviser to Sir Matthew Arundell;
Lawrence Hide is likewise Arundell's auditor; Anckitell, although
an honest gentleman, cannot be considered because "at this

tyme he was procured by Sir Mathewe Arundell to com unto me to perswad me to disolve or adjorne the musters, muste nowe there be examined, and therefore in this case not fitt to be a comissioner."—*Undated.*

On reverse : " Mr Trenchard, Mr Hannam, Mr Hyde, Mr Antyll, Mr Hawley, Mr Fra. Hastings, Mr Gibbes." 1 p. (P. 825.)

[See *Acts of the Privy Council*, 1589–90, p. 80.]

MR WARDOUR.

[*c.* November, 1589].—Reasons for the invalidation of the grant made to Mr Wardour.

" Ffirst, for taking it by the name of Clericus Thesaur, where in deede there was never any such officer since the erectinge of an undertreasourer, and he that was first undertreasourer was before that Clericus Thesaurar as it wilbe proved, and his office in truth at that tyme in another personne as by the ffee therunto apperteyninge will manifestlie appere.

Next, that it annswereth not in forme any of the grauntes made to his predecessors.

Further, that because he arougateth to hym selfe by his said graunte an authoritie to lay owt and allowe of the Quenes treasure for all kinde of necessaries expended in the receipt, the whiche he that graunted hym the patent coulde or wolde not dar with owthe the Quenes spetiall warrante.

Next, for that he taketh uppon hym by the said graunte the Tellers office to make contentes of the money, to put his seale to the bagges and chestes, etc.

Lastlie, for that he hath it with an expresse ffee that none of his predecessors ever had and under the Lorde Treasurers seale at armes, his predecessors having the same time . . . " [*partly illegible*].—*Undated.*

Endorsed : " Allegations for the annihilating of Mr Wardours patent." 1 p. (P. 2227.)

[See *H.M.C. Salisbury MSS*, Vol. XIII, p. 417.]

SIR THOMAS HENEAGE to QUEEN ELIZABETH.

[1589 or before].—"That your Ma^ty shold mislike me is my unwillynge fawte and my wurst fortune, which I finde by your wordes, must confesse by my lackes, and suerly wold faine forgoe by my labor. But nether any of my deserts nor all my desire hetherto hath enabled me to contynew your Ma^ts favor, or to avoyde the contrary. My bitter experiens prooves yt, specially in matters of Parliament whear nether heartofore my best speeche with my most burden for your Highnes coold be thought worthe thanks, nor now my silens can stand withowt blame. Moch more happy be they that by popular speeches can purchase credyt in the world and by partiall reportes procure favor from your Highnes. Howbeit, I wold never coome by happines with soch condityons nor seek ether ii strings to my bowe nor ii bowes for one marke. For I will never shoote but to serve your

Ma^ty alone, leavyng divers markes for conynger archers, whether I save or lose. To doe all thinges that might be most acceptable to your Ma^ty is that the honestest seeke but the wisest can not find. And yet my selfe that is so unsufficyent, if I wear some-tymes warranted of your Highnes will by your wordes, I coold doe better than offend you, thoe not so well as to content you. Which grace if it be thought to great for me, yt might yet please your Matie of your goodnes, when men of more consideratyon and of your Cowncell* shall say nothing with your favor, not to impute it as a fawte that I shew not my follye, I mean to speake sodenly in soch causes as by some experyens I can telle yow may be better served in with sylens. As for your Ma^ts sharpest speeches, I acknowledge with all humblenes it becoomes me to beare them, tho it be reputed to other a matter of prayes that was reckoned to me in way of reproche. And thus will I conclude: whatsoever be the cause that the dogge must be strycken, I can best assure your Matie he will nether breake cheyn nor coller but byde at your feete."—*Undated.*

Holograph. 1⅓ pp. (**114.** 38.)

Court of the Admiralty.

1591 to 1604.—List of names, possibly of those who were involved in legal proceedings in the Court of the Admiralty.
128 pp. (**243.** 2.)

Tenerife.

1593, April 1.—A letter from Captain Francisco de Arcola Vergara, alderman (regidor) of the Island of Tenerife and Gover-nor of the naval fortress of Santa Cruz, to Dr Pedro Farfan, judge, Florian de Mansilla, Dr Juan de Quesada and Fray Juan de Aguirra. They are authorized to arrange a meeting with the King at the Court with a view to recommending that Vergara be nominated Captain of Tenerife.—San Cristobal in the Island of Tenerife, April 1, 1593.
Spanish. 1 p. (**205.** 66.)

Palma.

1593, June 28.—A letter from Doctor Pedro Farfan in recom-mendation of Lope de Vallejo, alderman (*regidor*) in the Island of Palma.—Madrid, June 28, 1593.
Spanish. 1 p. (**205.** 66a.)

Henry Damstorff to the Lord Treasurer.

[Before September 25, 1593].—Mr Sebastian a Bergen has asked petitioner to approach him on his behalf to obtain " cas-sationem repressaliorum Georgii Leakii " under the Great Seal, accompanied by letters from the Privy Council, as promised by the Judge of the Admiralty, for the restitution of the £234 which

---

* In September, 1589, Heneage himself was made Privy Councillor.

Leake has already received. Leake's whereabouts are unknown and the plague is becoming more virulent from day to day. Bergen proposes to delegate full authority to Herman Langerman, merchant of the Steelyard, to prosecute Leake for the repayment of the money. Bergen also requests that no commission of reprisal be granted to Peter Gerrard against the Hamburgers, since the Judge of the Admiralty has informed him that Gerrard is not desirous of any such commission, nor, in the Judge's opinion, can he legitimately claim one. Finally, Bergen asks that both Leake and Gerrard be persuaded to rest satisfied with what law and justice shall award them at Hamburg.—*Undated.*

Endorsed : " The humble petition of Henry Damstorff of the Stillyard." 1 p. (P. 1973.)
[See *Cal. S.P. Dom.*, 1591–94, p. 373.]

WILLIAM BALL to the PRIVY COUNCIL.

[? 1593].—Three years ago petitioner married the sister of James Reynolds. He discovered that the greatest part of her estate was in ready money, but that it had been borrowed from her by her brother who had not troubled to give her bonds or receipts, or arranged for witnesses to be present at such transactions. Moreover he declined to make a full reckoning of his debts to her for more than two years. Eventually, at Lord North's house last Christmas, petitioner and Reynolds agreed to approach Lord North and request him to adjudge the matter between them. He showed himself willing to do so on condition that both parties stated their respective cases and demands on paper. This was done, and after due examination and discussion, it was decided, following upon pressure by Reynolds, that out of an estimated £341 he should be asked to repay only £230. Reynolds faithfully promised Lord North and petitioner on his word as a gentleman that he would implement the agreement. Now he refuses to honour it on the grounds that it was not formulated in strictly legal terms. Petitioner asks that Cecil oblige him to do so, especially as he obtained all that he demanded, and gave his word to an eminent person like Lord North.—*Undated.*
½ p. (P. 1790.)
[See *Acts of the Privy Council*, 1592–93, pp. 487–8.]

RICHARD YOUNG and JOHN ELLIS.

[Before 1594].—Certificate to the effect that Richard Young held a messuage in Stratford at Bowe in April, 1590 ; that his son-in-law, John Ellis, agreed to subscribe with him to a bond for the payment of Young's debt of £1200 to Reynold Tardiff,* and that in consideration of this Young conveyed the messuage to John Ellis. For the past two years Ellis has been residing on the estate, and to strengthen his title to it Young releases himself absolutely from all rights to the property.—*Undated.*
Endorsed : "Mr Ellis." ⅓ p. (P. 2340.)

---

* Probate of his will granted in 1594. [See *Prerogative Court of Canterbury Wills*, Vol. IV, 1584–1604, p. 407.]

BAYNHAM *versus* ASHLEY.

[? *c.* May, 1594].—A note to the effect that Baynham has been granted in reversion for 31 years the demesne of the manor of Allington, and the best part of the manors of Maidstone and Boxley. Ashley desires to purchase a part of the manor of Boxley, but will have to pay heavily for it " unles hir Matie please to have the more gratious consideration of him onely becawse he nor his children shoulde not be molested hereafter by his adversaries whoe pretended to further the Queens title and gett to him selfe this commodious grant ". Baynham has the manor house of Boxley and is alleged to have cut down some of the Crown's woods there, whereas it is denied that Ashley has felled any trees but those for which he has paid.—*Undated.*
½ p. (P. 2370.)
[See *H.M.C. Salisbury MSS*, Vol. IV, pp. 538–9, and *PRO. Depositions of the Exchequer*, Kent, 30/31 Elizabeth, Mich. 19.]

SIR WILLIAM DANSELL.

[? *c.* May, 1595].–Details of the allowance granted to Sir William Dansell, late Receiver-General of the Court of Wards, which amounted to £210.—*Undated.*
Signed : Walter Tooke, auditor. ⅓ p. (P. 2209.)
[See *H.M.C. Salisbury MSS*, Vol. V, p. 222.]

HUMPHREY PLESSINGTON to [SIR ROBERT CECIL].

[After October 25, 1595].—He has been given the wardship of Henry Farr of Burstead, co. Essex. Next Monday he is to bring a case in the Court of Wards against Pease and others for committing waste on his ward's property. He understands that Cecil will not be present in the Court that day, and asks him to speak to the Attorney on his behalf.—*Undated.*
½ p. (P. 1337.)
[See *PRO. Wards* 9/348.]

BERMONDSEY.

[? 1595].—Map of Redrith (Rotherhithe), co. Surrey between the River Thames and Long Mead. Certain places are shown, such as, " Pickeringes ", " Nashe ", a limekiln and other buildings and fields. In 1595 a lease was granted to Carpenter of Pickering, Nashe and Samshore. (*See* CP. Legal 24/16).—*Undated.*
Endorsed : " Bermondsey " *and in another hand :* " A survey or plotte of Pickeringe and Nashe, Redrith ". 1 *sheet.* (CPM *supplementary* 49.)

JOHN CURTIS.

[1595–96].—" The Sheriffe haveing her Ma^{ts} wrytt of execution to enter into a howse and to putt an other man into the possession therof (which howse is purposelie kepte with greate force againste him by manie desperate persons soe that he dare not enter), he requireth A.B. (A justice of the Peace) to aide and asiste him, and uppon theire approchinge unto the saide howse the said Sheriff readeth his wrytt unto them, and useth perswasions with them and all other the good meanes he maie by two longe howers that they shoulde avoid out of the same, wherbye he mighte make execution therof accordinge to her Ma^ts comandement; whoe obstenatelie refuse to doe the same and answere that they will sooner loose theire lives then the possession, and then they thretten the saide Sheriffe and A.B. of theire lives and throwe greate stones, shoote arrowes and also gonns at them, wheruppon the saide Sheriffe and A.B. sett uppon them, and a servant of the saide A.B. (beinge farre of from the saide A.B. and without his privytie) killeth one of them with a gonne.

The question is whether the killing of this rebellious person be murther or manslaughter or justifiable by the saide A.B. and his servant or by anie of them."—*Undated.*

Endorsed: "The case upon the deathe of John Curtys." ¾ p. (P. 2292.)

[See *Acts of the Privy Council*, 1595–96, pp. 228–9, 239–40, 247–8.]

WILLIAM CLAXTON to SIR ROBERT CECIL.

[September 1596 or later].—He is an apprentice in Newcastle-on-Tyne, and since April 13 last has been in prison, where he was committed by the Mayor and other magistrates of the town. Their reason for doing so was the suspicious arrival of a letter from France addressed to him but delivered into their hands, but of which he knew nothing until it was shown to him at his examination. He denies knowledge of the identity of the sender, neither was he ever at the place from which it was sent, nor knows any living person there. Petitioner can only assume that it is part of a conspiracy to discredit him in the town. After suffering five months of close detention, and despite the efforts of his master and others to have him released, the Mayor and other magistrates refuse to do so without instructions from Cecil. He begs that letters be sent to them authorizing a re-examination of the case, and that he be dealt with according to his guilt or innocence.—*Undated.*

½ p. (P. 1797.)

[His indenture as apprentice is dated June 24, 1595. He was transferred to a second master in January, 1596 and to a third on April 27, 1598. [See *Newcastle Merchant Adventurers*, Vol. II, p. 223. (The Surtees Society, No. 101.)]

—— to PHILIP II, KING OF SPAIN.

[? 1596].—A petition describing how the English forces took possession of the city of Cadiz, and seized a number of prominent men and women from whom they demanded a ransom of 120,000 *ducados.* Fifty of the prisoners, most of them clerics, were shipped to England because they did not pay the money asked of them by their captors. Petitioners request the King that

instead of sending the Fathers of the Order of Our Lady of Mercy
and of the Trinity to the territories of the Moors, he dispatch
them to England to effect the release of the above-mentioned
fifty prisoners.—*Undated.*

Spanish. Imperfect. 2 pp. (**205.** 65.)

ROBERT SMITH to SIR ROBERT CECIL.

[Before 1597].—By means of forgeries and perjuries Robert
Harrison, of Ely, with the connivance of William March* of the
same town, has succeeded in depriving petitioner of his estate.
Others have suffered the like treatment at his hands, and petitioner
proposes to submit a petition to the Privy Council since no course
by law is open to him. He asks Cecil to view his case with
sympathy and favour.—*Undated.*

½ p. (P. 364.)

SIR FRANCIS WILLOUGHBY.

[1597].—" My true and just conceipt, as farr as my understandinge can judge, of the valew of the wardshipp and lease of
her Ma^ts parte of the land duringe the mynoritie, protestinge
that I will sett it downe no lesse but rather more then I judge it
to be worthe, and would nott in that pointe abuse so honorable
a frend for x soche wards." There follows an evaluation of the
lands of the late Sir Francis Willoughby which have been conveyed to his heir Perceval Willoughby and to his widow, and
out of which an allowance is to be made for the maintenance and
inheritance of the seven daughters of Sir Francis. An estimate
is also given of the provision left to Frances Willoughby, the ward
and one of the daughters, who has been awarded no marriage
portion and very little inheritance in land. It is signed by
Michael Molyns, who adds the further information that Sir Francis
had sold much of his estate before his death and mortgaged a
certain portion of it to Lady Arbella, all of which is to be excluded
from the benefits which the Crown may expect from the wardship.
—*Undated.*

Endorsed : " Mr Fra. Willoughby. Richard Bolton of Little
Bolton in Lanc." 1⅓ pp. (P. 2298.)

[See *H.M.C. Salisbury MSS*, Vol. VII, pp. 233, 493, 545, and
Vol. XIV, pp. 27–8.]

WEST MARCH between ENGLAND and SCOTLAND.

[1597].—Map of part of Dumfriesshire and Cumberland referred
to as " the debatable ground between England and Scotland."
—*Undated.*

Endorsed : " 1597 ". 1 *sheet.* (CPM **1.** 3.)

EMBASSY TO FRANCE 1598.

1597–98, January 31.—" Mr Secretarie Cecill his negotiation
into Fraunce.

---

* Probate of his will granted in 1597. [See *Prerogative Court of Canterbury Wills,* Vol. IV, 1584–1604, p. 276.]

Althoughe her Matie, according to a resolution taken when Mounsieur de Maissie was last in England, had promissed to send to the Ffrench Kinge some servants of hers of good quallitie to conferre with his Ministers, both to be truely informed of the state of his affaires as also to understand how hee stood affected to the generall treaty of peace offred by the Cardinal Albertus in the behalf of the King of Spaine of the one parte and the Ffrench King, the Queene of England and the States of the United Provinces of the other parte : yet it was not throughly knowne whome her Matie intended to imploy in this service till the beginning or neare the middest of January about which tyme Mr Secretary, Mr Harbart and Sir Thomas Wilkes were nomynated and had instructions signed by her Majestie to this effect ffolowinge :

Instructions for Robert Cecill, our Principall Secretary, sent as our Ambassador to the French King, and for John Harbert, Master of our Requests, and Sir Thomas Wilkes, knight, Clarke of our Counsell, whome wee have likewise appointed comissioners for his better assistance in his present negotiation. Att our Palace of Westminster, the last of January 1597.

Fforasmuch as you our Secretarye are sufficiently accquainted with the substance of the late negotiation of Mounsieur de Massie sent to us from our brother the French Kinge to give us knowledge of an offer of peace made to him on the behalf of the King of Spain, and of the intentions of the said French [King] concerneing the same, it shalbee needlesse here to expresse the particulars of the said negotiation. But that the rest nowe imployed with you in our service may receave knowledge from you of the materiall points of that negotiation, whereby they may the better conceive the effect of these our instructions and the scope of our meaneing in the present ymployments of you and them :

You shall therefore with all diligence, after the receipt of your dispatch, repaire to Roane in Normandy, where wee suppose you shall fynde our brother the French Kinge, and there to him deliver our letteres of credence with all due salutations from us ; and shall let him know that (according to our promise signified) wee have sent you our Secretary and you the associates to conferr with such ministers as hee shall appoint on his part, and the deputyes of the Estates of the United Provinces if they shalbee arrived as wee suppose they are, ffor which purpose you may lett him know that you attend his pleasure and direction for tyme and place to bee appointed for conference to bee had amongst you upon the points propounded by Mounsieur de Massie.

Wee thinke it meete (if you see cause) that you have conference with the Ministers of the Ffrench King alone, and of them you shall require to bee informed particularly how the motions of peace from the King of Spaine or the Archduke Albert have proceeded, as well before the repaire of Mounsieur de Maissie to us as since his comeing thither and departure from hence, and what creditt may bee given to the motions, ffor that thereby wee have had cause to remember the disorderly proceeding held with our ministers sent to treate for peace in the yeare 1588 att Ostend and Burborough, wherein you shall relate unto them the manner of treating held at that tyme by the King of Spaine and his ministers, which hath and doth give us cause to doubt of the sincerity of the Kinge of Spaine at this tyme. And for that it is in reason likely that as well the King as his Ministers wilbee earnest with you to understand, upon such satisfaction as they will suppose to have bene given you in this principall point, our inclynation to a peace and what conditions wee will require of the Kinge of Spaine for a pacification with him, that hee may give knowledge of your disposition thereunto and so drawe from the Archduke a direct answeare concerneinge his power to treate in that case with us :

Wee are content you give the Kinge a tast of our inclynation thus farr, that wee shalbee content to hearken to a peace if upon this mutuall conference betweene his ministers and ours with the deputyes of the States wee shall thinke it convenyent to proceed to any treatye.

In this conference with the Ministers of the French King you may happily find whether there bee likelihood of plaine and direct dealing in the Spanish Kinge ; or whether the motions for peace are but baites laid to abuse us as in the yeare 1588. Whereupon you shall by conference with the Ministers of the Ffrench King and of the Estates, either severallie or joyntlie as occasion serveth, judge of all circumstances requisite tendinge either to the makeing of peace or contynuance of warre which is the principall cause for which you are sent.

After this conference first with the Ministers of the King alone, if so it happen you shall in the next to bee had with them and the deputyes of the States joyntly consider how farr forth they and wee may bee induced to assent to a treaty of peace on each part, and what reasonable conditions may bee required on either part if it shalbee found requisite to enter into treatye with the comissioners of the Kinge of Spaine :

Ffor you shall not enter into any conference or treaty with any comissioners of the Kinge of Spaine untill after report by you made of your severall conferences with the comissioners of the French Kinge and the Estates, wee shall consider of the advertisements and take a further resolution. And then if you shall determyne to treat of peace our pleasure herein shalbee signified hereafter by what persons wee shall thinke it fitt to bee dealt in.

And albeit as a Christian Princesse wee doe heartilye wish and desire peace for us and our estate, kingdome and people, and would acknowledge the same as a speciall blessing of God, yet are wee in wisdome and providence to consider how the same may bee of assurance to us and noe masqued peace whereby wee might bee drawne into danger to our irreparable hurt. And for that wee have had antient confederacy with the people of the Provinces United, for both our securityes, our speciall desire is that if wee shall discend to treate of peace they may bee concluded in the same with conditions sufficient of securitie, otherwise wee shalbee unwilling to accept of any peace for our selves.

Our meaneing therefore is that you with the comissioners of the Ffrench Kinge shall effectually consider of such conditions of peace as shalbee required by the comissioners of the States if they shall inclyne to a peace, and of what necessity they bee and how many of them may well bee forborne for the present. And in case the same demaunds or any of them shall seeme unreasonable, whereby you maye gather their inclynations to bee rather to warr then to peace, you, finding the offers of the Kinge of Spaine in reason acceptable for the security of the Estates, shall with the ministers of the French Kinge by conference with the said deputies travaile to perswade them to frame their demaunds agreable to honor and reason.

But if the comissioners for the Estates shall willfully refuse all perswasions to peace and to condescend to reasonable conditions such as ought to content them, then by common consent of you and of the comissioners of the Ffrench Kinge they shalbee informed of thinconveniencies that of necessity must followe their willfull determination, that is, that either the French Kinge or wee for the benefitt of our owne countries and people must accept of a peace with conditions for our selves, and leave them to theire owne fortune ; or els for standing for them the warre must bee contynued for theire respects onely, wherein they are to consider of the burthen of the charge they must of necessity undergoe, not onely in maynteyneing forces to defend themselves, but also to assist us and the French King to maynteyne a warre without certeinty of charge to bee throwne upon us.

Moreover they must advise how to answeare our charge for the succors already yeilded to them by the space of divers yeares past.

To conclude, when you shall throughly have enformed your selves of all particularities needfull, wherby to discerne the true purposes of the Spanish Kinge in the offer of peace, and shall have found by your diligente travaile and indeavors the direct intentions of the Ffrench Kinge and how farr he hath already proceeded with the King of Spaine (a matter which wee do speciallie commende to your care), and that you shall have seene the purposes of the Estates and their determination to have peace or warre, you shall with all expedition advertize your proceedings and what shall have appeared to you in every particular together with your opinions. And because it were a matter to us full of difficultye to prescribe unto you a way of proceedinge in this our service, considering the same will and doth consist of many points, wee must and doe referre to your discretions the manner and course you are to hold herein. Not doubting but you in your experiences and duty to us (haveing this light of instructions) wilbee carefull to furnish your selves with the knowledge of all other matters and circumstances whereupon wee may addresse our judgements and resolutions to imbrace peace or to contynue warre as shalbee best for our Royall safetie.

And forasmuch as in this conference there will many things
fall into consideration and debate amongst you which hath beene
heretofore handled on all sides, sometime betweene Spaine and
France and Burgundie apart from us, sometyme between England
and Spaine, and other times betweene the Low Countryes and
Spaine alone, and lately betweene us and the Low Countryes,
wee have thought fitt provisionally to instance you so farr by
this memoriall as yow may in no discourse bee found ignorant of
forme and proceeding in like cases, nor bee unfurnished how to
proceede now in the conferences in the discussing of this hard
question of peace or warre with consideration of all difficulties
riseing on every side as hereafter followeth :

Ffirst, yow shall declare to the Kinges Ministers that wee at
the first motion hereof had cause to remember the disorderlie
proceedings of such as treated with our comissioners in the yeare
1588 at Ostend and Burborrough, where long tyme was spente
of purpose and delayes used by the Spanish Councellors to give
tyme to the Kinge of Spaine to have his great navye in readines
upon the sea, and the Duke of Parma to have his army by land
in the Low Countries. And though they had given out in the
Dukes name that hee had sufficient comission from the Kinge of
Spaine to treat of peace, yet by proofe it followed that there could
bee shewed no such comission sent from the King. But after
many delayes a comission was shewed onely warranted by the
Duke of Parma. And for the proof of ill meaneing secretly hidd
under faire language, many points tending to make a peace being
offred privately by some of the Kings comissioners, the same at
publique treatyes was by the same particular persons denyed
against the oathes of credible persons produced by our comissioners to avowe the same.

And besides these disorders the Kinges comissioners finally
pretended to lack authority to assent to diverse speciall articles
propounded to them, being very necessary and indifferent to
the good conclusion of the universall peace both betwixt us and
the King of Spaine and the Estates of the Low Countries and the
saide Kinge.

With all which disorderly proceedinges none are more
accquainted and privye then the President Richardott whome
wee understand now to have bene specially used by the Archduke for communication att this tyme with the French Kings
Ministers. And for theis and such like respects, wee did doubt at
the first to answeare Mounsieur de Maissie, shewing to him those
reasons wherewith wee were moved to doubt of the sincerity of
the Spaniard at this time. Yet, neverthelesse, yow may say that
wee are well contented that after yow have heard of the manner
of the proceedings on the Archdukes part, how the same maie
bee waighed to bee good or badd, shall you by conference with
the Kings ministers and the comissioners of the Low Countries
consider of all circumstances requisite tending either to the
making of a peace or the contynuance of the warre. If the
Kinges Ministers shall urge unto yow their facillity to have a

peace, according to Maissies declaration agreable to that of Chastian Cambresie, you may then remember unto them by way of argument that in that peace the Ffrench King is to have restored unto him divers of his townes and fforts in Picardye as Callais, Arders, Chasterlet, and likewise his Duchie of Brittanie made free. But whether those things shalbee performed there is some reason to doubt, especially for Brittanie to which the Infanta of Spaine maketh title by her mother and the Spaniards in possession of divers townes thereof. Besides this it is to bee doubted how the warrs with the Duke of Savoy shalbee compounded.

And it is to bee considered that if all conditions shalbee performed that were included at Chastean Cambresye, there was at that tyme speciall provision made that wee as Queene of England should have after certaine yeares the towne of Callais with the members thereunto belonging restored to us, which conditions were as reasonable to bee graunted now by the Ffrench Kinge as it was at the same tyme at Chastean Cambryse, where consideration maye bee had, that by the consent of the Kinge of Spaine the same may bee nowe effected without contradiction of the Ffrenche Kinge, consideringe hee oweth unto us as great summes as the towne of Callais is worth.

But of this matter concerneinge the conditions for the Ffrench Kinge wee meane not further to enlarge unto you, though it bee requisite ffor yow to shew that you are not ignorant of such thinges if occasion bee offred. Ffor as for matters betweene him and us there may further communication bee had hereof to cleare such matters as remayne in suspence betweene us, especiallie concerneing great sommes due by the said Kinge unto us whereof at tyme convenient yow may give some remembrance by speeches without any manifest manner of demaundinge reimbursements. But if the Kinge himself bee not disposed to remember the same as his debt, you may object and as *ab improviso* make mention thereof therby to binde him to have regard to our state that hath bene engaged by our assistance of him, not onely since hee became Kinge of Fraunce but also for preservation of him to come to that Crowne.

Secondlie, for the state and condition of us as Quene of England with the Kinge of Spaine, yow are in your conference to consider as well of the difficultyes that doe arise both by the matter of the peace and by the warre.

Ffor the first, in the matter of peace are to bee considered a multitude of thinges requisite to bee had, amongst which cheiflie are theis which were propounded in Anno 1588 at Barborough.

That in makeing of peace the antient treaties of peace betwixt the Emperor Charles as Duke of Burgundy and King Hen. 8, our father, may be remembred and confirmed both for amitye and for the entercourse, with abolition of all that passed contrarie to the said treatyes from the beginning of both our raignes. And when tyme shall serve, especiall provision to bee made and added to the same treatise that our subjects maie use theire

lawfull trade of merchandize in all the Kings dominions that were
in the possession of the Emperor Charles at the tyme of the said
antient treatye without any trouble by reason of the ecclesiasticall
inquisition, so as they give no open occasion where they shall
traffique for merchandize to the contempt of the Catholique
religion ; and when tyme shalbee to add any thinge to the antient
treatye, it shalbee necessarie to have speciall covenants for mutuall
traffique betweene our subjects and the subjects of Portugall for
the common benefitt of thcm both, for that at the tyme of the
treatise betweene the Emperor and King Hen. 8, the kingdome
of Portugal was not subject to the Kinge of Spaine, but was in
good amity by antient treatye betweene the King of England
and the Kinge of Portugal.   And so it shalbee good for the subjects of both countryes to have such treatyes renewed as hath
bene betwene the kingdomes of England and Portugal.

Of all these thinges, if the Kinge should discourse with you,
wee thinke it fitt you bee provisionally informed.

Furthermore, wee have also just cause to demaund satisfaction
for great sommes of mony lent to the Estates that were att
Bruxells holding the part of the Kinge in Anno 1577, who being
destitute of money to mainteyne them in the Kings obedience
did at that tyme by sundry ambassadors require to borrow great
sommes of moneye in the Kinges name, which was willingly for
the Kings service delivered to such as are now in creditt for their
service to the Kinge of Spaine, as by their obligations, when
tyme shall require, shalbee manifest.

Item, it shalbee also most necessary to bee thought of for contynuance of peace, that the Estates of Holand and Zealand and
other provinces united to them may be restored to quietnes and
to bee made free and possesse all the antient liberties which hee
[sic] held at the Kings entrye, for without the restitution of them
to theire antient libertyes and to bee free from all oppression
of strangers, it is so necessary for us to see the assurance thereof
as without it noe good peace for us is likely to bee contynued.

And for matter to bee considered to the benefitt of the Estates,
though their comissions are most sufficient to remember the particularities requisite for their owne assurance, yet for your remembrance (whereof you cannot bee ignorant) the most ordinary
meanes for their assurance are these :

Ffirst, that the pacification att Gaunt made in Anno 1576 is
necessarie to bee observed, which pacification was ratified by
the Kinge of Spaine and the prelates, nobles and townes of all
the provinces obeying the Kinge representing the Estates of
the said countryes in November 1576; and after that confirmed
by Don Juan de Austria at his entrye into the goverment at
La Marchffame in Ffebruary 1577, at which tyme is to bee
remembred that in the 18th Article of the peace there is a speciall
provision that all the obligations made by the Estates with any
that did assist them shalbee answerable to furnish money to serve
for such as did aide them, and principally by name thus expressed :

—The most high and mighty Princesse the Kings deare sister, the Queene of England,—which speciall provision is to bee remembred when time shalbee to treat thereof.

Secondlye, that all the forces of strangers being souldiers may bee sent out of the Low Countries, as well out of the provinces nowe obeying the Kinge as out of the United Provinces of Holland, Zeland and the rest. And therefore if peace may bee graunted to the United Provinces, it is most necessarie that the Estates may bee warranted to levy so much money as by their bonds unto us they owe ; and for some part of the said money the townes of Antwerpe, Burges, Gaunt, Newport, Dunkerk and Brussels are also bound, for the which they are to contribute for theire portions. And upon satisfaction made to us the two townes which wee have for our assurance may be delivered into possession of such as held them when we entred into them.

Many other conditions there are to bee considered for the benefitt of the Estates which wilbee manifested unto yow by themselves at your conference, without obteyning wherof to the said Estates wee shalbee very unwilling to accept any peace for our selves. And upon the discussions of those conditions will rest in good likelyhood the finall successe of this cause now comitted to your charge. So as either peace may bee accepted with such reasonable conditions for the Estates, or if it shalbee thought that such reasonable conditions canott be by any treatye obteyned, then the said Estates must yeild to beare of greater charge for the warre to be contynued by the French Kinge and us then hitherto they have yeilded, which onely for theire benefitt and assurance shalbee contynued though to our great charges without anie profitt to our selves ; consideringe if it were not in respect of the surety of the said States and their countryes wee mighte both have peace upon reasonable conditions betwixt us and the Kinge of Spaine, and so thereby wee should bee free from all callamityes that the warres have brought and may bring both to our countries and people.

And upon the consideration of these difficulties which concernes the Estates, both of the Ffrench Kinges ministers and yow, you shall use the best reasons you can to perswade them to hearken to a peace and to make their demaunds for conditions with the Kinge of Spaine soe reasonable as in honor may bee required of him, and maye also bee sufficient for their assurance to live in peace and to enjoy all theire libertyes, and namely to have the freedome of theire religion, which they now professe. And in the debateing hereof they may bee remembred what thinges were agreed upon before tyme in the tyme of the Prince of Orange, speciallie by the Pacification at Gaunt Anno 1576, and by the Colloquies after that in the tyme that the Kinges Councell of Estate att Brusells tooke armes to expell the Spaniards, which act of theires was allowed by especiall placcarde of the King dated at Brussells in December 1577. And the same placcarde also confirmed by the Estates Generall at Brussells the same day, and which also was by a confederation made in January 1578 solemnely accorded by the prelates, men of the church, Lords, gentlemen, magistrates of townes and castles representing the States of all the Low Countries and being under the obedience of Kinge Philipp.

After which also followed in July 1578 a solemne publique Act both by the Councell of State and the Estates Generall of the Low Countries assembled in Antwerpe by which a generall peace was established for all the Low Countries, and besides the ratifieing of the pacification at Gaunt a great number of articles were there allowed in the reformed religion professessed [sic] in Holand and Zealand. The review of which Acts and other the like soe passed in favor of all the provinces of the Low Countryes may seeme at this tyme to make reasonable projects for the demaunds to bee made for the Estates of Holand and Zeland and thother Provinces United.

And though at the treaty begunn 1588 at Ostend the Estates of the Low Countries were not then ready to joyne without comissioners for the treaty of peace at that tyme, yet (as you John Harbert doe best knowe) upon your sollicitation in our name the Estates of Ffrizeland by deputyes of Ostergo and Westergo, the 7 Silve comonly called the 7 wolden and cittyes did assent and determyne to enter into treaty by meanes of us or our deputyes upon reasonable conditions with the Kinge of Spaine and his deputyes, which act of theirs was ratified the 6 of December 1587 and signed by sundry of the Estates of that province comonly called the land of Omland, the remembrance wherof may serve at this tyme as a good induction for yow to perswade the comissioners of Estates to assent to the like.

And if hereupon, notwithstanding all the perswasion, the comissioners of Estates shall not bee induced to hearken to a treaty of peace, or though they should agree therto yet if they could not condiscend to require reasonable conditions such as ought to content them, then by common consent of the Kings Ministers and yow they may bee informed of the inconvenience that of necessity must thereof [follow], that is :

That either the Ffrench King and wee shall for the benefitt of our owne countries and people accept of a peace with conditions for ourselves and leave the Estates to themselves at their owne wills unprovided for, and still subject to a civill warre ; or els by standing for them and forbearing to accept our owne peace the warre must bee contynued onely in respect of them, which if it shalbee so resolved the Estates are to consider what charges they ought to bee at, besides the maynteynance of their owne forces, to assist both us and the French Kinge to hould out such a warre as wilbee uncertaine what the charge thereof may grow unto aswell by sea as land.

And likewise they are to consider how wee may bee reimbursed of our great sommes of money and other charges theis many yeares yeilded to them without any manner of satisfaction or gratuity for the same. And if the comissioners of the Estates (being charged to beare the burthen of the warres which shall contynue for their sakes) shall seeme desirous to understand wherin their charges should be required above theire former expences and actions, it may bee said, as to the charges by them to be borne for the Ffrench Kinge, yow will leave it to bee answered by the French Kings ministers.

But for answering to them to satisfy our charges, yow may alledge that although it bee a thing uncertaine to be esteemed, yet in two things wee doe thinke to bee releived of our former burthens.

The one is to have some good portion of money expended by us and sent to them, to bee repayed towards the maynteynance of our charges in the warres that shalbee contynued.

The second is, considering wee are like onely to bee burthened with the mightye forces of the Kinge of Spaine by sea, that wee may bee assisted at all times, when wee shall prepare our navye to the seas to withstand the Spaniard, with some good number of shipps and soldiers of the Lowe Countries to joyne with ours, which charges they may with more reason beare.

Ffor the first, consideringe that they have had so long tyme and so many yeares the benefitt of our aide both with money and men without any repayment of anie sommes or any manner of helpe untill those two late journeyes by assistance of shipping wherein they are able to doe great things, considering both their abundance of shipps and that the King of Spaine, the common enemy, hath and doth only attempt to offend us and our country by sea without any hostillity used against them by sea :

Yow, the Secretary, if yow shall see Mounsieur de Lencye [sic], may as of yourself remember him of his bonds joyntly with the Duke of Bulloigne, and both their promises for the payment of 20,000 crownes which oughte to have bene paide more then twenty monethes since.

Yow may also at the same tyme remember him of the contract made at his beinge in England for the payment of the charges of certaine forces lent to the King at the seidge of Amyons, for the answering whereof the Kings bond under his great seale is here in England for the payment of 66,000 crownes and odd money which was for thentertainement of the English forces only for 6 monethes, and yet the forces have contynued there above 15 monethes. If by this remembrance unto him the money may bee gotten, you shall doe good service.

And if upon the allegation of these thinges which may bee fitt for us to require (if a treatie should bee begunne the French Kinge shall require some memoriall of our demaunds) you may privately deliver them unto him for his remembrance though not signed authentically as our comissioners.

Finallie, considering there are like to arise soe many difficultyes upon those your conferences, for to induce all parties to enter into a publique treaty and an accord for a peace, as the same cannott without some length of tyme bee well discussed and resolved or reconcluded, especiallie considering the distance

M S—C

of place of the King of Spaine from France, England and the Low Countries, to which three he is the principall enemy : for that purpose it wilbee necessary that reasonable tyme bee given to have us all, the three Kinges and States of the Lowe Countries, to bee fully and largely from tyme to tyme informed of all the circumstances of the said difficulty [*sic*? difficulties] concerneing us all, both severallie and jointly, as, by common concord of conditions of peace may bee assented unto. And therefore yow, our comissioners (if such difficulties and doubts shall arise as cannott at this your being there bee discussed) shall consider with the French Kinge and the Estates comissioners, either by speech joyntlie or severallie as you shall see cause in respect of the three causes aforesaide, how a truce may bee made betwixt the Kinge of Spaine and his Leivetenant the Archduke on the one parte, and the French Kinge and us, as Queene of England, and the States of the United Provinces on the other parte. So as the same truce may have contynuance for no lesse tyme then 13 monethes after 28 daies to a moneth, and bee graunted and confirmed by every party interchangeablie, not onely by writeing subscribed and sealed in authentique manner but also by oath to bynd every of us to the observation of the said truce. And if this shalbee allowed of, then by the French Kinges meanes as of himself the same may bee propounded to such of the Arch-dukes Ministers as have occasion to deale with the Ffrench Kinge, and to proceed therein as shalbee found necessarie to determyne the same ; wherein upon knowledge from yow how the same shall proceed, wee will let yow understand our further deter-mination before yow grow to any conclusion.

And if it shall happen that after all these forcible arguments used to dissuade the French Kinge from makeinge peace with the Spaniard in either sort then by comprehending his allyes, the King shall urge yow to make him some offer of assistance against the common enemy, seeing wee doe not allowe of his falling from us to any pacification yow may then in generall tearmes thus answer him :

That as wee are still in eminent expectation of invasion by the Spaniard (a matter wherwith the whole world is filled) besides our charges in Ireland by the rebellion there maynteyned, wee cannott in any just reason be invited to any auxiliary charges wherby to weaken ourselves. So by the experience of our former proceedings with him hee shall not need to doubt but if wee see the blow to have likely his lighting place on him, wee will bee ready as ever were to assist him by all such meanes as shalbee agreable to the condition of our affayres.

Subscribed heere in the foote by Mr Secretary himselfe.

Ffor the finishing of this dispatch there were also written diverse letters of creditt from her Matie to the King, to Madam his sister, to the Constable and Duke of Bouillon, besides a Privy Seale for the comissioners dyetts.

Whereby Mr Secretary was to have for himself iiii^l *per diem* allowance. And the rest 50^s *per diem* a peice.

There was also one other letter of speciall importance written with her Ma^{ts} owne hand.*

Though these instructions and whatsoever els belonged to the negotiation were soone perfected and made ready when once her Ma^{ts} pleasure was knowne whome she intended to imploy therein, yet there was some protraction used both before the dispatch was presented to her Majesties signature and likewise afterwards onely of purpose, as it should seeme, that the Estates Deputyes, Justitian Nassaue and Mounsier Barnevelt, might bee past by in the Narrow Seas towards France before her Ma^{ts} comissioners did set forth.

Att length it being well perceived that the Estates used extraordinary protraction thereby discovering their unwillingness to enter into conference, especially seeing it tended to pacification, it was then resolved no longer to attend their comeing, and the rather because the Ffrench King, whose presence in Brittanie was necessarily required, grew impatient that the conference was so long deferred. Therefore the dispatch being ready, all provisions shipt and gone, and Mr Harbert and Sir Thomas Wilkes with most of the company gone to Dover, Mr Secretary himselfe followed the tenth of February, being accopnayed with the Earle of Southampton, the Lord Thomas Howard, the Lord Cobham, Sir Walter Raleigh with diverse others.

Hee tooke barge at the Duchie House and went to Gravesende by water. Then he tooke coach and horses and rode the same day to Sittingborne, being mett in the way by Sir George Delves and Mr Cromer who accompanyed him to the *George*, being the Postmasters house where hee was lodged.

Heere Mr Merediths man overtooke us and delivered to Mr Secretary a jewell from the Queene.

[*Marginal note:* 11 Ffebr.] This day being Satterday and as stormy weather as ever was travayled in, hee rode to Canterbury where he dyned at the *Sarazens Head* being the Postmasters house, and wrote some private letters by the ordinary post to my Lord Treasorer and some other of his freinds.

In the afternoone hee rode to Dover, and was mett at Barham Downe by Sir Henry Parmer, Sir Thomas Wilford and some other gentlemen, both of Kent, and such as were gone before to Dover with purpose to accompany him over. Hee was lodged at one Kemps house nere the Castle.

[*Marginal note :* 12 Ffebr.] This day Mr Tomkins arrived with letters from my Lord of Essex whereunto Mr Secretary made answere by post at seaven of the clock of the eveninge. Hee likewise sent his servant Shepeard to London this afternoone by whome he writ a private letter to my Lord Treasurer.

This afternoone order was taken for placeinge the gentlemen in her Ma^{ts} shipps in this sorte :

---

* For a copy of this letter, see PRO, S.P. 78 (France), Vol. 41, p. 195.

Vantguard

Mr Secretary	Mr Thynn
Earle of Southampton	Mr Beeston
Sir George Carew	Mr Doyley
Mr Norris	Mr Maynard
Sir Alexander Ratcliffe	Mr John Ratcliffe
Mr Wroth	Mr Meredith
Mr Harbert Crofts	The Chaplaine with some of
Mr Warburton	Mr Secretaries servants

Answeare

Mr Paget	Mr Maurice Berkley
Mr Stanley	Doctor Crompton
Sir Charles Blount	Mr Cope
Sir James Wootton	Mr Tufton
Mr Throgmorton	Mr Studdall
Mr Slingsby	Mr Hubberd
The Swedland Gent.	Mr Cooke
Mr Daniel	Mr Philipps
Mr Crane	
Mr Harbert	

Quittance

Sir Thomas Wilkes	Mr Cuttes
Mr Ffrancis Mannors	Mr Turvyle
Mr Vane	Mr Corbett

Tremontane

Mr Cannon	with most of Mr Secretaries
Mr Smyth	servants.

The *Moone* her Ma^{ts} pinnasse served to transport Mr Secretaries trunks and other provisions which were shipped the xiiith of this instant Ffebruary.

[*Marginal note:* 13 Ffebr.] This day one Russells, a French gentleman, being sent from the French Kinge to the Estates, arrived at Dover from the Lowe Countryes, by reason of contrary wynds. Mr Secretary had long conference with him.

Hee received letters this evening from the Lord Treasurer, the Earle of Essex, Sir John Stanhope, Mr Grevill, and Mr Wade brought by John Symonds.

[*Marginal note:* 14th] The 14th my Lord Thomas Howard, my Lord Cobham, Sir Walter Raleigh with others retorned to the Court. Mr Secretary wrote a letter of thankes for the jewell hee received from her.

My Lord Cobham had the letter to deliver. Hee (Cecil) writ by post to my Lord Treasurer and a private letter to my Lord of Essex for a supply of xx daies victualls for the 800 soldiers sent out of Picardy for Ireland, and driven to the Downes by contrary winds.

The same day Peter Browne arrived with a letter from Mr Edmonds conteyneinge some speech betweene the Marshall Byron and him concerneing the treatye. The letter was forthwith sent to London to my Lord Treasurer, being dated at Paris the 17th of Ffebruary, and it conteyned in effect this much :

[*Marginal note :* The effect of Mr Edmonds letter.] That the King did comunicate with him the first dispatch which hee received from Vervin which conteyned great offers of the Cardinalls part shewing his necessity and his feare. And that they intended conference with Mr Secretary, and the comissioners of the Lowe Countries may further engage the French King into a warre against him.

That therefore hee doth seeke peace at any hand, promising the delivery of Callais and Ardrees within two monethes after the conclusion of the treatye, and within another moneth following to restore thother places, Douelans, le Chasteylett and La Capelle and to rase Blavett.

That for assurance hereof sufficient hostages should be delivered.

And that the accord should be reduced to the same state and conditions as it was last made in the yeare 59.

That the Cardinall pretended to demaund that tearme onely to procure money to withdraw the garrison.

That the Spanish comissioners were willing to have signed those offers, and urged those of the Kinges part to have also subscribed, thereby to have concluded his owne treatye, promiseing that they would afterwards treate with her Majesty and those of the Low Countryes, but it was refused by the French Kings comissioners to advance the one before the other

And because it appeared they are not as yet sufficiently authorized to treate with her Ma^{ty}, they demaunded pasport to send into Spaine for more ample power.

That the King had given pasport in name of the Legate, and had answered that hee would resolve of nothing till the comeinge of Mr Secretary and the comissioners of the Estates.

It was also said to bee moreover promised on the behalf of the Duke of Savoy that Bresse shall remaine to the King in exchange of the Marquisitt of Saluce.

This was the substance of that letter concerneing this matter.

[*Marginal note :* 15th.] The 15th of this moneth Mr Secretary receaved letters from the Lord Admirall conteyneing an advise of a fleet from Spaine discovered about the mowth of the Silve.

To this letter hee made answer the same afternoone by an ordinary post.

This day Shepheard retornd and brought with him letters from Sir John Stanhopp to Mr Secretary with an advice from Brittanie sent by Captain Prynne. Hee brought also the copies of ciphers betweene Mr Secretary and such as hee doth ymploy for matter of intelligence in forreigne parts. This advise came that xxxvii saile of shipps were to come for Callais with 4000 men from

Spaine, whereupon notice was given to Sir Robert Crosse, being
at the Downes, to the end he might plye over in the morneinge
with her Maties shipps which was done accordinglie.

The next morneing, being the 16th, Mr Secretary himself rode
to the Downes with an intent to have gone over with the shipps,
but they had all weighed before his comeinge, whereupon he
retorned to Dover where he mett with Captaine Poore, by whome
he was advertized that the Spanishe fleet entred into the harbor
of Callais yesternight.

The same day Mr Secretary writt twice to the Lords at ten
in the forenoone and three in the afternoone.

[*Marginal note:* 17th.] The 17th, after hee had made a
dispatch to the Lords, hee imbarqued himself in the afternoone
and sett sale about 5 of the clock.

[*Marginal note:* 18th. Deepe.] The 18th arrived at Deepe
about fower of the clock in the afternoone, where Mounsieur
de la Boderie, a M^r d'Hostell of the Kinges did attend his comeing
and delivered him a letter from the King.*

[*Marginal note* : 19th Febr.] To this letter Mr Secretary made
an answere the next day, being the xixth, in this sort following,
and sent the same by a French carrier which attended Mounsieur
de la Boderie.†

Mounsieur de Chate who comaunds this towne was absent
when wee entred it, being buisyed at Kilboufe about his sea
preparation. Howbeit his lewetenant enterteyned us very kindly.
And in the eveninge the comaunder himself came home.

This afternoone Mr Tomkins, a gentleman of the Earl Marshalls,
was dispatched for England by him. Mr Secretary writt to the
Queene and likewise a joynt letter from him, Mr Harbert and
Sir Tho. Wilkes to the Lords to this effect :

[*Marginal note:* 19 February. A joynt letter to the Lords.]

May it please your Lordshipps. Being now arrived here at
Deepe after a good and convenyent passage from Dover by Gods
favor, wee thinke it our part to advertize your Lordshipps of
the same as desirous to omitt no circumstances that may concerne our cares and dutyes in this service.

Att our arrivall wee found Mounsieur de la Bodiere, M^r d'Hostell
of the Kinges, a gentleman of very good fashion and understandinge, by whome I the Secretary received this letter which
here I send your Lordshipps. And to the intent yow may receive
what course wee meane to hold, I send your Lordshipps the
coppie of that answer which I have returned to the King, being
moved by this gentleman to write some thing because he was to
dispatch away a carrier presently towards the King. [*Marginal
note :* The 2 precedent French letters.]

How the same may like her Matie I know not, only this I
may say as wee finde thinges here disposed, it is such as wee
have all thought fitt to returne, ffor as wee doubt not but her

---

* For this letter *see* PRO. S.P. 78 (France). Vol. 41, p. 159.

† For a copy of this letter *see* S.P. 78 (France), Vol. 41, p. 161, with English
translation appended.

Matie would thinke our imployments to little purpose if wee should not beginne with the principall head to whome wee are addressed. So to the intent that our advancements further may give the King lesse collour of excuseing his absence, though indeed wee find that the estate of Brittanie did violently presse his owne presence, wee doe resolve by easie journeyes to passe to Paris where wee doe meane to forbeare any formall colloquy with any of his ministers other then by way of discourse untill we shall heare from himselfe what course hee will then direct us for our accesse to him. And beinge now come over hither, wee are most willing to remove rather then to abide at Roan where wee shall dispaire to speak with him and live in darknes without any manner of meanes to understand thinges to any purpose ; there being on this point no other difference consider-ing her Ma^{ts} honnor then our further paine and charge, which to mynds that are desirous to undertake all things which may deserve her Ma^{ts} acceptation, no such second considerations can move any difficulties. And forasmuch as by the last letters that came to Mounsieur de la Ffountaine it seemed there was some course resolved on to draw to the Cardinall new powers from Spaine, wee thinke this course of ours fittest which, notwithstand-ing, wee doe humblie submitt to your Lordshipps favourable interpretation of our desires at all tymes and in all things to doe the best wee can.

When wee are at Paris, if wee bee drawne further, it shalbee unto a good country and where wee shalbee better accomodated, in which case two hundred miles rideing were better bestowed to deale with the King personally then to passe as farr as this place onlye to treat with subjects.

Besides wee shall have this other advantage to speake with him before the deputyes of the Estates have flattered and raised him, and shalbee returned to Paris by that tyme they come thither, who being members of a popular state have not so much cause to value themselves as wee that are the humble servants of so great and glorious a monarche, they happily not meaneing to presse accesse to the King but resolveing to content themselves with conferences with his ministers. They are not yet arrived but to [*sic :* do] attend the firste puffe of wynde, diverse of their bagages being landed and (as wee heare) they meane to follow the Dutch bravery by comeing with 60 horse all of a colour.

Wee have certified the Kinges M^r d'Hostell of the new discent of the Spaniards thereby to give the King some alarum to draw him neare, ffor after his owne presence in Brittanie hath disposed the mynds of those that have voluntary purposes to become his servants,

It is conceived that the Constable, who was left for us at Paris, shall remayne with the armye in Brittanie (where force shalbee needfull), and the King returne to have aydes to the Low Coun-tryes army where he shall finde another manner of avenge.

Although it be very true that the same was in great misery before theis last supplies came to Callais, which are notwithstanding a miserable company but that they are naturall Spaniards for the most part, and so more trustie to reinforce two garrisons.

The Governor of this towne haveinge longe attended for us was constrayned to goe to Kilbevy where hee hath much of the sea preparations which are intended for Brittanye, and is appointed to be Admirall there. But hee hath left his Lewetenant Governor heere who is ready to afford us all good usage.

On Tuesday wee meane to goe to Roan to bedd, where likewise Mounsier de Montpensier remayneth. Wee are informed that there are ten or twelve thousand men left ready to defend the ffrontiers. How true it is wee know not but by the Marshall Byron, Generall of those troopes in his government of Burgoigne.

Thus haveing troubled your Lordshipps long wee doe humbly take our leaves, being desirous to take the first comoditie of sending back as wee doe by this gentleman towards my Lord of Essex, who came over with Sir Allexander Ratcliffe for company and is returned from Deepe the xixth of February.

Directed to the Lord Treasurer, the Earl Marshal and the Lord Admiral of England.

The xxth of this moneth there was another written by the comissioners to the Lords wherein was sent another letter of Mr Edmonds brought from Paris by old Painter, by whome the dispatch following was sent into England. 20 Febr.

May it please your good Lordshipps. In the enclosed addressed to me, the Secretary, from her Ma^{ts} agent at Paris, there is expressed a discourse delivered unto him by the Marshall Byron, whereby your Lordshipps may perceave how necessarie it wilbee for us to present our selves to the Kinge before any conference had by us with his ministers, and how unwillinge the Kinge seemeth to bee wee would have speech or discourse with the Constable untill wee shall first have spoken to him.

Moreover wee thinke it fitt in our owne opinions and agreable with our instructions that wee take our ymediate light first from the King whose disposition wee shall best discerne, and by the meanes of our aboade unto him shall have meanes the better to discover the trueth of thinges, therby to direct our courses in this.

The furthest places of our travaile (as wee conceave) wilbee Towers or Argieres, and both in good countryes ffor the comodity of passage by waters, victualls and other necessaryes for our present uses.

The other part of Mr Edmonds letter wee humblie leave to your Lordshipps grave consideration, haveing thus breiflie noted unto you so much as doth confirme our resolution to passe with as convenient diligence as wee may to the Kings presence as most availeable to her Ma^{ts} service, hopeing, though our journey bee further then wee thought yet beginning in the right place, first that wee shall drawe our selves and others afterwards nearer to finish in some other place as much as by our instructions (which specially tend to matters of inquisitions) wee are directed.

Att Deepe xxth of February.

[*Marginal note:* 21th]   The xxlth the comissioners and all the gentlemen dyned with the Governor, being therto solemnly invited.

[*Marginal note:* 22th]   The 22th wee removed from Deepe to Roan and dyned by the way at Tobas, to which place the Governor of Deepe brought us.

Heere Mounsieur Villers mett with us and brought us to Roan, being accompanyed with some 20 gentlemen well horst, being sent of purpose as it should seeme by Mounsieur Montpensier, who did himself meet with the comissioners halfe a mile out of Roan, and conducted them to their lodgeinge, being L` Hostell Vanderell, where the Duke Montpensier had caused a chamber to bee hung with very rich hangings of his owne with a faire bed for Mr Secretary.

[*Marginal note:* 23th.]   This daie the comissioners and all the gentlemen dyned with the Duke, of whome they had great enterteynement.   And in the evening the gentlemen were invited to a banquet and danceing.   The Premiez President of this towne came to visitt Mr Secretarie.

This day Sir Henry Davers and Mr Edmonds arrived in this towne from Paris.

[*Marginalnote:* 24th]   This 24th a dispatch was sent to the Lords.

[*Marginal note:* 25th]   The 25th Sir Thomas Wilkes fell dangerously ill of a feaver.   Mr Edmonds retorned to Paris.

[*Marginal note:* 27th]   The 27th the dispatch following was made to the Lords and sent by Jasper, Sir John Stanhops man.

[*Marginal note:* Dispatch to the Lords the 27th February.]

May it please your Lordshipps.   Since wee did joyne in letter to your Lordshipps of the fower and twentieth, being ready to depart from hence to Paris, to which Sir Thomas Wilkes subscribed, it hath pleased God to our no small greif to visitt him with a very sharpe feaver full of badd accidents and sweatings, contynuall sleeping and great decaye of strength universallie.

Hee hath beene ill disposed ever since our comeing to Dover, but since our landinge in appearance throughlie mended.   By this accident our stay hath bene here very longe ever since Wensday, at which tyme wee resolved to have parted on Friday towards Paris.   But now that it appeareth that the best that can bee lookt for is a slow recovery, wee have thought it very necessary to depart.   And if it bee Gods pleasure that hee doe recover, wee hope hee may come after us to Paris by that tyme wee are returned from the King, and then assist us when all such persons shalbee assembled that must joyne in conference.

In the meane tyme wee have caused consultations of physitians and have left a very honest man of his acquaintance named Breasda for to attend him, though his estate in such a nature must more shew itself then medicine.   Wee are right sorry of this misfortune and pray to God to alter it, to whose pleasure and providence wee must committ it.   And soe wee humbly take our leave.

From Roan xxviith of Febr.

This very day, after the finishinge of this dispatch, Mr Secretary and Mr Harbert removed from Roan towards Paris. They lay the first night at Margene and Mounsieur Villiers accompanyed them in the way some 4 or 5 myles.

[*Marginal note :* 28th. Pontois] The 28th they came to Pontois and were lodged att the Archbishopp of Roanes possessed by Mounsieur de Allen Court who is sonne to Mounsieur Villeroye, the Kinges Principall Secretary.

The Governor of this towne was said to bee here though he shewed not himself. And his wife lay sick in the towne. Mr Secretary sent Mr Phillips to visitt her.

Here the carrier that was sent from Deepe to the Kinge mett with us and brought a letter to Mr Secretary in answeare of his the xixth.*

There was also at the same tyme another letter of the King written to Mounsieur de la Bodire with which Mr Secretary was made accquainted.*

March 5. Paris.

The first of March wee came to Paris and dyned by the way at St Dennys, where some tyme was spent before dynner in veiwing the monuments of the church.

Mr Edmonds mett us on the way betweene Paris and St. Dennys, and conducted Mr Secretary to his lodgeing, being a faire and spacious howse of the Duke Montpensiers in the streete called Rue de Cock.

[*Marginal note :* 2] This day Mr Secretary was visited by divers as Mounsieur de Maissie, Seigniour Cantorini, Agent for the State of Venice, Anthony Peres and Mounsieur Madeny, Agent for the States of the Lowe Countryes.

[*Marginal note :* 3] The third of this moneth Mr Secretary writt to the Lords the dispatch following :

May it please your Lordshipps. Wee are now arrived at Paris soe farr onward on our way to the King, haveing made our journeys the lesse because wee were desirous to find some answere there of the letter which I, the Secretary, writt to the King upon my arrivall at Deepe, which hath fallen out accordinglie as may appeare by this letter inclosed, as also by the coppy of a letter written to his M^r d'Hostell which attends us this voyage, which wee have thought good alsoe to send to your Lordshipps because it conteynes some particulers.

It is very true that the nearer wee draw to the center of this kingdome, the more wee gather of the state wherein th'affaires doth presently stand, of which for the present your Lordshipps may assure your selves of this one thing : that this country that hath endur'd a warre of that perpetuity both needeth and affecteth peace universallie. And howsoever it may bee well argued that the makeing of peace will give Spaine breath and meanes to prevaile in any enterprize against all his enemyes hereafter when his appetite shall serve him to breake out into warre, yet this is

---

* For these letters, *see* PRO. S.P. 78 (France), Vol. 41, pp. 185 and 186.

firmely stood upon by all here (and not without reason) that by the same repose Ffraunce, of any country in the world, will soonest flourish upon laying down of armes. So as if the consideration of breaking ffaith with her Mat^ie and others were no more dangerous then it is for any enequallity betweene the good that Spaine and Ffrance shoulde gett by being particulerly conferred one with another, there is no questestion [*sic*] but France should receive good by concluding a peace upon any equall conditions, though it were sure to fall to warr againe within few yeares.

If therefore your Lordshipps now observe how likely Spaine is to bee weary of French ffaith when Marcurye upon excesse of the King personally in to Brittanie with small force is farr onwards to become the Kinges servants all, that every particuler towne and place makes hast to acknowledge him, Dynan and Vaneez being reduced, and the composition of Ansennys and Rochforte, one of the Duke of Mercuryes principall fortresses, with many others being yesterday ratified by Parliament, so as even in that province, to which the King of Spaine may pretend most right, hee is abandoned and onely thrust into one coyne at Blavet.

Wee doe then thincke your Lordshipps will gather, seeing each of the partyes that have infested him can never now trust one another, that if Ffraunce had ever collor to urge his allyes to beleeve that Spaine will conclude, hee is now best provided.

Wherin I for my part, I, the Secretary, have bene bold at all tymes to deliver myne humble opinion, that whensoever Spaine will come to any reason, no consideration of former promises, oathes, benefitts or obligations of honoor should make it to bee refused here. Not that I imagine so of the Kinge in whome there is great virtue and sincerity, but for other respects which your Lordshipps can judge, and whereof I have in my dispatch from Roan spoken freely to her Majestie, being bold onely to affirme thus much :

That when the match is to bee playd between the Councell, the Nobillity and the Popular of Ffraunce on the one side, and the Kinge onely on the other, the odds is rather to be laid on the plurallity then the unitye.

And therefore the more wee looke into our imployment wee thincke wee may the more renewe to your Lordshipps memoryes that, fforasmuch as concernes the preparation to a treatye, conteynes :

Ffirst, wee are like onely to make this fruit of our negotiation, to justifie the Queene to the world that she is not alienated from a Christian disposition, wherein your Lordshipps will hardly imagine how sinisterly the generallity are possessed to the contrary, wherein our comeing hath done her great honoor. Although by all our discourses and our compaynes wee doe divulge that, seeing God hath blessed her Mat^ie with so greate successe against her enemyes, shee will never heare of any conditions but such wherein both honor and safetie above all thinges shalbee concluded.

Secondly, wee shall take from the King his advantage to say

that if her Matie would have harckned, shee mighte have bene included.

And lastly, wee shall doe that which can never bee expected by his ministers (who are compounded of nothinge but severall partiallityes) namely, to discover and distinguishe him from them, especiallie takeing this course, though to other provinces, to bee nearer with him, and to learne that, by often discourseing and abrupt speeches, which by a formall artificiall speech will be disguised, ffor whosoever knowes him must know that any man of meane judgment may well distinguish his art from nature. But for any hope that wee can make preparation to a second treaty with the Spaniard for peace and truce, it is not to be looked for, seeing such is the mixture of her Ma^{ts} estate with the Estates fortune. And such is their constitution and resolution (although the Spaniard shall have power and all authority) as I, the Secretary, doe particulerly knowe it, that they come instructed to refuse to treate if they were offred *la Charta Blanche.* Soe as wee doubt not but your Lordshipps see for that point that theis are matters *opposita in subjecto.*

The case therefore is plaine that wee shall temporize it and shall make a journey of inquisition to see what may bee expected of France, whether it will leave his freinds either nowe or here-after, wherein as wee might feare by externall circumstances to bring present newes of peacemakeing in France. If wee did not suspect that the Cardinalls treatye will breake out into some enterprize in Picardye upon Monstreal or Bulloine, or if wee lapped not in that helpe with which the Estates may disswade him, wee should little trust to that which our just arguments or our enumeration of benefitts past or true representation of her Ma^{ts} present estate in her affaires could be able to doe with him and his Councell. For where wee might justly argue that the King, being now soe farr onward as he is, need not now hearken to a peace but upon condition of honor and advantage, I, the Secretary, know it already by good meanes that there hath bene consultation already, what is like wee will not say, who they suspect are onely come to wynne tyme with them, and therefore that his ministers are provided to say to us (if wee urge that) *Alons donc faire one armie pour chaser les,** a matter to which I know the States care not to inflame him and meane to ayde him.

To which if your Lordshipps will say that is true, it is wee shall reply, as wee intend to doe, that the King of himself is now provided better then ever and that his necessities bee now diminished. His ministers will answere flatly negativelie that without some depose or great assistance theire possibillityes are not able yet to keepe an armye together, but by eating out the people who will not longer endure it.

Wherein, though wee intend to give little way to their argu-ments of necessityes, yet your Lordshipps may please to beleeve

---

* The original despatch in PRO, S.P. 78 (France), Vol. 41, p. 214 reads: " Alons donc faire une armee pour chasser les Espaignols tout a un coup hors du pais bas."

that although it is meerelie the disorder of France that increaseth his wants, yet an argument that God will have it soe, your Lordshipps may understand this for certaine that, now that an allarum is come hither of the gathering of forces to some head and drawing of artillery together by the Cardinal of Picardye (supposed for Monstruel and Bulloigne) the Constable is not provided of any body of an army worth any thinge, nor able to give one dynner to any of the garrisons to releive them.

Compagnelle for Bulloigne and the Viscount Auchye for St. Quintines telling him and the Councell here, since I came to the towne, that neither of them had bread, munition or men, to keepe a place 5 daies.

Here was also with me, the Secretary, a French gentleman of the Religion, Lewetenant of La Nouee his regiment which is in St. Quintynes, and with him one Deale that came over with Mr Sackville that dyed valiantly in Normandy, who hath a company there, who both vowed unto mee that if the Cardinall sett downe before St. Quintins hee would carry it in ffower dayes, that more then one monethes bread neither captaines nor souldiers have had this 5 monethes day, that of 1500 there are not 600, and that because they are of the Religion and those whome the King ever sends soonest to a place of danger, they were answer'd hee could not lett them to have a lyvre.

They that treate doe lye at a place called Vervin, which is six leagues of St. Quintynes, a newtrall burghe, and 5 leagues about it there is a truce whilst they sitt, the Legate being at the boards end. A pretty distance from the table is a moderator. Hee lay in St. Quintynes when hee went thither, and had much speech with this French gentleman which shall serve for another dispatch, hee haveing beene with me, the Secretary, two or three tymes, and being well affected and a wise gentleman, and one that is not ignorant of many particulers.

Wee thinke by our next letters wee shall give your Lordshipps the newes that the King is in Nants, in which respect wee doe slacken our journey because wee may have thereby to meete him about Towers, which being the quarter in which the Duchesse of Beauforts wilbee brought a bedd, and here wee are surest to have him oftenest.

Besides wee hope that the Estates deputies will not be long after us or at least, if they bee contented to treate without comeing to the King, wee may come back to this place by that tyme they are here, and hope to find Sir Tho : Wilkes able to come hither.

Wee meane to goe out of this towne on Wednesday at the furthest, and to be rather in travaile in the heate of theis devotions then to tarry heere in this greate citty, being so insolent a place where nothing but robbing and cutting of throates is practised every hower of the night.

Besides on Sunday sennight is the Kinges Easter whome wee will not trouble before that ffeast.

Wee have bene very well used everyewhere by all Governors

where wee came and in this place, though wee were not mett by the officers of the citty, who have the priviledge never to meete any but the Kinge, yet have they bene in the howse where I, the Secretary, am lodged (being L'Hostell de Montpensier) with us and made a solemne oration how the King recomended the good usage of us and how much Ffrance is bound to her Matie, for all which wee have thanks. And I, the Secretary, tould them that as it was a contentment for her Matie to have been able so much to have steaded France, soe it would be very agreable to her to have it confessed of their mouthes.

Thus have wee laid before your Lordshipps for her Ma^{ts} satisfaction where wee are and what wee purpose, wherein (though it bee true that rolling stones gather noe mosse) yet wee hope your Lordshipps shall finde that wee shall make some profitt by the way, and that wee will effectually urge what is conteyned in our instructions, though wee thinke it not amisse to let your Lordshipps knowe both what is provided to answere us and how thinges are disposed.

Yesterday Mounsieur de Maissy was with us and the Venetian Ambassador afterwards with many complements with whome I, the Secretary, had much speech at his owne desire, to whome I used all good formallity in which they stand much. And for his satisfaction spent tyme in discourseing of her Ma^{ts} actions by sea against the Kinge of Spaine, and of the reasons and successes wherewith hee was much pleased, and by which hee told mee how much honor shee had gott in the world.

And for the matter present I ledd him as I could from it, onely I used such generall discourse of her Ma^{ts} purposes now and of her indifferent affections as were fitt for the world to know, finding it a decorum to doe so least I should have beene to dry to one that was so large in protestinge the great affection the Seigniorie bare the Queene, and seemed to speake soe playnelie of the King of Spaine, wherewith (as since I understand) hee remayneth very well pleased and said to Anthony Peres hee meant to make a dispatch to the State presently of the corrospondency of her Ma^{ts} Ambassadors held with him.

Anthony Peris hath also beene with mee, the Secretary, and hath very good respect and gratefully acknowledgeth all the Queenes favors to him, and his obligation being truely in all his words very respective to my selfe, and very freelie and kindly discovering his mynd, neither is hee ignorant of many particulers of the mannors and humors of this court, of which I may make some use, the gent[leman] deserveing courteous usage and thanks of mee.

Thus have wee for dutyes sake delivered your Lordshipps an accompt of our proceedings wherein wee must and doe submitt our selves to her Ma^{ts} acceptation, of whose saftie and your Lordshipps well doing it wilbee great comfort if wee may heare, for which as wee are bound wee daylie pray. And so most humbly take our leaves.

From Paris 3 Martii, 1597.

Postcript. Wee must here also add this one thinge to your Lordshipps, that the Cardinalls lack hath beene this one yeare infinite, and that even with those men here that are wise and yet are apt to undervallue the Queenes succouring of the Kinge of late yeares to any purpose, wee find noe one thing more to stopp their mouthes or with lesse impudencye denyed then when wee shew them the notable fruit which hath risen to the King by the late diversions which her Ma^tye hath made by invadeing the King of Spaine and namely, the last keeping from him of his treasure this long : D. Maissie himself confessing to mee, when I reckoned that in the number of her Ma^ts other helpes to the King, that Richardott talking freely with Mounsieur de Villeroy, who urged him to deale plainly with him whether the Kinge meanes good faith if England would treat, used theis words :

[*Marginal note :* Richardottes words] Blame not my M^r to bee tractable if their [*sic*] bee good meaneing, for shee most galles him and his in keeping his treasure long from him, and spends him half in fetching it home wherein though shee take it not, yet it fareth with him (that hath so many mouthes to stopp and people to releive and cannott) as it doth with a phisitian that finds his patient in a feaver burneing for drouth and sends him a weeke after store of drinck to coole him.

The Provost of the merchants who governes this towne is called Anglois. Hee was in it all the time of the troubles and governed in the pride of the league, and after over-ruled them, and is very remarkeable for his wisdome in this kingdome and betraid the Spaniards with Brisack. Hee hath bene with mee this day and hath discoursed very long with mee, being passionate against the peace out of hate to the league and the Spaniard whome hee would be sorry to trust having betraid them. Hee hath shewed me a letter from Bewlgen, the Secretary, where hee writeth that the composition which D. Mercury is like to have is 200,000 in money and 50,000 franks pension, but to quitt the goverment whollie. They that came to the King were the Queene Dowager, Madam Mercury and her sister Madam Joyeuse, who fell downe att his feete in Towers.

This Provost is very wise and practised in affaires of state and, I see, harkens after them. He told mee privately that theis three ladyes were also with the Kings mistresse, and they hoped by her to prevaile for the goverment of the province hereafter, though in no sort for Nants.

Ymediatlie upon the finishing of this dispatch Mr Corbet arrived with the infortunate newes of Sir Thomas Wilkes, and because noe scandall might rise about his buriall wherein those of Roan were very scrupilous, Mr Secretary gave order for the imbalmeing of his body to be sent into England.

Mr Vaughan, a principall servant of his, writt to Mr Secretary signifying that his necessityes were so great that his servants had not money to defray the charges of his phisick and other nececessaries [*sic*] for which he was indebted there, whereupon

Mr Secretary gave order to one Willaston, a merchant of Roan, to furnish Vaughan with 200 crownes and sent Vaughans letter to the Lords inclosed in their packett.

[*Marginal note:* 6th] The sixt of this moneth Facondar the post arrived with some private letters out of England from the Lord Treasurer, the Earle of Essex, Sir John Stanhoppe and others.

[*Marginal note:* 8th] The viiith another dispatch was made and sent to the Lords by Mr Cannon, agent of the Earle of Derbys, to this effect :

May it please your Lordshipps. Haveing now the opportunitye of this messenger who goeth voluntarily for England, wee have thought it not amisse to move your Lordshipps that, forasmuch as wee cannott yet heare any thing of the Estates deputyes wherein there can bee nothing as the wind hath served but a voluntary slacknesse, it will please your Lordshipps to move her Matie that, if they have resolved of some such artificiall delay, that wee may not be tyed to their grosse comeinge, but haveing dealt with the King according to our instructions and seene what language doth hold, to come our wayes into England whereby the affayres may be still kept in dispute, which can bee noe losse to the Queene to contynue, and the scandall of unwillingnesse to treate, if faith bee meant by the Spannish Kinge, may yet bee taken from her Matie and laid upon them, who haveinge made this sweete of theire sower are fittest for the obloquie of practise and private partiallties.

Thus much doe wee write now out of jelousie of this stay and with desire to receave some provisionall direction because the dependancye on dispatches (when seas are to bee passed) are neither safe nor speedy, if otherwise it happen before these letters come it was but our labour to write, and that for which wee would not have dispatched expresslie any bodye to your Lordshipps.

This day wee cannott stirr till noone in respect of the processions for the reduction of Brittanye which are soe solemnely performed. And soe wee humbly take our leaves of your Lordshipps.

From Paris 8º Martii, 1597.

This letter was noe sooner written but Mounsieur Resels arrived with a letter from the Kinge which (albeit the Comissioners were ready to take horse when it came) was forthwith inclosed in another letter and sent to the Lords.

[*Marginal note:* Chatree. Estampes] This day the Comissioners removed from Paris and came that night to Chatree to bedd. The next day to Estampes to dynner and to Egervaile to bedd.

[*Marginal note:* 10th] The 10th they came to Arteny to dynner and to Orleans to bedd. The Marshall de Castre who governes this towne met with the Comissioners about a league out of the towne, being accompanyed with divers gentlemen of good quallity to the number of some 50 or 60 horse.

Mr Secretary was lodged at a comon inn called the *Escue* in the markett place.

[*Marginal note:* 11] This day Mounsier Ansell came to visitt him, and the townesmen presented wynes and sweetmeates.

[*Marginal note:* 12] The next day being their Easter Day the Marshall Byron himself, de Chastre and Mounsieur Margaosie came to Mr Secretaryes lodging to visitt him. John Wells was sent post from hence to Mounsieur Villeroy to signifie the arrivall of the Comissioners in their towne and their intent to come to the King with all speed.

[*Marginal note:* 13] The 13th of this moneth the Comissioners tooke boate on the river of Loyre to passe to Angiers where the King was the first night.

[*Marginal note:* Bloys] They lay at Bloys but came in something late. Mounsieur Mantignye is Governor of this towne.

[*Marginal note:* 14] The next day they removed from thence to Lowers [*sic*] where Mounsieur de Saverye is Governor, who enterteynd them with all shew of kindnesse, and the towne presented them with wyne and sweetmeats.

[*Marginal note:* 15] The 15th at night they came to Lawmore Saresmore [*sic*] where Mounsieur de Plessis doth governe. Hee was with the Kinge at their comeing thither, but his Lewetenant, who is called Mounsieur Peerfets, entertain'd the Comissioners and brought them to theire lodgeing, being a gent[leman's] howse, wherein the King useth to lodge when he comes to this towne. Madam Plessis sent a gent[leman] of hers to salute the Comissioners and her coach to attend them, because they staid there the 16th all day.

[*Marginal note:* 16] This day Mr Edmonds was sent to the King. And Mr Phillips and John Wells sent to take up lodgeings at Angiers.

[*Marginal note:* Pont de Sey. Angiers] They came to Angiers the 17th but landed at Pont de Sey where the Governor gave them kind enterteynement untill such tyme as theire baggage was landed and horses made ready.

The Governor of the province of Anam [*sic*] whose name is Mounsieur Rochpott of the order of the St. Espitte [*sic*] mett with the Comissioners at Pont de Sey, being accompanyed with some 40 or 50 horse, and conducted them to their lodgeing at Angiers. They came to the towne about 5 of the clock in the afternoone.

[*Marginal note:* 18th] The 18th of this moneth the agent of Geneva, who is one of the Sindigz of that citty, came to visitt Mr Secretary at his lodgeing, and so did Mounsieur Villeroye with whome hee had long conference, and after him came Mounsieur de Inquervills.

This day did the Duke Mercwes make his entrance into the towne.

[*Marginal note:* 19th] The King came from a place 3 leagues off where he had hunted and sent Mounsieur de Roquelaure att 11 of the clock of the night to visitt Mr Secretarie.

[*Marginal note:* 21th] The 21th Mr Secretary writt to my

M S—D

Lord Cobham and sent his letter to Mr Willingstone to Roane to bee sent over by the next.

This day the Comissioners had their audience of the Kinge, who had conference with Mr Secretary alone at least 2 houres in his garden. They were brought to the King by the Duke of Bouillon and Mounsieur de Maissie who came to their lodging for them.

After Mr Secretary had done with the Kinge he went to visitt Madam his sister, and delivered her a letter of credence from her Matie and had speech with her neare half an hower.

When they came back to their lodging they found their [*sic*] Mr Bussie, John Symonds and Peter Browne newly arrived out of England.

[*Marginal note:* 22th] The 22 they had their second audience and were brought to see the Kings mistresse, La Duchesse de Beaufforte. Mounsieur le Premer came for them.

[*Marginal note:* 23th] The 23th they had another audience of the King as hee lay in his bed. The Admirall brought them unto him.

[*Marginal note:* 24th] This day the dispatch followinge was made to the Lords and sent by Painter the next day.

[*Marginal note:* Another dispatch to the Lords. 25]

May it please your Lordshipps. Being arrived at Angiers on Ffriday night last, the 27th (i.e. *N.S.*), wee thinke it fitt to give your Lordshipps present knowledge, haveing before bene driven to write such rapsedys as wee take upp *par la rue*, wherein wee thinke your Lordshipps better liked our diligence then if wee should have wholly used silence untill wee had arrived here where the subject of our charge was to bee handled. From the tyme wee landed att Deipe till our recovery of this place there passed 30 dayes over our heads, wherein your Lordshipps may be pleased to take knowledge that wee onely spent in travaile 10 daies of the same, it being more then 310 miles from Deepe hither. The rest was all spent in attending the issue of Sir Thomas Wilkes unfortunate accident, and in expecting answere from the Kinge whome wee were not a little vexed to follow into Brittanie, if wee could as well have avoyded the notorious inconvenyence to her Ma^{ts} service as wee were willing to save our selves an ill journey, the youngest of us both being not humersome now of noveltyes, and neither of us to bee spared where her Ma^{ts} honor and service is in question.

To have hoped for the Kings returne had bene strange and hopeles to us that knew his presence in Brittanie onely made his fortune.

To have treated with his subjects had bene of all the most absurd.

To have retournd without doeing anye thing (if that had bene convenyent) was more than wee durst doe without comission. And therefore after wee came to Paris upon a joynt resolution (when Sir Thomas Wilkes was liveing), wee thought alsoe to stay by the way and at Paris, as wee did that from our landing 19th before wee could stirre our foote from that place being still to have heard from England. But when wee saw noe winde brought us anie direction, and knew the French King would not hazard Brittanie to leave us an ill journey, hee being then to strike *le coup de partie* in that province, where her Ma^ty may bee glad to bee ridd of ill neighbourhood, wee did resolve to neglect all our owne incomoditye and soe came on thus farre where wee arrived the 27th of this moneth (i.e. *N.S.*) whether as many reasons ledd us as there was reasons to send us over.

Tuesday wee had accesse to the Kinge whome wee did finde accompanyed with the Dukes D. Mercury, Despernon, d'Afonse and De Monthusson, the Marshall de Retts, Saverdyn [*sic*] and Boysdolphin, the Chancellor, the Admirall, the Secretaries and divers others of great quallitie.

Wee were brought to him by the Duke of Bouillon and Mounsieur de Maissie and others. I, the Secretary, did deliver him her Ma^ts letters and kind salutations with all due complements, and assured him of her great contentment to heare of his good fortunes, and told him how her Matie had charged me particulerly to informe my self of his good health to the end to advertize her by my next comoditye whereof I was glad to bee able to send soe good newes.

I told him further that forasmuch as princes, whose jurisdiction and dignity hindred them from personal conference of their affaires, were constrained to serve themselves of some confident ministers by whose mouth they might discover their inward meaneing, it hath pleased my soveraigne out of this consideration (that those ought ever to be faithfull whoe were tyed in straightest bonds) to make election of mee, though otherwise of little meritt, whome she had made her creature to comunicate unto him her secrett and princely thoughts when it should please him to discover his owne disposition and judgement of this project of a generall treatye, wherto shee had beene so invited by Mounsieur de Maissie his propositions.

This I did tell him was the generall subject of our legation, wherein wee were comaunded precisely to addresse our selves to his owne person before any further conference with any of his subjects, to the intent wee might govorne our selves in all things with all others according to his advise and councell. Ffor howsoever shee had yeilded for his satisfaction to engage herselfe thus farr as to depute us hither, and whatsoever assurance Mounsieur de Maissie had given her of the inclynation of the comon enemye, yet shee was soe farr from beleife of any good meaneinge in the contrary partye as shee still thought it fitt to resolve all resolutions untill shee had fetcht her true light from himself, who can best tell how great a stranger shee was to this cause. And forasmuch as in a matter of this weight it was very necessary that their advise and judgement should be used whome longe experience had well instructed in affaires of state, it pleased her Matie to honor mee at this tyme with the company of two of her ffaithfull servants whome I then desired to associate and assist me in this service, whereof Almighty God hath taken one to my extreame greife, and left mee this other, whome therewithall I tooke by the hand and did present according to the substance of my letter of creditt, which he did read very curiouslie.

Hee did receave us with very respective forme and did pronounce in all theire hearings his thancks to her Majestie for her great favor, which though it could not make her affection great beinge such alreadie (said hee) as speech could not deliver, yet did this manner of dealinge with him both in the forme and substance multiply his obligation. Hee had bene longe her servant, and hee held himself and his estate next under God confirmed by her, who would acknowledge it in whatsoever quallitye fortune should bestowe him. For the care of his health hee humbly thanked her, and thought himselfe unhappie in nothinge more then in that hee had not seene the same perfections which meane men (whose fortune he did envy) had to their contentment beheld with admiration, desireing mee to tell him truely in what disposition of body I now did leave her.

Whome I did answer that (God bee thanked) shee was when I came out of England according to her custome *come ceste Princesse qui na jamais senty que ceste de maladie.*

Thus much being passed and our resolution being for the first daye to passe noe more then a complementall audience, where all the princes should approach soe neere him whome wee wished should bee the witnesses of nothing els but his sensible and publique acknowledgment of his obligation and respect towards her Majestye.

I, the Secretary, made request unto him because the tyme and place was now improper for any further particularityes, that hee should yeild mee some other accesse where with more freedome hee mighte understand what wee had in comission, beseeching him for this tyme onely to permitt mee so much favor as to present the Count of Southampton who was come with deliberation to doe him service.

Hee said I should with all his heart the next morneing have accesse, and then embraced and welcomed him. And afterward, when I presented to him all the rest whome I described to be most of them her Ma^ts servants of very good place and all gentlemen well borne, hee did the like to them, and soe suddainely tooke me by the hand contrarie to myne expectation, saying hee would walke with mee downe into the garden *en qualitye de amy*, where he entertayned mee an hower and a halfe with many pleasant and familliar discourses of his opinion of diverse of his subjects and other particulers not fitt for paper nor of necessity now though fitt to bee related at other tymes, wherein when he had pleased himselfe hee brake forth very abruptly into theis words, (eh bien) I have bene sorry to find that it hath beene soe confidently beleived amongest yow that the Kinge of Spaine despiseth to compound with mee as being a poor prince, my subjects halfe masters, and I therfore contemptible. And that it hath not pleased her Matie to hold more comon councell and corrospondency with mee in her designes upon the Kinge of Spaine, wherein hee doubted not to have done her service. For hee must deale plainely with mee that, notwithstandinge they were noblie begunn and ended, yet unlesse her Majestie did make the warre of another fashion and followe it with a more constant resolution, the greatest purse in tyme must ever spend the lesse for himselfe. Though hee were naturally affected to armes and had made it his profession, yet hee was by Gods ordinance a kinge of people and made it a conscience needlesselie to waste them. Neither was hee of soe meane judgement as not to discerne how great a scandall it were for him to beere the imputation of such an ambition or irreligion as when it was offred him by peace which could not be bought with blood, that hee should disdayne to heare of it for his owne good and his allyes, assuring mee that howsoever the power of other princes was absolute over theire subjects, yet durst not hee adventure their suspicion of being carelesse of what became of his kingdome, either in respect hee wanted children or tooke a glory in the fortune of armes, in the which hee confessed on his soule hee tooke more delight then in all the professions of the world. Howsoever, said hee, I am censured amongst yow to bee sould over to idlenes and delight wherin I will confesse God hath made me a man. And as I know my frailty to bee a scarre in my forehead, soe the circumstance of my misfortune considered, if I bee not guilty of other villanyes I doubt but I may be numbred (if not among the better sort) yet not amongst the vilest ranck of princes.

I told him that for the first report, it might easilie bee answeared with trueth itselfe which needed noe other helpe, ffor I could assure him it was soe farre contrarie to my hearinge and knowledge as I durst avowe the relator to him was the first and only author. And for any conceipt that hee should bee despiseable for his poverty I must use libertye of plainenesse that it was a paradox to others that a kinge of Ffraunce should bee in such necessity, haveing now noe one subject unreduced ; assureing him with humble suite of pardon that the comon discourses of tyme did feare that some who governd his affaires did represent his owne lacks the greater to the intent to drawe him into some other courses more to theire likeinge. Att which hee smiled and told mee hee knew whome I meant.

I told him so did not I, but thus I further proceeded with him that all that looke with single eyes upon the Kinge of Spaine handling this matter (in seekeing him alone) doe fully thinke that as hee would bee glad by single contract with him to have the lesse to doe awhile, so should it bee with noe other finall purpose then to worke his ruyne by the meane of such seperation. And for her Ma[tie], if shee had not held him deare when he was weakest, shee would not have sought soe much to restore him. Neither needed shee nowe have bene unreconciled to Spaine if either her ffreindshipp or judgment had bene soe weake as to have forsaken other quarrells. For the second point of her Ma[ts] not comunicating with him her designes in particulers :

Ffirst, I must bee bold to remember him, haveing had the honor to understand somewhat of them, that her Majesty did ever accquaint him in generall with her purpose of makeing warre on the comon enemye. Although under his pardon I must bee bold to say that hee was never pleased to allowe of any thinge to bee done upon the Kinge of Spaine but in Ffraunce onely, where although I could not deny but her Ma^{ty} by enjoying great numbers with him might have furthered some of his particuler desires, yet had shee thereby wholie kept herself exposed to the fleet of Spaine ffrom which no action of his in Ffraunce would have secured her. And as it pleased God to prosper her in the first action at Cales, where her forces did bring awaye of his greatest shipps and utterly consumed all the rest besides his infinite magazines of sea preparations, soe could it not but [*sic*] be denyed but by that very action of diversion hee was mightily assisted to his owne enterprizes whilst the Cardinal was kept here in weaknes by reason hee was forced to keepe all at home to defend himself, desireing him to remember this last yeares action also, so fresh in memory, whereby he had so good successe at Amyens. And whereof also the Estates of the Lowe Countryes made theire advantage by encountringe an enemy who was the more infested with all manner of lacks and miseryes by her Ma^{ts} diversion and occupation of his treasure and forces.

So as her Majestie had given sufficient proofe of her contynuall care and labor to assist him, though shee had lent him never a man to serve him, which shee did still notwithstanding to her greate charge in the tyme when her affaires at home in both her kingdomes were in termes of greater difficultye then they had bene at any tyme since 88.

Att this he did a little change his manner and said abruptly, *Mounsieur Cecil, je le confesse tout vouz avez raison. Je men acquietray envers ma seur et facon d'home de bien.* And soe haveing heard before that wee desired to see Madam hee said, yow shall now goe to my sister, and soe departed.

Wee went thither and I, the Secretary, delivered her Ma^{ts} letters with all complements and assurance of her good will, lettinge her understand that I had charge to crave accesse to her to informe her more particulerlye of any thing at her best leisure, and to assure her of her Ma^{ts} readynes to employ herself in any thinge wherein shee might stead her, with divers other French ceremoniall phrases which are now soe usuall as they will make mee forgett my Paternoster.

All was accepted from her Majestie with very great affection and wee were courteouslie receaved. Shee was well painted, ill dressed and strongley jewelled, but well accompanyed with a number of great ladyes, the Duchesse of Mercurye, Madam Longuevill, Madam de Roan, Maddam Mombasson, Madam Mountaban, Madam Belisle and divers others.

The next morneing, being Wednesday, hee did send to mee to excuse himselfe till after dynner, being ill disposed, and then sent Mounsieur de Premier about 4 of the clock for us, who waites in the place of Mounsieur de Grand. The King did much intreat mee to goe in to see his mistris and his sonne. Shee is with child and truely a faire and delicate woman. I stayed little to speake with her, and yet shee is very well spoken and courteous, and spake of her Matie with very great respect and wished shee would once comaunde her.

Then the King tooke mee into the garden and told mee hee would crave pardon for speech of any matter of state that night but onely minister matter of sport because it was late, but the next daye I should have a cabinet audience, and nowe onely talke and bee merry. Hee then did tell mee all the particulers of Mercuryes proceedinges, how the Spaniard and Mercury brake about Nannts which they would have had, which hee refused, and so all fell in peices. Hee told mee also that hee had putt off Mercuryes entry hither till our comeinge, whose presence hee was sure did vex him. I answered that hee needed not bee offended with us, for wee were glad hee did soe well. True it is that all the people, when he came in, cryed out upon him, *Voycy la queue de la ligue, vooycy le petit roy de Bretaigne.* Afterward hee passed the tyme in familliarity both in discourse of the Queene and her court, showing to diverse the picture of her Matie that I wore.

After two howers stay wee returned and the next day hee sent for us into his cabinett where he was in bedd, and then att very great length gave audience ; haveing heard before I came hither that the King called those which spake sett tales *les harranguers follastres*, and finding in my discourse with him what forme was to bee used towards him, and being above all other thinges desirous to make advantage of driveing him to open himselfe by first speakeing, I did shortly and provisionally resolve to beginne myne audience onely with a short preface and to confine my selfe to these heads followinge :

Ffirst, that it was not my purpose to trouble him now with long discourse or formallityes, for as I might well thinke in that to doe wrong to the judgement of a prince, which could judge so well and was charged with soe many affaires, soe was it little needfull seeing I came from a prince that hath given proofe of her amitye by effects and not by words and protestations.

Secondly, that the Queene our soveraigne had not sent us to diswade him from makeing a peace without his allyes because shee should thereby doe her self wrong as well as him, insomuch as once to doubt him, for besides that shee knew his owne wisdome would foresee the ill of it, shee was sufficiently reposed [upon] an assurance that he was a prince of honnor, faith and gratefulness. Neither was it other then injustice for any prince to suspect that in another which they would be loath should be doubted in themselves.

Thirdly, that shee sent us not hither with perswasion that any offers which came from the fraudulent enemyes carryed any trueth, but onely to satisfy the straight amity betweene them, and to make him see how much shee would repose herselfe upon

that which should passe the ffyle of his judgemente, haveing not
a little ventured her honnour to send us thus farre, whereby the
world might conceive shee sollicited him to mediate a peace for
her, being also not assured whethere there were such sufficyent
power or noe as shee should thinke to treate with the Kinge of
Spaine if hee would inclyne to it.

Ffourthly, that shee had not a mynd alienated from generall
peace for anye particuler interest, haveing justly satisfyed herself
with revenge sufficiyent on her enemyes and not extending herself
to any further desires then to conserve her owne right and honnor
to preserve her freynds.

Ffithly, that shee desired now particulerly by him to bee
cleared what the offers were, and what in his owne judgement
hee did beleive of them, and how hee did deliberate to embrace
the peace, and finally, above all other thinges, to knowe how
they could thinke the Estates might be proceeded withall in case
they refuse to bee comprised in the treaty, seeing they deserved
especiallye to bee cared for, both for the honor and obligation
of ffaith given them, and alsoe for the interest which both theire
realmes have in their conservation.

Hee heard mee all this with great attention and answeared
mee :

Ffirst, that hee was gladd I was not a Venetian, and that hee
loved to negotiate with the Earle of Essex for hee leaves circumstances, soe as hee saw wee served a wise prince. Rethoriques
was for pedants. Hee could now truely and freely answere mee
and not as hee answered ordinarye ambassadors, seeing the
Queene had sent her tabletts.

Ffirst, hee did thanke the Queene that shee would not mistrust
him, for what any creature possible could doe hee would doe by
her councell. And if hee were to loose nothing but life, hee
would quitt it for her. As for her feare to bee scandalized by
sending soe farre especiallie to him, hee desired mee to thinke
her Majesty in that did runn noe danger, for shee sent not to
her enemy but to a freind, to a Kinge and her brother, to one
that made it knowne to all the world that hee honored her and
that hee desired it. If hee had drawne us after him for pleasure,
it had beene another matter, but hee protested hee did tarry for
us ffive weekes to the perill of all Brittany, soe as the world saw
his necessity. Ffor yet neither had hee or would hee bee neg-
ligent to shew in us the respect hee bare his sister before all other
princes liveing.

Ffor the power of Spaine hee doubted not but by Sonday it
would bee certified for the carrier was returned to Fflaunders.

Ffor her Ma^{ts} suspicion of the enemyes offres hee had so long
so thought himselfe, for he knewe nothing but necessity drave
him to seeke him, and thus malice would never cease.

But now hee told mee upon his honor and as he desired absolu-
tion of his sinnes, hee would truely tell mee all. The enemye
offred him all but Callais, and that onely now of late hee stuck
to deliver untill some triall, but presently to contract for it,

which hee said was not a matter one way or other that ought to make or marre the matter.

And for the Spaniards meaneing towards the Queene, hee made this judgment, neither did the contrary side conceal, that his losses were infinite. Ffor, saith hee, her interrupting by sea doe mightily charge him and consume him, a matter for which the Queene is to bee comended. Ffor I confesse the Queene hath hurt him and not I, but hee mee. And therefore if hee can with good conditions make an end, hee were madd not to bee contented. And if I make him shew a power to treate with the Queene, shee haveing given none to treate with him, doe not I an honest worke?

Beleeve (saith hee) I pray yow, that though his affaires by private faction and disorder doe not prosper, yet if there bee no remedy his councell and his purse will eat out the Queene of England and us all. And therefore now is the time to consider. I have dealt faithfully with my sister, and the more because I see shee doth in this sending respect mee, ffor if I would beleeve what hath bene beaten into myne eares, I am told that your drift is to amaze mee to leave mee in the warre ever, and to accompt that your safety. But I am not of that ffaith. And yow doe see that though I may have good offers, yet I have forborne till I may bring in others.

I answeared him that for these calumniations theye were ever used by malitious spiritts but never creditted by princes against those whose actions were soe contrary.

Ffor the offers hee had her Matie beleeved it, as I told him before ; but for any forwardnes for others, ffirst, I say it failed in the originall beginninge for his freinds because neither the power was seene nor the conditions yet seconded.

Hee answered, that was true, but I should here [sic] now furthwith. And for conditions betwene England and Spaine, they were easily agreed. The difficulty was for the States for whome (saith hee) must wee bee still miserable in perpetuity.

I told him that was the knotty question and untill that were decided, there could bee no sure resolution, in which I left them that were wise men to speake for themselves.

Hee asked mee this, but what thinke yow. I made difficulty till hee pressed mee. And then I answeard that I heard many wise men hold it for infalliable, that it were a strange apprehension to all his neighbors to behold a Kinge of Spaine by conquest or contract owner absolutely of all the seaventeene provinces.

Hee rose upp to mee and said I was an honest man, hee loved mee for myne opinion, but, saith hee, use no such speech to my councell that I say so.

I then asked him what his judgment was how thinges should be carryed.

Hee then told mee that the Estates would bee with him on Satterday, that hee and I should meete as onely to passe the tyme, and that hee would tell mee what they said and what

Barnavelt would doe, who is myne. (Saith hee) there is but two wayes, either I shalbee driven to all necessity and fury of my people who are ready to rebell for peace, or my frends must helpe mee, which I see yow meane not, by maynteyneing the warre and in helping mee. Heare I pray yow therefore (saith hee), seeing you will have warre, speake with my councell, heare there [sic] reasons. I will assign yow Villeroy and Massie. Shew them what the Queene will doe for a warre.

I answered him that I feared I had already passed my comission to speake openly. But his favourable usage and comandement made me bold and forgetfull. To meet with his counsell I and my fellow were ready at his pleasure. But to deliver the Queens mynd for a warre was not the ground of our comission, wee being sent to see the bottome of the likelyhood or safetye of a treatye. And yet I desired him to consider that the Queene was in a warre and soe reckoned her charges and her expenses at large, which I thinke he had never patience to heare before himselfe, neither should I have told him now but that hee was in bed.

Hee denyed many of theis particulers, in which I answered him. And then he said. I was sonne to the Treasurer.

I told him also that my soveraignes case was worst of all the three, for his fortune by her helpe encreased, the Estates grew rich, and she had newe fires kyndled still, and yet new importunityes, so as her trouble was *infinitum*.

Well, saith hee, it is a strange message, when a man is in need and wants, to heare of others lacks and former helpes. If the Queene will propound her minde what warre shee would have to be made (saith hee) I will urge nothing but upon good consent. And because yow told mee yesterday I never liked anything but my owne warres, I say this ; if my plotts be not allowed good, lett the Queene of England, if shee be alyenated from a peace, set downe the way of a safe warre, in which the Spaniard may be beaten indeed. And then will I bee found reasonable. But to loose my self and my kingdome, to bee mutined against by my people, it is hard for mee to bee put to it.

I told him that our comission was to deale in that which was propounded by Mounsieur de Maissie, which the Queene was borne in hand should not now have bene unready. For the warre makeing in another fashion wee had noe power to deale with it here.

Well, saith hee, I see yow come to wynne tyme. For my part, I would tyme could be wonne without losse of my kingdome. But if I stand on the defensive now, I loose my reputation. If I lett goe my hold and my offers, my people will rebell against mee, ffor though I have honor to bind mee, yet the feild misery [sic they feel misery]. Collours I have none to breake it. Ffor I can have any thing and if I have my owne, what honor will it bee to mee if it breake after.

I told him that point of a single peace was it which must not bee disputed of, ffor then all leagues were ridiculous. And with

pardon, I must speake it, that if thinges should bee so carryed
(as when one ffreind had helped another to equall his enemy)
hee should then compound with the third enemy for his own
particular advantage without his confederates, I must make
princes take heed of assumeing others quarrells, and make us
that were her Ma^ts poore servants wishe, that if any such strange
accident should followe of which wee never dreamed, that the
Queene had but her money in her hand which shee hath spent
in France and the Lowe Countryes. Wee doubted not but with
the assistance of God in her juste quarrell, Spaine should gett
as little at her Ma^ts hands as hitherto it hath done.

Hee told mee hee liked mee well for my pleynesse, and that
her Ma^ty might trust mee to dispute for her. But seeing then,
saith hee, that yow will not have mee make peace alone, nor
yow may not make peace without the Estates, what is the third
way yow would wish. (Saith hee) propound it.

I told him againe wee came not to propound but to heare and
argue of that which was propounded by Mounsieur de Maissie,
and to consider of it with his councell and the Estates Deputyes.

No, saith hee, then yow will, I perceave, push mee to the wall
still to speake. How would you like it to have us two that are
monarches to make peace with Spaine and make the Estates
make a truce?

I told him it were good to heare the Estates. But if his Matie
would have mee to tell him my poore opinyon, I have ever found
them as jealous of a truce as of a peace, and so I told him the
reasons.

Well then, said hee, what if wee could make a temporall peace
and lett them bee in warre.

I told them [? him] so they might not perish by it, it was least
harmefull.

Well, saith hee, what will meetinge content the Queene. I
desired him to pardon mee, when it came to conference on all
sides it should bee debated.

Hee would needs have mee speake. I told him I saw no cause
why hee that had little to defend but one ffrontyer, and might
bee assisted by the Estates for the present, should not weare the
King of Spaine out of Picardy by little and little, who was old and
tyme would discover what the Cardinalls marriage would prove
to in the Low Countries. And if the Queene might but once
have quietnes in Ireland and have recovered in some of her
owne meanes, if hee were once overpressed, shee would bee the
same that ere shee was to him. Otherwise, if a generall peace
with honor and safety might bee wrought, her Matie was (as I said
before) not alyenated.

Well, said hee, I see that the devise is that I must bee tossed
still, my countrie must be miserable, and no end must bee had.
But, sir, said hee, yow see I deale with you not like an Italian
upon punctoes nor with devises. And the Queene shall see I
will trust yow and negotiate freely with yow for her sake. I
will speake with yow agayne within two dayes. I shall then

know more and I will strive to bethinke mee with yow what course wee maye take which the Queene shall not dislike, unlesse I must smart for all. But I pray, saith hee, use this speech to my councell, that you came not to disswade mee from peace but to see upon what termes of honor and safety the Queene shall venture ; and to see how the Estates may bee included and that the Queene will not abandon them ; but if they may bee safely brought in, that yow doe know the Queene will not bee unreasonable. And the rather because yow find mee soe truely to discover my impossibility to maynteyne a warre and my passionate resolution to comfort my people with a peace. And so heare what wilbee said to yow. And keepe yow on these grounds still which I direct yow with myne, for the Queene your mistrisse will like it well that you should bee rul'd by mee and so hath shee written to me.

Whereat I could hardly forbeare smileing when hee would tell mee what my soveraigne had written. Much more passed but it is impossible to write all. Wee are sorry to bee thus tedious. The affaires of the religion are setled, wherein hee hath much complayned to mee of them. They have sent mee thanks ffor her Matie confessing that they were dispatched more speedilie at our arrivall in tenne dayes then in 40 before.

The King himselfe meerly told mee that when he heard a Hugonite was landed, hee was sure I would bee a spokesman.

I told him her Ma^ty knew Hugonetts were honest men, and I did hope that they should neede no spokesman to him, seeing ffaith and merritt did plead for them.

I [sic? Ay], said hee, I would they had more discretion and patience. The Duke of Bulloigne is here not well contented in some private suite. Hee hath Espernon for his freind who is very sound with the Kinge and counted one of the most able men of France. Hee useth to us great respect and protesteth to owe unto her Majesty obligation for her wishing the Kinge to deale well with him in his late prosecution in Province. St. Aldgone hath broken the matter to the King for Count Maurice to marry Madam. [The] Estates, wee can assure your Lordshipps, came to offer the Kinge contynuance of the former 4000 paid and to increase that charge further.

Whether your Lordshipps or they have informed her Matie of this wee know not. But of this I, the Secretary, have particuler knowledge. They wilbee here to morrow, with whome wee will hold all good corrospondency ; yet Barnavelt is wholy French.

Those of the religion much honor the Queene, but all their counsell is this, the Queene must roundly helpe the Kinge.

Thus have wee now delivered to your Lordshipps an accompt by way of narration of the substance of our accesse. Wee thinke it therefore best becomeing the meane conceit wee have of our owne slender judgment to referre the censure to her Ma^ts wisedome, hoping att our retorne to deliver some such accompt as may justifie our duty and diligence and, if under her Ma^ts gratious pardon wee shalbee comaunded to speake what our weake understanding shall have gathered, wee shall doe it more confidently when wee are, where wee may strengthen our arguments by verball replications better then by letters which may bee intercepted under other collours, and what toyes (for the most part) cipheres are. Seeing the Estates are at hand wee shall have uniformity in our negotiation. Wee doubt not therefore but within ten dayes after to have finished our conference and to bee at the sea side within six dayes after. If your Lordshipps will say that wee were instructed to advertise before wee conclude, wee wilbee bold to lett your Lordshipps knowe that wee neither have or meane to take any liberty of conclusion ffor as your Lordshipps knowe wee came but to enquire, to conferre and to advertise whether wee that heare by common conference find that a treatye may be thought expedient for all parties. Wee thinke therefore that wee shall doe our dutyes sufficiently to advertise personally all such resolutions, ffor seeinge wee are now at Angeirs instead of Roan and that wee have never heard one word from England of fresher date then the xxv[th] of Ffebruary, wee hope your Lordshipps will conceive that wee have small hope of effecting any thing by answeres to any dispatches. This is therefore that which wee intend, and that which wee thinke agreeable to our comission to informe ourselves of the power which the Kinge of Spaine doth send to a generall treatye, to heare the Estates reasons and see what they will doe, to find also by conference with all three partes whether the King will leave them or noe.

To the States also wee meane to use noe language but of all corrospondency, and yet to lett them knowe, howsoever either their reasons or their wills shall divert peace makeinge, that if for their cause the warre bee contynued, they must thinke to beare the greater burthen and not to increase or contynue her Ma[tys] insupportable charge of them.

Lastly, for the better justification of our retorne, wee doe thus conclude, that if treaty with the enemy shall goe forward, it must bee in some place neere England, for contynuation whereof in speech shalbee carryed on still betweene the French King and them whilst wee, in the meane tyme, have informed her Ma[ts] judgment, and shee hereupon resolve, which is the furthest of our comission. If wee find that the Queene shalbee forced to charges of a warre, then must the warre be advised and resolved on by her Ma[tie]. Of which two many points, God forbid wee should presume either to advise or your Lordshipps, if you would attribute anything to the small knowledge which wee have gathered in this negotiation, fall to any resolution upon our letters, which are maymed and barren informations in such intricate questions in comparison of personall relations. Our suit is therefore to your Lordshipps, that seeing tyme cannott prejudice the Queene to like of this course, that her Ma[ty] wilbee pleased to send us shipping for Caen, whereby wee shall save allmost 200 miles ryding, the coast being as fitt as Diepe in all respects, and that they may bee there by the xii[th] of this next Aprill.

Angiers, this Thursday, the xxiiith of March 1597.*

Your Lordshipp, my Lord Admirall, doe knowe that Esterham is a very good road hard by Caen, where if wee might have the *Answeare* or the *Adventure* with Captaine Reignolds, wee should bee gladd.

[*Marginal note :* 24th] This day the deputyes of the Estates arrived.

[*Marginal note :* 26th] The sixe and twentieth Mr Secretary and Mr Harbert had conference with the Kinges councell and were mett by Chasteau Vieux, Captaine of the Guard.

This day was the affiance made betweene Cesar Mounsieur and the daughter of the Duke of Mercury in the castle of Angiers.

This evening Mr Mole arrived with letters from her Matie bearing date the 27th concerneinge the intercepted pacquetts of the Cardinall.

This night the Comissioners, the Earl of Southampton and Sir George Carew supt with the Kinge.

This afternoone the deputyes of the Estates had audience.

The xxviith they came to Mr Secretaries lodging to visitt him, with whome they had conference neare 3 howers.

This day also this dispatch following was made :

May it please your Lordshipps. Haveing had this day and yesterday our conferences in the castle of Angiers with the Kinges Counsell, and to day morneing with the Estates Deputyes, wee thinke it fitt to send your Lordshipps this accompt by this bearer whome wee have cause to send into England. Wee have also receaved her Ma^{ts} letter by Mr Mole, and your Lordshipps that night att xi^{en} of the clock, with answer whereunto hee shall retorne, haveing sent this day to have audience to morrow but cannott get it because the King is in physick. Wee are promised it the next day, and then will wee both together deliver the substance of her Ma^{ts} royall instructions to himself in private.

Hee receaved the Estates Comissioners in the castle yesterday, where hee kept his court, his owne towne lodgeing being straight.

They that treated with us were the Chancellor, Duke Espernon, Duke Bulloigne, Monsieur Sencye, Villeroye, Maissie, Plessis and Shamberghe.

When wee did assemble I, the Secretary, was placed at the boards end, and the Duke Espernon on the right hand and the Chancellor on the left.

I, John Herbert, next Espernon on that side and the Duke of Bulloigne was over against mee, and so the others in their places.

I, the Secretary, did declare unto them the like language which I held to the Kinge.

Ffirst, to shew the substance of our legation was onely to satisfie the King that hee might see thereby her Matie would neither discreditt any thing which hee should beleeve nor sever herself from him att any tyme either in counsell or action of importance according to the obligation of faith and honor betweene them. Ffor otherwise wee both had charge to protest in her Ma^{ts} name that shee doth nothing with any beleif in any thing which should proceed in soe corrupt an enemy, in whome shee hath discovered soe notorious practise and collusion. And so it was declared unto them how the treaty in the Duke of Parma his tyme was carryed and how Richardott then did use himself. In which respect her Majestie, when Mounsieur de Maissie had shewed the inclynation of the comon enemy in respect of his great necessityes, and when hee seemed so much to assure her Majestye of a power already given to comprehend her and the Estates in the treatye, her Matie notwithstanding, when shee heard from what a broken trumpett that was sounded, did so little expect to find any thing of substance followe on in conclusion, as hee could not forgett with how great earnestnes shee did contest it with him that even in that originall circumstance wherein Richardott was used it would bee found, if it were tryed, that they were not soe provided but that they [*sic*? there] would bee found abuses. Nevertheless, things being here conceived otherwise, and her Ma^{ty} being loath to bee scandalized to have interrupted such a good intention for the publique good of Christendome, shee had thought it fitt by this publique sending to make tryall of the probabillityes to come to that whereof there was conceived so generall an expectation, desireing to bee cleared by them in particuler how all things stood in the firste point and in all other, and what was returned by the carrier which I, the Secretary, by the Kings owne speech, perceived was returned to Bruxells.

The Chancellor made a studdyed speech amplyfieing in generall the Kings sincerity and his necessity, and how acceptable a thing it was to save Christian blood. And therefore wished that wee would deliver the particuler of that wee had to say or to require in that great action.

Wee answeared againe that as the question did now consist whether it might bee likely by treaty of peace to make good conclusion of good conditions to all parties interested, such as in honor and safety might be accepted of by all, so till this first point were cleared it was hard to discend into other particulers because her Ma^{ts} honnor was too much engaged already by this which shee had done.

Hereupon Espernon (who is a reserved spirit) looking upon Mounsieur de Bouglon, and hee looking downe to Villeroy (as though the Chancellor had said what he was capeable off :

Villeroy tooke the tale and did reduce from the beginning how the matter had bene carryed, that the enemy had long reserved the Kinge, that the King was offred all his places which the enemy held, according to that which Maissie had told the Queene, and that the King still persisted :

That it was in vaine to thincke of any composition except his allyes were included, whereby the matter was trayned into length untill the losse of Amyens, and then it was renowned. And soe Richardott had assured it since that tyme that there was power very authenticall to treat in generall, if it were soe intended on all sides, whereupon hee said Mounsieur de Maissie was dispatched and deteyned there six weeks about it, and another sent to the Estates to advertize them accordingly. And since upon her Majesties makeing question of that power which the deputyes had, the King had given charge to examyne the power. And to the intent they of the Spaniards part should shew that which they had, the Kinges deputyes were comaunded to shew theire comission from the French Kinge, whereupon they shewed theirs.

In conclusion it appeared only a comission for Fraunce authenticall. But for the Queene and the Estates there was onely a power from the Cardinall, which being refused it was said that her Majesties sending to his Islands made them in Spaine desperate that shee intended to treate, which was the charge of it. And therefore moved the French Kings ministers for leave to send into Spaine for a new comision The answer wherof was now retourned though not certifyed hither but every hower attended.

It was answeared by us that for her Ma^{ts} armeing to sea it might have bene well replyed that in that point hee would have done otherwise though shee had bene engaged in a treaty, for shee should then have differd from the Kinge of Spaine and from the French King and all others. But for the estate of the affaires now in present, wee were sorry that by miscarriage or *male intend** the Queene had bene no sooner admonished that shee might have staid our journey, and that it happned ill for her Matie that Mounsieur de Maissie did no better beleeve the Queenes doubts.

Whereupon because that speech was directed to Mounsieur de Maissie, and that Espernon and all the religion side lookt on him (as who would say) it belongd to him to speake, hee tooke upon him then to answere.

Ffirst, hee confessed that the Queene did shew her wisdome in the doubt concerneing the peace, but that shee needed not to have embraced peace except shee pleased, for his comission tended as much to perswade her to make warre as peace, and that his M^{rs} causes and fortunes stoode at that tyme upon more then a formallity of sending to this end only. Neither needed it to bee made such a matter as whoe would say that never king had sent to another, ffor truth of princes actions stood not upon rumor which follow passions. Neither was the treaty at that tyme otherwise to have bene carried, and if her Matie would have resolved particulerly of a warre, shee would not have followed soe precisely the overture of peace. But her Matie was absolute and might draw on her causes att her pleasure and her resolutions. The Kinge was pressed to take opportunityes when they were offred, and the Queene hath done herself honor not to refuse to send. Shee medled not with the Spaniards

---

* *mal entendu* is meant here.

but tooke off the publique scandall, and therefore it was to much urged that the Queenes honor was dyminished in doeing what shee did.

To this point most of them agreed with one voice that her sending was most honorable and most necessary.

Hereto wee answered that wee could not dispute that circumstance further whether her Ma^ty had good or harme by sendinge.

Neither was it urged as if her Matie would have thought too much to send to the furthest part of his kingdome to doe him honor. But this I must say under his favor, that I, the Secretary, never understood it, haveing had the honor to waite upon her Ma^ts councell when hee was with them. But that his whole scope was to shewe the great offices of Spaine and how fitt it was now to end warre. And that the Kinge presumed he did a great worke in it, and that it was now to bee taken when the King of Spaines necessityes were so important. So as when her Matie found by the discourse, and that notwithstanding the Spanish King was in great want, yet a peace was necessarie, her Majesty thought of no other subject to bee handled then to informe herself what apparance there was of comeing safe and honorably to that pacification.

The point of inviteing the Queene to a warre was of all points most necessarie, for the Queene was then in warre more then ever before tymes. Shee had an army newly retorned from the sea, shee had her troopes in France maynteyned nyne monethes beyond promise, her forces in the Lowe Countryes, eight or ten thousand men in Ireland, and now preparations to sea. So as for any such matter, if that had bene the purpose onely of his comeinge, her Matie might have resolv'd without sending us hither.

Wee told them also that it seemed strange to us that the King, who wee know would not have the thought to conclude single, would soe farr shew himselfe in this befoore hee had sounded the conditions for the Queene in some particulers, ffor this was enough to make the matter suspected that there was noe sincerity, and that the enemy would raise himselfe reputation by it.

Then Villerou answered that without a beginninge thinges could not bee sounded, some one must speake, else nothing should be knowne. And this hee would protest, and knew that the King had also protested it to us, that hee was still *La Charte blanche* in that matter, and had ever resolutely told them that they did speake to a dead wall as long as they went to sever him from the Queene. And therefore that there was nothing but just proceeding and such as no way ought to displease the Queene, which hee was willing to speake there before good witnes. And that the French Kinges deputyes had bene fayne to use art to please them and keepe them together, the Legate being in person on the ffrontiers now five monethes and the Spanish deputyes, who were apt enough to thinke by the length of the matter that the French King did but worke them about the Queene of Englands consent. So as in the meane tyme, if wee would either stay 2 or 3 dayes or enter now into particulers what the Queenes conditions were, either to demaund in the peace or els what the Queene would doe to helpe the King by warre, they would heare it and it would wynne tyme against the answer arrived.

Wee than that saw to what end this tended, and saw what wee should get at his Councell by reason or disputation, haveing nothing to offer for the warre but onely the laying before him her Ma^ts former great charges with France and his great debts to her which wee are sure Espernon and divers there never heard of before, wee did for the rest and for the present thinke fitt to have the aid of the Estates, who wee knew had both arguments to disswade peace and had gott offers to present the King, which weighteth downe all benefitts past in this corrupt tyme and councell.

Wee replyed further that as wee were particulerly charged ;

Ffirst, to make especiall inquisition of the peace in which the Queene had beene so often dealt with, and that wee understood the Estates were arrived with whome in councell and motion wee were to hold correspondency, seeing that first matter would soe shortly bee cleared that wee did thinck it an ordinary way to conferr with them and that they might bee alsoe heard (all parties present), by which meanes thinges might bee expedited and the answere of the power attended. Or especially considering the respect which ought to bee carryed towards them and haveing soe freely called them into a league offensive or defensive, whereof none could better tell then Mounsieur Bouyllon and Plessis Cenoy [sic] whose instance in the Kinges behalf made that to bee done which the Queene did, for what was their need for her to tye herself with new formallityes when her Matie already (onely under God) and without any manner of utillity by any contract, had soe royallie and fortunatelie assisted him and the Lowe Countryes. So as if this should be violated, they that were least touched whomsoever could not but runn the hazard of scorne and infamye. They all allowed of the course propounded and so wee parted.

And afterward, it being very late, wee were brought to the King in the garden. When wee came to him and that hee had done with the Estates Commissioners, the King told mee, the Secretary, that hee had caused this number to assemble with us at first because this was an affayre which touched his whole kingdome, and that hee had made a mixture of all such as were of severall dispositions to the intent that every one of them, on whome depended so many severall parties, might know his manner of proceedings and so give satisfaction in grosse to the multitude, each of them haveing a quantity of people who do move no further then as their heads doe sway them.

The Chancellor, that *bon home*, and Maissie, hee said, were ministers of his justice and associates with his courte of Parliament. Espernon no leaguer but affectinge the reputation of a devout Romanist and very froward to them of the religion.

Senoy [*sic*] and Villeroy with Scomberghe affecting the peace as knowing his extreame necessities. The Duke of Bouyllon and Plessis, hee said hee need not describe for we knew them. This censure hee gave mee, the Secretary, in his garden of them when wee retourned from our conference with them. And the firste question which hee asked mee when I saw him was whether I had not told his Councell that the Queene was no way against any peace or purpose to keepe him in warre and misery, pretendinge to have a desire to putt that out of his peoples heads. And thereupon recounted to mee very badd offices and conceipts which had bene wrought into his head, which I did satisfie I hope and found necessary, the accompt whereof may bee fitt for another tyme.

I told him I should have much injured her Matie if I should have said otherwise, and soe gave him an accompt of all that had passed of which hee seemed to allowe.

And when this was done hee retyred and sent us into a banquetting house where musique was and so wee spent the tyme.

I, John Herbert, sometymes conferring with the States deputyes, and I, the Secretary, with the Duke of Bulloyne, with whome by Edmonds I doe hold privat corrospondencie, hee beinge one whome hee trusteth, besides private speeches when hee is appointed to walke with me and accompany mee.

This day the Estates Comissioners had conference with us for the space of two or three howers, wherein wee did acquaint them what course wee had held with the Kinge and his Councell, how much wee had bene in paine for lacke of their company, and with what straight comaundement her Ma^ty had enjoyned us to publishe to the world in what estimation shee held that State, a matter whereof wee neede not to use large protestations seeing they did dayly feed upon the fruits of her Ma^ts extraordinary protections. Onely least some should, as they did desire to sever them artificiallie, might have sett on foote some bruits that her Majestie meant to seeke her owne quiett without respect of them, I thought it fitt to assure them to the contrary, and for proofe of it to appeale to the Duke of Bulloine who could well tell what course wee held in our conference yesterday with the Councell, desireing them to bethinke them how to disswade the King from treaty with Spaine, if they could not bee reconciled to their doubtfullnes of harkneing to a peace.

Mounsieur Barnevelt did thereupon very formally yeild us thankes in her Ma^ts behalfe, protesting assured confidence in the Queene with acknowledgement of all her former benefitts, as also for that which they had understood since they came to this place, how her Matie had demonstrated the favor towards them, thankeing us very much for the particuler corrospondency which wee held now in communicating with them what had passed of late ; as also in haveing certified them before they came into this towne of such thinges as were convenyent by those confident persons that were used betweene us, whereof one is Mr Edmonds, who is very trusty and sufficient. The other is one Aersens whome they doe trust, and resolve to leave us this agent.

After this they went plainely to worke that their State might not hearken to a peace or treaty of peace, and that theire commission was resolutely to protest against it; that they found all the Kinges Councell, with whome they had any conference, passionate for it, and that the King himself did plainely tell them that though in his nature hee did not desire it, yet by the importunitye of the people and necessity of his affaires hee should bee forced to accept it for some tyme unlesse he were better assisted. And therefore they concluded to us that all his trust was in the Queene of England who onely had power to alter it.

Wee told them that wee had laid before the King the strictnes of the Tripartite league, and the danger for him to trust to Spaine whoe would onely serve himself of him against others thereby to ruyne both.

They answeared that these thinges were in vayne, they had said them often. Leagues between Princes had civill constructions, and benefitts that are passed helpe not future things. Neither are present necessityes, wherein it is in vaine to contest with them that must be judges of theire owne lacks, remedyed with enumeration of good turnes past. They therefore come fully resolved to obstinet any treaty, and doubted not but by this tyme theire fellowes had bene in England and had procured us authority to doe as they would doe, namely, to divert the Kinge by presenting to him the present extremities of the Spaniards, which made them so willinge to treate, and by presentation of some other manner of project to helpe him to beate the Spanishe army out of the Low Countries.

To this we answered them that wee had no such dispatch, but onely were to follow our former instructions as wee had already informed them. Ffurther, wee held some discourse with them why they should not hearken to a treaty if those conditions with bannishing of strangers might bee made by treaty that were to bee desired by a warre, which was subject to adverse successe.

Hereunto they answered that it was the way to theire perdition ever to acknowledge one person whatsoever for their soveraigne, either as Kinge of Spaine or Duke of Burgundy, that monarches might bynd or loose as they saw cause, but the composition of theire State being once altered it would resolve of itselfe, saying it was not onely the condition of removeing Spanish forces and strangers but all such natives of the Provinces as were now Spaniolized, which was farr greater in number then the Spaniards were.

Wee told them they best knew their State but many wise men were of another opinion. Yet seeing they did so resolve, it was not wee that could alter it but rather yeild to them the power to know themselves better then any other could doe. Onely this wee thought, they should not find it an easie worke to doe in hast though for our parts wee wisht it were soe. And therefore, if they could divert the Kinge from the course the Councell

had trayned him in by arguments or offer, wee should bee very
glad. And did indeed conceive that if they would joyne with
the French King in making the warrs, who now had need but
to make warre in one place, and not increase those enterprizes
in places more remote, there might come good of this interruption. They told us that it were reasonable her Ma^ty should
send over an army of 12 or 13000 men which would make way
into the heart of all hee possesseth. Wee findeing in them this
speech did plainely lett them knowe that her Ma^ts ffleetes at sea
and armyes that had bene sent out to make a diversion of the
enemyes forces, besides manye other greate charges in Ireland
and elsewhere, have soe much increased as her Majestie would bee
well advised how to engage herself suddenly for others, especially seeing in leiwe of old [? all] that shee had purchased for them
shee was never yet reimbursed of one half penny. They shifted
off that with their ordinary excuses, and still insisted whether
wee had heard out of England since the arrivall of their deputyes
or noe, ffor they did hope by that tyme her Matie had heard
them shee would take some such resolution. And if an army
were once kept together in Picardy or Artois, England need not
to bee in doubt, no, if France should leave the Queene and them,
ffor it was cheiflie they that need to feare and not the Queene,
for she might ever be mistris of the seas.

Wee told them that it was true that if there were nothing to
bee expected but such a mayne invasion as was in 88, her Majesty
might prepare well to defend by strength at sea. But whether
that were a charge supportable or no, wee left them to judge.
Besides, wee saw that the enemy tooke unseasonable tymes in
winter, when a navy could not bee ever maintein'd at sea, and
that by the meanes theire shipping was never from Spaine, by
which hee might transport a convenyent army on a suddaine.
Wee told them also that experience last yeare shewed us that
they durst come in the winter, and that they meant to make
the warre of another fashion and further then ever from Callice.
With Callice an army in calmes might bee suddenly transported
if they had nothing to feare of France, which might save an
army in spight of all the shipps that should bee kept at sea. And
therefore as wee went not to perswade them more then wee would
our selves to any perillous resolutions :

So wee must then require them to bethinke them how to ease
the Queenes charge if the Queene must bee kept in warre for
them. Mounsieur Barnevelt seemed a little awakned with this
and then fell into protestations of their necessityes, and withall
dislikeing the diminution of her Ma^ts forces that ought to bee
in the Lowe Countries. But wee told them her Matie had done
but for theis late enterprises and theire good, but that her Majestie
must bee forced to summon them to some better reckoning by
reimbursements of those great somes which they did owe the
Queene. Whereupon they incited on the contract and other
arguments. Wee told them plainely that must bee no answere,
and that they must stand no more uppon theire contract without

civill interpretation then by their former speeches it appeareth other princes meant to doe in the like occasions. Much more there passed both with them and on Sonday with the French which [we] cannott not [sic] advertise all att once but leave thus much humbly to your Lordshipps judgements, and hope to give her Majestye an accompt of the rest of this our hard negotiation hereafter. Ffor that dispatch which is come by Mr Mole wee doe thank God both for the publique and our particuler that God hath given her Majesty the fortunate discovery wherby her Majesty may now by dealing plainely with him make judgment what to trust to, wherin wee will not vary from that princely and prudent direction which wee have received but each bee witnes of the others words to the Kinge. Thus have wee yeilded your Lordshipps an accompt truely of all that hath passed and hope that your instructions bee examined, which wee trust shalbee our tryall and not our successe, that wee shall not receave her Maties disfavor the diminution whereof is more precious to us then our lives.

The Kinge goeth to Nants and from thence towards Blavet the 8th of Aprill to leave it blocked, soe as wee shall have our dispatch before he doe depart one way or other. Yf hee do satisfy under his hand this last matter wee will proceede further ; if hee doe not wee will come away. Soe as wee beseech your Lordshipps that our shipps may bee att Caen, and to thinke that wee are not so rash as to doe any thinge without reason. If the Kinge part from Nantes hee will not bee back in 6 weekes. Whatsoever wee finde wee will keepe all things still else till wee may wayte on her Majestie. If the power come wee will then informe the Queene whether wee and the Estates deputies finde it fitt here in our poore opinion that a treaty bee prepared, for if not best a warre must be. Wee will alsoe without giveing finall answere one way or other take our leaves and promise them her Maties resolution.

This is all wee can doe with our lymitations which wee may not exceed. Though wee have made great difficulty to followe the Kinge to Naunts, yet is it not prejudiciall for us to goe, though necessity for her Ma^ts service did not require it. Ffor though it bee somewhat further from Caen as it lyes then Angiers, yet it is a safer way to Caen then this from Angiers and Rhemes without any other good townes are by that way to bee had to lodge in.

Besides wee shall have a cornet of Montgomeries horse which wee may trust that will not cutt our throats or betray us when wee come neare the scattered troopes which must march towards Blavett. And thus haveing singly and truelye delivered the particulers wherein wee could not avoid length, which is no pleasure to either of us, wee doe most humbly take our leave.*
Angiers, March, 1598.

[*Marginal note :* March 28.] Because wee have so urged to heare whether the power were come or noe, the King hath sent

---

* See *H.M.C. Salisbury MSS*, Vol. VIII, pp. 104–12.

a carryer expresse to Vervyn, and by the 30th hee shall heare with particuler certeinty.

[*Marginal note:* March 29.] This day they had audience againe and imparted to the King the effect of her Ma^ts letter of the 17th brought by Mr Mole. They were brought to the King by Mounsieur le Grand.

[*Marginal note:* 29th.] The 29 Facondar was sent for England with the letters of the 27th.

This day Mr Secretary went to Mounsieur Villeroy to the Estates.

This day also Romane the Post arrived with letters from England and coppies of the Cardinalls intercepted pacquets.

[*Marginal note:* 30th.] The 30th the Estates Deputyes came to Mr Secretaryes lodgeing and had conference with him and Mr Herbert.

[*Marginal note:* 31th.] The last of this moneth the Kinge departed from this towne of Angiers towards Nants, but being in hunting hee lost himself and returned back to Angiers where hee made little abode but went thence early in the morneing the first of Aprill.

[*Marginal note:* Aprill 3.] The third of Aprill wee removed out of Angiers towards Nants and lay the first night at Ansenis.

[*Marginal note:* 4th.] The next day about 4 of the clock in the afternoone wee arrived at Nants.

[*Marginal note:* 5th.] The 5 of this moneth Mr Mole was dispatched with letters in answere of her Ma^ts of the 17th of March brought by him, the tenure whereof here followeth :

[*Marginal note:* Aprill 5, 1598] Most gratious Soveraigne. After wee had receaved your Ma^ts letters so full of princely and prudent directions by Mr Mole, wee founde nothinge left for us but to apply them to our present negotiation with our best diligence and discretion according to the circumstances of the tyme. How wee had proceeded formerly till the hower of his arrivall wee have delivered your Ma^ty an exact accompt by long and particuler discourses sent to our Lords, being driven to husband our tyme and vallue our instructions as much as wee could untill wee mighte see whether the Spanish comission were come or noe, whereby your honor at least might bee thus saved, that if yow had pleased yow might have treated. On Monday the 27th the King rode forth very early and came in very late.

That night I, the Secretary, sent to have audience. The next day hee sent mee word hee must take phisick, but in the afternoone I should bee welcome. About 3 of the clock on Tuesday wee both went to him and found him in bedd, where I, the Secretary, did desire him (because the matter was weighty) that hee would [*discharge* deleted] that hee would bee pleased for my discharge to heare us both together. Hee yeilded to it very willinglie, and so wee sate downe by his bedd side where wee warmed him soe well, as whether it were his phisick or our message, Mounsieur le Grand was faine to fetch drinke for him.

Before our comeinge to him wee had considered how much wee should disadvantage soe playne a matter if wee should speake unto him in other stile then with assurances that his deputyes had done so much as was discovered by the letters, though with such reservations to himself as became us ; although wee must plainelie tell your Majestie that inwardly our hearts so boyled that wee held our selves accurst to tread upon the soile. Wee considered further that wee should no sooner touch upon a part of the quick but that hee (who knew all hee had done) would straight conceive wee knew more then wee speake, and therefore thought it unfit by temporizeing to give any leizure to studdy or advise with others for his answer. Wee have therefore thought it good to sett downe here precisely the same language which I, the Secretary, used, for wee that know your Ma^{ty} to bee in all languages *mieulx disans** must justly thinke that your Ma^{ty} hath cause to bee very jealous whether your meaneinge hath bene delivered in the French to the same sence which of English repitation should now expresse. And therefore I, the Secretary, beseech your Matie to pardon myne errors especiallie who have come so short of that significancye and propriety which in your pure stile doth allweyes flourish.

Sire, Depuis que jay eu l'honneur de voir vostre Ma^{te} jay receu une depesche de la Royne ma Souverayne, et suis infiniment marri de ce que par son commandement (sur l'exigence des affaires) je suis contraint vous faire ses plaintes tresinstantes pour le grand regret et mescontentement qu'elle a d'avoir occasion de se mesfier de la syncerite de vostre affection en son endroict qu'elle a tousjours tenue pour fidelle et inviolable ; aiant eu notable indice que les procedures de vos ministres en ce present traicte de la paix avec l'Espagnol portent desseing et promesse que vostre Ma^{te} se laisseroit en fin aller a rompre la foy publique que vous luy avez juree. Elle ne peulte, Sire, croire chose si indigne de vous, mais les lettres mesmes qui sont tombez entre ses mains des Deputez d'Espaigne et d'aultres portent clairement telles asseurances. Elle ne peult aussy que le supporter avec beaucoup d'impatience jusques a ce qu'elle soit au vray esclaircie par vous mesmes de la verite, et que vous lui aiez faict paroistre combien il vous desplaist que vos ministres aient tenuz telles procedures en son endroict.

Ces lettres des Deputez d'Espaigne escrites au Cardinal contienent qu'ils sont acertenez et par le Legat et par vos ministres que vostre Ma^{te} este resolue de leur donner pouvoir de conclurre son traicte particulier si il y a empeschement en l'accord de vos confederez. Et que vostre Ma^{te} consent que vos deputez signent de part et d'aultre les articles convenus pour vostre accord particulier lequel seroit baille pour quelque temps entre les mains du Legat. Et que vous ne vous attaches maintenant a la formalite de leur consideration que seulement pour l'acquit d'honneur.

---

* The original letter in PRO, S.P. 78 (France) reads : '' one of the *mieulx disans* of Europe ''.

Dont sil plaist a vostre Ma^te avoir plus particuliere cognoissance, je luy remonstreray l'extrait de quelques unes de desdites lettres. Pour aussy asseurer vostre Ma^te qu'il ny a aulcun artifice ou simulation de la part de la Royne ma Souverayne en ce que je viens de vous representer, je vous proteste sur mon honneur et devant le Dieu vivant comme Monsr Herbert icy le pourra tesmoigner, que l'extrait que je vous exhibe est le fidelle abrege des lettres qui ont este prises, escrittes en chiffre par le Cardinal au Roy d'Espaigne, dont les originaulx sont entre les mains de sa Ma^te. Et la Royne ma Souveraine prend merveilleusement a cueur le scandale que ces declarations apportent au prejudice de l'estroicte amitie qui est entre vous.

Pour lever lequel soupcon elle m'a commande de vous semondre et conjurer (sil vous plaist) de luy ouvrir en cecy fidellement vostre cueur, quelles sont vos intentions, et si vous avez faict signer tels articles, et l'en esclaircir vivement par l'asseurance expresse de vos lettres ; m'ayant commande de ne le communiquer qu'a vous, et ne voulant croire que vostre Ma^te seule, sur la conscience et integrite de laquelle elle se repose, qu'elle fera plus equitable jugement de ses merites que ne pourront ou ne vouldront faire ceulx de son Conseil.

Et pour ce que sa Ma^te ait envoye ung gentilhomme tout expres pour porter quant et luy nostre responce, nous vous supplions bien humblement que vostre Ma^te se vueille esclaircir sur ce sujet, afin que nous pourrions juger comment nous avons a nous gouverner pour nostre descharge.*

After hee had heard this first speech without other interruption, saying in this kynde—*Ah ! cela est faict in Angleterre, la royne ne me trouvera pour tel*, with diverse other broken speeches, sometymes smileing in scorne of the invention and sometymes rapping out an oath all tending to absolute denyall, hee made this quiett answere :

Ffirst, that on his honor and by his part in Paradice hee never gave anye such comaundement, and that hee was sure his ministers durst not for theire heads commit any such act, but still inferring that it was either an artifice of some in England or of the Estates.

To this wee replyed, ffirst, that as assuredly as wee know the light from darknes so truely wee did both know that this was no devise of England, of Holland nor of any creature liveinge, but the worke of the Cardinal himselfe whereof my self in particuler, the Secretary, had so perfect knowledge, as if hee would beleeve me as a Christian I did protest upon my religion and faith that it was nothing but a true letter and a cipher of the Cardinals wherewith I had reason to be well acquainted, haveing had diverse of them fall into my hands. And therefore it greived mee to see him passionate in distrust though I joyed to see him passionate in deniall of it, assuring that I did wish my armes and leggs broken for comeing hither untill I had heard him. This we spake both to him with feelinge. Well, saieth hee, I

---

* Copied from the original despatch. *See* S.P. 98 (France, Vol. 42, pp. 18b–19b).

am satisfied, but I did allwayes quitt your Mistriss. And now goe on, I pray you, saith hee, what bee these further particuler great presumptions.

Whereupon I, John Herbert, read unto him this extract enclosed wherein wee used those cautions which I, the Secretary, received also from my Lord, my father, in his great letter to mee.

Ffor, first, wee left out many of those articles which shewed the Kinge of Spaines readines to yeeld him all his desires, because that would have made him proud and raise himself towards us. Ffor though wee thinke hee knowes too well what hee shall have of Spaine, yet wee would not have him thinke that wee know it out of the Spaniards mouth.

Secondlie, wee left not any thinge unto him that might shew him that the Spaniards meane to offer any injurious conditions to England, for then he would also have thought your Maties state the more irreconcilelable [sic]. And therefore onely acquainted him with the reports of Villeroys speeches, of the Legates speeches, of Bellievre his speeches and other things, which wee have further sett downe in the inclosed.

When hee had heard this hee did make this answer very sensibly and orderly without study or without advise, for he little dream'd of such an overture, wee can assure your Matie it beeing not the least worke to procure audience so private and setled as wee have had no small number.

Hee said that in this matter he observed three thinges.

Ffirst, the instructions from the Cardinal to the Spanish Deputyes.

Two speeches of the Legate.

The discourses, speeches and promises of his ministers.

Ffor the first, hee had nothing to doe to answer him, the Cardinal might presscribe what he listed, and it was no other like but hee would bidd his comissioners propound the hardest.

Ffor the Legates speeches of him, true it was that hee had ever shewed himselfe to the Legate to bee desirous of a peace, and so had reason for his honor was engaged in it. And the Pope had travelld in it, and hee must not loose his reputation with them howsoever others contemned peace, wishing us to thinke whether it bee not a pretty tyme that he hath kept le bon home, the Legate, at the beggerly towne of Vereine 5 moneths day by day, and only of purpose to see what the Queene of England would doe.

Ffor the rest, true it was that his comissioners wrote to him when hee went into Brittanie, that the Spaniards said hee meant but to abuse them and make his profitt, and that they offered to bee gone. And that the Cardinal himselfe protested that hee knew the King of Spaine would taxe him for that facillity which hee had shewed already. Whereupon, saith hee, I directed him to use all art to keepe them together whilst my affaires were accomodated in Brittaigne. At which very tyme, when I had greatest need, the Queene drew awaye her succours and left my frontiers naked.

This, saith hee, may have bene the cause that my ministers in private discourses have used large speeches of my resolution. But that all is not true that the Spannish Deputyes report to the Cardinal and that the Cardinal writes to the King. God and I know that they have not done it nor dare not. No, the Queene must think that the Low Countries affect peace with the Cardinal for his private. And yet hee is accomptable to a M^r that wonders why nothing is done. And therefore the Cardinal, seeing that Brittany is reduced, that I will have the Queene and States included, with those ffynenesse hee is well accquainted, being yet desirous to bring as well to passe if it might bee, hee hath written thus to the Kinge that hee may see his carefull instructions to his deputyes, and what cause his deputyes give him still to contynue. This it must needs bee and nothing els, said hee, and soe certify the Queene, I pray yow, for shee shall never finde mee *trompeour ny pipeur*. And when I have a mynd to doe such an act, I will never denye it ffor I had as willingly it were knowne today as to morrow.

Wee told him wee were glad to heare his Ma^{ts} words so absolutely. Wee hoped his Ma^{ty} could not find but her Matie had cause to doe what shee did, and that in thus doing she did like to her owne franke and royall spiritt.

Hee confesseth it was true : but now, saith hee, that yow are satisfied, what doth the Queene say, tell mee to satisfie mee. Will shee joyne with mee to make peace or no with Spaine, now power is come. Or will shee assist mee in such sort as may bee for our safety and comon profitt. Yow speake nothing directly to mee. If shee could make mee a good offer, she should see whether I were soe tyed as I would not breake the treaty.

Wee then answered him that for your Ma^{ts} drawing away the troops at the instant, your Ma^{ty} had kept them there 15 monethes, and that shipping had bene sent for them 3 monethes before. Besides they were sent for Ireland. And yet if de Maissie had importuned for them soe much as hee sollicited the peace, her Ma^{ty}, wee know, would not have denyed them.

Ffor the power which hee said was come, now that the Estates might know so much, wee would doe our best to perswade them. And as wee found them, so should hee heare more.

Well, said hee, must you to Nants for I must needs be gone to morrow.

Wee told him wee had comaundement, even as wee would beare the perill of it, not to proceed further in any matter till wee had such satisfaction in ourselves by his answere as might warrant our judgment in not suspending the negotiation. Being men better brought upp then to doubt such a religious and princely vowe of such a prince, yet wee could not discharge ourselves entirely without it would please him to satisfye her Matie by a letter to herself what hee had done and what hee will doe.

Well, saith hee, though shee writt not to mee, and that I am sure shee will not distrust yow two, yet will I write that which

is fitt for a letter as things stand now. And therefore, saith
hee, yow shall have my letter. Besides I will send Villeroy to
yow to satisfie yow particularly what hee [hath] said or done,
for this is true, I repeate it againe, no such thing is done nor
ever was comaunded to bee done. And where they say myne
did move them to send for a new comission and that I did say
I will write to the Queene to be content, the Queene knowes herself
I never writt so to her, nor never did it proceed but from their
motion to send for a new [commission] when my servants disliked
the former, baile upon it, saith hee.

Wee then departed, and by that tyme wee had bene at our
lodgeing an hower the Duke of Bulloigne. . . .* As wee were
talking, Villeroy and Maissie, who had bene with the Estates,
came to my lodgeing and found the Duke with mee who offring
to goe away they staied him and said hee mighte remeyne. Hee
then in short begun to tell us what the King had said, and following ever the same course which the Kinge did, in making shew that
it was onely the Cardinals devise for his owne justification, did,
in the hearing of the Duke and us, vow by monstrous oathes
that there was neither any such thing done as signeing nor any
authority given to signe any thinge.

Wee did then desire him to hasten the Kings letter that wee
might fall to some resolution, for wee waste tyme here and saw
that others affaires went on apace.

Hee told us wee should and so wee ended. Beeing desirous,
now that wee were thus driven to the wall to advise with the
Estates and with the Duke of Bouyllon what to doe, wee must
assure your Ma^{ty} that wee found the Estates resolute not to
hearken to treaty.

Wee find all them of the religion absolutely of the opinion the
King will make peace, and can have no other councell of them
but that your Ma^{ty} must offer him great helpe, such are the necessityes of Spaine, such are the greedynes of France and such is
the unremoveable resolution of the Estates not to treat any way.

Wee have now delivered your Ma^{ty} a true and plaine narration,
though diverse other arguments have passed which wee cannott
set downe being ashamed to have thus detayned your royall
eyes. Yow know our power that wee cannott promise treaty
with the Estates, neither may wee discover ourselves to have
come over for nothing but for inquisition, ffor then shall wee
confirme that wee were sent onely to gaine tyme. Soe as being
driven to us the best of our poore slender judgements, wee have
resolved of this course and not without advice in part of the
Duke of Bulloigne and the Estates.

Ffirst, to the intent to keepe him in expectation, wee will tell
the King that wee are sure that when your Matie is informed of
all these particulers, yow will quickly resolve either to helpe him
or concurre with him in the treaty to which belongs choice of

---

* The original despatch reads : " . . . the Duke of Bouillon came to me,
the Secretary, to see me, I having bene the day before with the Princesse of
Orenge and the Duchesse of Bouillon."

other Comissioners, place and other forme. For the helpe in particuler wee cannott speake it, but therein would bee glad to know what hee would desire and for what purpose, that the common utility of it may be discerned by your selfe and your Councell. For such it may bee as hee had as good tell us in plaine tearmes hee doth meane to conclude without your Majestye.

Secondly, wee will privately tell him that although wee have so sufficient understanding of your Majesties mynde as that wee knowe most of your Ma^ts conditions in which yow will stand with the Spaniard for the peace, and that wee might give the Kinge presently liberty to assure the Spaniard underhand that hee doth finde by us noe other likelyhood now but that your Matie will send comission to treate according to the power which is come from them ; yet finding now that the Estates were so resolved which your Matie beleeved not when wee came from yow, wee are constrained to desire the King in respect of that circumstance that hee will give us leave to repaire to your Matie and that wee might carry the Estates with us, who do contest with us that they doe knowe howsoever France would use them, yet that your Ma^ty would heare them alsoe howsoever afterwards your Matie resolved to proceed.

To this request of theires wee meane to tell the Kinge that wee dare not but condiscend, it being past our rules that his Matie can thinke it safe or honorable that they should bee left out, and therfore wee must have new instructions. If wee should say wee would write home, hee would thinke wee would but waste tyme. And your Ma^ty shall lack such light as wee can give yow by way of information, though wee are farre from presumption of thincking to give councell. Besides your Matie may well thinke that att our parting hee will speake in his last and clearest voyce to us, whome if hee finde still content to tarry hee will still hope to draw us on by little and little.

The good that your Matie shall have by this is this : if hee doe not followe the greedy and corrupt councell of this nation who comonly answere, even the best of them, when there is speech either of faith or honor breakeing, that necessity hath no lawe, that every man ought to provide first for himself, your Matie shall then wynne tyme here. Yow shall have these two, which are of the best ministers the Estates have, humble petitioners to yow in England upon whome your Ma^ty will worke more in an hower then all your instruments can doe in a moneth. Wee have also had opportunity to try them now and can guesse somewhat by Barnevelt what may bee looked for. They are past their old rules and doe plainely confesse that they see what trust to give France, and have observed what her Ma^ts direct proceedinges are. By this course, if your Matie shall finde it fitt, by taking some good resolution to disorder the present facilitiye of the French Kinges peace which being once disjoynted will not bee so easily sett together, your Ma^ty will see they will do as much in it to ease yow as can bee found reasonable rather then your Ma^ty should leave them.

If, on the other side, your divine judgment resolve that it is better to suffer France to make peace alone then further to helpe him, then is your Ma^ty by this meanes eased of sending any to the Estates with whome, howsoever thinges goe, wee thinke your Majestie will newly consult, for things stand to our poore understandinge now but rawly, come peace or warre. And therefore wee will so use it as Barnevelt shall voluntarily come creeping to yow, who wee assure your Matie is wise, and with whome wee have had soe many and particuler conferences almost once a day since wee mett, as in many things your Majesty shall make verie good use *in omnem eventum* of their comeing to seeke yow and not the worse when yow have heard our poore informations. For wee must plainlie lay before your Majesty that although the King hath said in both our heareings as much as wee have written, and that if hee bee not a monster hee hath said true of that which is past, yet both of us and I, the Secretary, especiallie, whoe have hadd accesse many tymes and have heard him in many humors, sometymes upon sudden in liberall speeches and sometymes in serious, discover himself to mee his ends and his natureyll disposition, dare not say other to your Ma^ty then that I feare France wilbee France and leave his best freinds, though to his owne further ruyne, to which I thinck God hath ordayned it.

The Estates have bene with the Kinge since our audience and have made him direct offers to contynue the former 4000 and more to any good purpose, and have plainely laid before him that neither the law of God nor man will suffer him to leave them. They have return'd to us and have passionately reported his answere to bee this, that his freinds have helped him long and that hee hopes after two yeares peace to order all things and to bee able to helpe them if they need, soe as they are in despaire, and now onely attend what hee will say to us, to whome hee yet never used any such language. If your Majesty conceive that it may bee hee doth this to merchant upon us and them, wee submitt ourselves to your opinion. But your Matie sees too well by the intercepted letters how neare hee is to his owne conditions. And there (? therefore), if your Matie should thincke wee doe this to have further instructions from yow to make him some particular offer, wee doe protest against it, for wee should but abuse your Majesty to desire it. But wee will come provided by way of discourse, withoute engageing yow, to enforme yow what it is that they would have, and how they would offer it should bee used for any good to your Ma^ty, which when wee have told yow then tis fitt for yow and your Councell there to advise of either way, whether your Matie shall doe anye thing for him in the warr or leave him to the peace and stand upp your self with the Estates.

Of both which wayes bee it farr from us to judge, not doubting if yow shalbee driven to the last way of proceedinge but God and your cause will defend yow, though your Ma^ty cannott but consider that the state of Ireland and Scotland are greatlye changed since 88, when France was not in warre with Spaine.

This doe wee humbly represent to your Matie as an argument that wee are neare our furthest inquisition, haveing found more then wee wish. And therefore meane now to labor onelie to this end, that when wee have enquired and informed and used all the strength of our instructions wee may leave thinges unconcluded, soe as yee may have the libertie of election.

This, if wee can doe, wee hope wee shall doe yow noe ill service, which is that for which wee were borne.

If his answere shall either bee directly partiall to himself or such as wee find hee is content wee should so construe them, in that case, as the Estates have already spoken plainely unto him according to our agreement with them and meane to pursue it when they are upon dispatch from Nants, so I, the Secretary, will finally lett him know that your Matie, before he was King and since, when all the world had abandoned him, did royallie assist him and thereby brought him to bee capeable of those conditions which now have made him change his language, and notwithstanding all contracts before and treaties since, your Matie never receyved performance of any thinge.

And whereas hee doth still insist upon the necessity that presseth him, your Matie must needs take that as a faire evasion out of that which both publique ffaith and infinite benefitts by greater necessity doe bynd him.

And because hee seemes to say that your Ma^ty drawes things to length, and that wee are come over to gaine tyme, I will likewise invert it upon him that his drawing us hither from whence wee can have no speedy returnes for our dispatches hath bene the onely cause of our protraction.

And if hee will say that wee ought to have had a provisionall comission, which is common in their mouthes, wee will tell him that provisionall instructions are allwayes by princes left to the judgment of their ministers to declare them upon new accidents or circumstances ; and that in this case judgment doth teach us to bee in some things reserved untill wee see how your Matie can satisfie the Estates to treate without them if hee shall once have given them such a finall answere, your Ma^ty haveing never before receaved into your thoughts any conceipt that hee could thinke it lawfull or expedient. And therefore that your Matie must heare them as hee hath done, before yow would like that wee should give him the *dernier met* [?*mot*] Besides wee will tell him playnlie that without a sight of the coppie of the comission your Matie cannott send any body to the treaty, ffor if the King of Spaine speake of the Pope in this comission which hath relation to her Matie or use any other punctilio which may carry away inequall sense, your Matie will disdaine to send any comissioners thither.

So as I will let him see plainelie that if his demaunds for the warre bee so exorbitant as your Matie shall find they bee but motives to bee denyed, or if hee or anie other of his ministers can thinke your Ma^ty wilbee carryed post into a treaty wherin soe many new circumstances are to bee considered, they wilbee deceived. And his Ma^ty will never bee able to justify his seperation from yow before God or man. When hee doth, either wee consider his sacred vowes of which the Earle of Shrewsbury is witness or remember how many mens lives and what somes of treasure your Matie hath spent for his conservation, wherein wee wilbee bold as wee shall see cause to know of him alsoe what course your Matie shall expect for the present payment of all those debts which hee doth owe your Matie, seeing now his new amitye will free him from all his necessityes.

Wee doe send your Matie herewith his letter which wee requir'd to warrant our report wherein, when wee noted the stile to bee bare and did insist to have it mended, wee were playnly answered that many wayes letters are intercepted, that hee hath spoken to us at large already whoe he thought your Matie would trust, hee was a prince soveraigne and desired to bee beleeved as other princes would bee. And that if the Spaniards should intercept his letters, it would putt no small jealousy into theire heads, and then your Majestie might happilie care lesse for him.

But to tell your Matie truely I, the Secretary, know it affirmatively by good meanes that hee was perswaded that such a letter it might have beene as I would have caused to have bene conveyed to the enemyes knowledge by some meanes or other.

Now hath your Matie all which wee have done, can doe or thinke fitt to bee done, wherin if your Ma^{ty} thinke it shalbee done without discretion, wee have then enjoyed (and I, the Secretary, especiallie) to much of your Ma^{ts} former trust. I humbly beseech your Majestye therefore to bee in no payne through any such apprehension, ffor I thanke God Nature hath not made mee lavish nor violent. Though I protest to your Matie if his ingratitude shall now appeare when it shall come to tryall, I shall in my heart abhorr him, for hee hath both witt, conscience and meanes to doe otherwise, although as a carnal natural man it may bee said that it is *prima facie* the longest way about to seeke that by warre which hee might have by peace.

And thus beseeching the everliveing God to blesse your Matie with perfect health and eternall happines, wee most humblie take our leaves from Nants, 5 April. 1598.

Postscript. Your Ma^{ty} shall finde by the letter from the King how he doth bauke the deniall of his ministers speaking to signe the articles, though he writeth plainlie they have not signed nor never had comaundement to signe.

I desired to see the coppie of the letter and did plainely expostulate why hee did not aswell in the letter disavow that point as thother, having so fully forsworne both.

I am term'd to curious, and that the King had said enough if reason would serve, and so much as any Christian would beleeve. But for the King under his hand to disavow his ministers doings, to whome hee gave leave to use large words in extremeties to keepe them from breaking off at that time, hee would not doe it by my leave. For so might this use bee made of it, that the Spaniard finding that they would say that for which they had noe warrant in one thing, might well thinke they would say soe in others.

To tell your Matie my replyes were to bee more tedious, but in short I must either take this or nothing, for it hath made mee stay this dispatch 5 dayes, for I could not forbeare to let them see that it was necessity and not my simplicity that made it to bee accepted by mee. For in my conscience the Kings ministers speake of it either by warrant of himself or Mounsieur Villeroy, but which party hee meant to disguise withall I dare not judge because he is the Lords annoynted. April 5th.*

John Symonds was sent into England this afternoone with a coppie of the former dispatch, being comaunded to passe through Normandy by land, where Mr Mole with the original went by St Mallowes there to imbarque himselfe for England, which course was thought fittest by the comissioners to bee taken to the intent both the pacquets might not miscarry.

This afternoone Mr Secretary had audience and was brought to the Kinge by Mounsieur le Grand. When he was retorned to his lodging Mounsieur Villeroy came to him and had conference with him neere an hower.

[*Marginal note :* 6th.] The 6th in the morneing came the Duke of Bouyllon to visit him, and in the afternoone the Estates deputies and the comissioners conferred together.

[*Marginal note :* 9th.] The 9th the dispatch following was sent to the Lords by Jasper, Mr Edmonds man, who was staid till the next morning upon some occasion.

[*Marginal note :* Another dispatch to the Lords of the Councell.]

Maie it please your Lordshipps. Having had audience the nexte daye saveing one, after our comeing to Nants, in the Kinges Cabinet, wee thinke it our part to advertise your Lordshipps of such particulers as passed, each of us distributing our portions to speake as should bee cause.

Ffirst I, the Secretary, told him that as at my first comeing I declared unto him that the Queene my soveraigne had imployed mee to him to discover her mynd and to understand his, and to resolve with him about this great affaire, so I desired him still to beleeve that shee had the same meaneing still, and that hee would not suffer himself to bee transported by those who would perswade him that shee desires only to amaze him thereby to make him loose his opportunityes, that it was now tyme to shew the effects of that ffaith which hee had sworne to her whose meritts had neither bene small nor unknowne. And to the intent hee might see that she would leave him no ground of jealousie, I desired him to resolve mee clearly whether hee did desire warr or peace, which hee should do no sooner then I would open to him her Ma^ts purpose to either way.

Hereupon hee replyed that hee was sorry to find himself in this extremity that either he must ruyne himself or offend the

---

Queene. But he must plainely tell us that his necessityes were such as hee could not stand out, for hee should gett by the hazard of a warre no more then hee should have with assurance by peace. And if hee once were able to stand of himself, hee then might bee a stay to the Queene and his freinds.

I told him that this was strange that his necessityes were such as that hee must bee forced on a sudden to compound with the common enemye, and to doe it to the prejudice of the confederates. There was difference betweene his estate now and before, ffor hee could then recover his kingdome with the helpe of his freinds, and now hee could not defend a part of it but must out of greediness of suddaine quiett make such a peace as must prejudice his confederates. And so wee fell into the arguments that his necessityes could not bee soe great, and that it was but his servants disorder who made it great of purpose to engage him as they had done.

Hee answeared it might bee true and might bee false, but what it was he knew best, and that howsoever wee might take upon us to understand or judge of others estate, that hee knew it himself and felt it ; and that if Brittany had not now come in hee had bene ruyned utterly, for the seige of Amyens had made him miserable.

Wee answeared him that if the Duke Mercury had not come in wee durst saye the Queene would not have denyed to have helped him by sea as soone as her shipps had bene fitt against the Kinge of Spaines ffleet, whome as shee had beaten in other places by land and sea and had helped to pull him out of Croyden by land, soe nowe shee would not have suffered him to have kept Blavet. But if hee had brought a navye thither shee would have helped to have removed him thence.

Also hee answeared plainlie that the Queene denyed Maissie directly any such succor. Wee answeared him againe that when Maissie was there his onely language was aboute peace, but at his parting hee asked for some shipps to further the seige of Blavett, and that answere was made that her Ma^{ts} shipps were new come home and wether beaten and could not presently bee made ready to goe out in winter.

But I, the Secretary, should come to him with satisfaction for all things.

Well, said hee, it is now past, and I am like a man cloath'd in velvett that hath not meat to putt into his mouth. Your comeing hath bene welcome, but your long stay after Maissie and the Estates lingueringe hath drawne on the tyme soe farre as I am in extremity. I hope the Queene will not looke I should undoe my self for that could bee no pleasure to her.

Wee answeared that his Ma^{ty} might use the worde of ruyne as often as he would, but the word would never justifie his arguments. Neither would his Ma^{ty} save breach of the treaty without being content to sustaine difficultyes or prejudice for the Queenes sake as well as shee had done for him.

Wee (? He) said that for the worlds satisfaction hee cared not, his conscience was witnes. And whensoever the world should calumniate him hee would justifie himself. For the Queene, shee had done very favourably for him, and yet her succors might have bene better imployed then they were, for hee neere had them in tyme nor half the number.

Wee desired him to excuse us, for although there was never yet by him one penny paid nor one promise kept, yet hee had them still contynued, and had them sooner then the tyme appointed and att Roan before he was ready, where hee had the bravest troopes that ever were sent to kinge.

Hee said they were brave troopes indeed, and his necessities only made him breake all promises.

Wee told him also that where hee said the numbers were decayed, it was not the Queenes fault, shee paid them. If any captaine deceaved it was a comon disease. But they that comaunded them would say that they were never accomodated but putt to all extremityes and abandoned, even in this province especiallie, to theire destruction, it being the first defeyt that ever any English troopes in our M^{ris} pay received.

Hee said in that hee could not remedy it, for hee lost his owne and a prince of the blood was one here taken prisoner. Wee told him wee would faine knowe in what matter to deale with him.

Ffor although wee had noe power presently to offer him satisfaction, in particuler if hee would leave the treaty, seeing the Estates could not bee comprised, yet wee could assure him that the Queene would aid him, and therefore desired him to speake plainely what numbers hee would aske and to what end. For if the designe were fitt and good for all parties, as wee knew the States woulde ayde him, so when her Matie should undertake it wee were sure that the Queene would also strayne herself upon any reasonable probabillitye to accommodate him.

When hee answered that he knew the Queene did much affect Callais, for to every body that spake with her shee shewed great passion for it, and so did all her Councell to, but it was in vayne to thinke of it nowe for hee might loose an army before it, and when hee had it hee should have no more then hee should have by peace.

When wee heard him say so after wee had so disputed with him in that conceipte of the matter of Callais, wee told him it was in vayne, as now wee saw things, to dispute of any thing but his peace. For as both his enemyes had written that all conditions were agreed on, so wee saw it now by his Maties owne conversion in 14 dayes, for hee that spake nothing but of particuler affection to warre when wee came, now would hearken to nothinge but peace. Wee would therefore proceed with him in that pointe. Hee said it was the best.

Then wee askt how hee would dispute with leaveing out the Estates either in honnor or safety.

Hee said hee had told them his mynd, ffor that necessity had no law, they might defend themselves a while well enough till their freinds reposed. But (saith hee) you sett a shew that yow came to satisfy. What can yow doe in the peace, now power is come and I have engagd myne honnor in that I have kept the Legate so longe. What will yow treate, or can yow or have yow any comission. It hath bene otherwise a strange legation, and must confirme that which the world say, that the Queene meanes no peace herself but to keepe mee in warre. And with this speech hee turned himself to mee, John Herbert, who answered him that wee came over with such comission as the Queene thought fitt, and that wee had power to doe more then wee sawe in duty wee ought to entend. Ffor the Queene, who entred soe lately into a confederacy more strict then before with such a state as the Low Countryes and at his only intreaty, did not dreame that his Matie would so suddenly have left them. And therefore, although wee know sufficientlye her Ma^{ts} meaneing for all particulers of the treaty of peace, yet were wee not warranted to say more without further knowing her Majesties pleasure for that mayne point concerning the Estates comprehension which are the third partie. Besides, I told him that if the States would have joyned, yet wee in our instructions would be well advised, without knowing her Ma^{ts} pleasure, to yeild that any treaty should bee kept so farr from England. And that wee would knowe more certainly of the power, assuring him that the Duke of Parma did by his letter before her Ma^{ts} Comissioners came over, write that hee had *una comissione testantissima.** Soe as hee must not finde our delay strange, especially seing the place of assembly at Roan was changed so as wee could not heare from England once in thirty daies.

Hee asked us whether did ever any man thinke that an enemyes comissioners would shew their power to treate before they bee assured that the other side will treate, or that it shalbee shewed but upon the place. My Comissioners, saith hee, were sent thither and with my power, and so both were shewed; and soe dare I say that yours shall see one if the Queene do send any thither, for, saith hee, both Taxis [and] Richardott doe say now to my servants that it is come, and in the same forme that the other is for mee. And for that point it is but in vaine to stand on it, for it is to mee a scorne and not to the Queene if the power were not sufficient.

And, besides, I know it that they doe desire a peace with all their hearts. I, John Herbert, said the Queene must know thus much, and that hee might in the meane tyme write to his deputyes to get a sight of it, least when her Ma^{ts} Comissioners should shew a power to treate, there should bee anie more respect shewed to the Kinge of Spaine in the fourme then hee doth shew her Matie in his. And that now his Ma^{ty} had thus farr opned himself that noe warre must bee made and that hee would leave the Estates, her Matie beinge informed of it hee should heare what shee would answere.

---

* The original despatch in PRO. S.P. 78, Vol. 42, p. 1 has *bastantissima.*

Hee said then, O, but I cannott tarry it. Withat I, the Secretarie, said, Sir, why then I beseech yow, let us have our pasport, if that bee the point, ffor if her Ma^ts benefitts past and your honor tye yow onely to respect yourselfe, the Queene knowes what to expect hereafter.

Hee was with that and many former contestations of ours much chafed, and said unto mee that hee had not used mee like an ordinary embassador to dispute thus freely and particularly.

I answered him that I took myself to bee sent from a prince that ought to bee extraordinarly respected. And, if without arrogancy I might speake it, I might take my self, consideringe my place, for no comon ordinary embassador.

Hee said it was true, and soe slubberd upp some speeches of kyndnesse againe.

Ffrom thence I told him of his letter last written, and how farr it was short of his speech delivered to us both together.

Hee said that for that point hee was too curious, hee would not bee taught to write, hee had said enough to us both of all that and had good reason to write no more.

I answered him that if any body had told him that I desired to appoint the stile hee had done mee wrong, for I was not so ill bred to doe it. And yet I had not kneeled at the foote of such a prince as my soveraigne scaven yeares but I could guesse what letters usually passed betweene princes when they meant to give satisfaction, and what in other letters.

Well, saith hee, as much as I do meane to committ to a letters perill my letter carryes. If the Queene trust yow not, why did shee send yow.

Wee answered that it became us to gett as much satisfaction as wee could from himself, finding that her Matie had so much cause of doubt, and that wee must bee content now that his Matie was so resolved. But if hee will have mee to expound his letter more effectuall then it was, I must crave pardon, and that I did contest cheifely that with his ministers that by his letters the King did dissavow nothing but that he had not given them comaundement to signe any thing, where in speech hee both dissavowed the haveing given them warrant to promise it as well as not to doe it.

Well, said hee, I have said enough for that matter, and where yow presume with benefitts past, the world will say that the Queene did herself no harme in it, and shall find me her faithfull and kind brother to the uttermost of my life.

I answered that howsoever partiall men might construe her Ma^ts helpe of him to bee out of her owne respect, sure I was that if her Matie had had a purpose to have served herself of the tyme and his necessityes, shee might have served her turne upon France when it was in soe many cantons with the same charge which shee had bene at with him. And for my part I humbly did beseech him to pardon mee, though I had for that speech no warrant as an embassador to speake it from the Queene:

Yet seing France did so partially regard itself as whensoever by the helpe of others it was made able to procure good conditions of the enemy, they must presently bee taken without respect of his allyes or giveing liberty to such a prince as myne was to bee informed or to understand and advise what way to take for himselfe, that I would pray to God that England might never have need of France though I would ever thinke reverendly of his Majesty, hopeing that hee would bee more respectfull then to loose so great reputation and the hearts of so many by doing so great an injury to her who never had fayled him, who notwith-standing that shee had shewed herself thus farre to bee contented at his intreaty to hearken too [sic] an enemy, yet shee would lett the world see that shee disdayned to seeke peace by any mans meanes in Europe.

And that, I durst avow it, shee was resolv'd at this tyme, as much as ever, to maynteine her honor against her enemy, howso-ever her freinds should use her.

Well, well, saith hee, *je combattray contre nous sacreete querelle.* Wee will advise further, and I will appoint the best of my Councell, whereof Villeroy shalbee one, to speake further with yow. And then wee will grow to some further resolution. For I would bee as loath to discontent my sister as any body.

Thus have wee sett downe this daies journall truely as our memoryes serve and with all his circumstances, here beinge nothing amongst them talked of but that the Queene may have a peace, that the States are onely self-lovers, that they will do well enough with underhand assistance, and that it is dis-honorable and ungodly to refuse that may sett publique quiett in Christendome.

Not knowing therefore in what tyme wee shalbee dispatched, and finding this opportunity of writeing, wee have thought it not amisse to acquaint your Lordshipps with so much as is past.

The Councell that should meete with us, as wee are informed, shalbee the Duke of Bouillon, Espernon, Villeroy, Seney [sic] and Scomberghe, who is a very wise man, with Plessis and Maissie, to whome wee doe resolve to speake plainely to the intent those persons, whereof diverse of them are free from gredinesse of peace, may know truelie what her Majesties intent hath bene in this legation, which the King himself, being every day more then other transported with desire of ease, is content to calumniate under hand. And, although hee bee never so plainely spoken unto, yet hee and the secretary slubbers [sic] it upp together and deliver but halfe to the rest, to the intent that it may bee thought if he had bene otherwise dealt withall or had any offer, that it would have stayed him from this course which his nature and humors doe draw him unto.

From Nants, the xth of Aprill, 1598.

This day the King did invite the Comissioners and divers others to dyne with him, and at evening did solemnize the ffeast of St. George in St. Peters Church in Nants.

[*Marginal note :* Aprill 13.] This afternoone they had audience in the Kings cabinet.

Att night Mounsieur Villeroy came to conferre with Mr Secretary at his lodginge.

[*Marginal note :* 14th.] The 14th Mr Secretarys servants were embarqued in a Scottish shippe to goe by long seas into England.

This morneing the Duke Espernon came to visitt Mr Secretary in his lodgeinge. The Estates deputyes had also conference with him.

In the afternoone Mr Secretary took his leave of the King, Mr Harbert and he haveing had audience in the Kings cabinett. And after that Mr Secretary had private audience in his innermost cabbinett an hower together. They should have taken leave of Madame the Kings sister, but shee was at a sermon.

Mounsieur Tremonall had this day private conference with Mr Secretary.

The Duke of Bouyllon presented Mr Secretary with a faire jewell wherein was the Kings picture.

[*Marginal note :* 15th.] Chastean Breean. The 15th of this moneth wee removed from Nants in our journey homewards, went to Chastean Brean to bedd, and by the way mett with Mounsieur Montbarrett, Governor of Rhemes.

Neere to Chastean Breean the Governor of the place met twith us. His name was Sieur Giles. The towne and castle are both belonging to the constable.

[*Marginal note :* 16th.] Here wee staid Sunday all day being our Easter Day.

[*Marginal note :* 17th.] Trois Maris. The 17th wee removed from thence about 10 in the forenoone and came to a village called Troys Maris to bedd. In our way wee mett with the Duke Montpensier travailling to Nants to the Kinge.

[*Marginal note :* 18th.] Rhemes. The 18th day wee came to Rhemes and were lodged at the Seneschells howse.

The sonne of Montbarrett mett with us without the towne very well accompanyed, and towards the eveninge his brother came to visitt Mr Secretary at his lodging.

[*Marginal note :* 19th.] Vitrey. The 19th wee came to Vitrey, where the next day after our comeing the preacher of those of the religion with others came to visitt Mr Secretary and the townsmen presented him with wyne.

[*Marginal note :* 20.] Fulgiers. The xxth wee came to Fulgiers at the house of one Mounsieur Jenure, who is sonne to the Kings secretary.

[*Marginal note :* 21th.] Anaranches. The 21th wee came to Anaranches, but stayed a little while by the way at a village called St. Gelun.

[*Marginal note :* 22th.] Vill Dreir. The 22th wee came to Vill Dreir where wee lodged the same night.

[*Marginal note :* 23th.] Thorigny. The 23th wee came to Thorigny, where the Marshalls de Anmonts widdow and Mounsieur Thorigny invited Mr Secretary to supper.

[*Marginal note :* 24th.]   Caen.   The 24th wee dyned at a village called La Masson Bland, and came to Caen to bedd.   There wee mett with Jasper the Post with letters out of England.

[*Marginal note :* Aprill 27th.]   The 27th being Thursdaye, wee parted from Caen towards Estreataon, a port some 3 leagues thence where the *Adventure* and the *Moone*, a shipp and pinnace of the Queens, the one comaunded by Sir Allexander Clifton, the other by Captaine Willis, did attend our comeing, being accompanied with the *Lions Whelpe* of my Lord Admiralls and two small barks, being men of warre of Weymouth.   Wee had not stayed there an hower but the marryners brought word that the winde was good.

Whereuppon Mr Secretary himselfe imbarqued with some few of his company in the *Adventure*, leaveing the other shipping for Mr Herbert and the rest of the company.   The wynd contynued good att our putting out of the harbor.   Howbeit, in the night, by what mishchance [*sic*] it is unknowne, the marryners did mistake their course and tooke the Hogge head for the Isle of Wight. By meanes whereof and the calmes and contrary wyndes wee stayed at sea Ffriday all day and night.   And Satterday in the morneinge, being the 29th, wee arrived at Landham castle in the Isle of Wight, where wee dyned, and after dynner came to ride att a little port in the Island where [*marginal note :* Portsmouth.] wee tooke passage to Portsmouth arriveing heere about ffower in the afternoone.

The xxxth in the morneing wee sett forth towards London, dyned by the way at Altham, and came to Staines about 9 at night, where a coach of my Lord of Essex attended for Mr Secretary, and brought him to the Court betweene 10 and 11 of the clock at Whitehall.   Mr Secretary went presently to the Queene, not stayinge longe with her, but retorned to his howse in the Strand.

210 pp.   **(351)**

SURVEY.

[Before March, 1597–98].—A description of the extent, value and bounds of the demesne land of Walterstone, and of certain pasture and arable closes adjacent to the property of Lord Abergavenny and William Cecil* of Altyrynys.—*Undated.*

Endorsed : " Mr Hopton ".   1 p.   (P. 2251.)

PAUL DE LA HAY to SIR ROBERT CECIL.

[*c.* May, 1598].—About a year ago petitioner's father-in-law, William Cecil, was given to understand that his son, Matthew, had agreed with his brother-in-law, John Parry, for the reversion of Cecil's lands to the latter, upon which Parry had named his child Cecil.   William Cecil therefore offered to come to terms with petitioner about the land, but he had preferred to postpone

---

* Buried on March 6, 1598. [See *H.M.C. Salisbury MSS,* Vol. VIII, pp. 82–3.]

the matter until Sir Robert Cecil had expressed his views concerning a previous bargain between him and William Cecil. Meanwhile, to prevent the rifling of his goods and the spoliation of his house by Matthew's wife, William Cecil made a will appointing petitioner as his executor. However, upon Cecil's death, Matthew's wife and her brother-in-law, Valentine Pritchard, encouraged Matthew to contest the will. Petitioner went to Lord Burghley who ordered him to procure the will, and wrote to Matthew that its stipulations should be observed. Matthew chose to ignore this order until petitioner had surrendered to him goods worth 500 marks, and it was agreed between them that the copyhold lands belonging to the demesne of the house at Alt-yr-ynys, as well as the household goods, should come to Sir Robert Cecil. Under the influence of his wife Matthew transferred the copyhold lands to her, and when he died he was " obscuriously buried ", and the cattle taken away by his widow's brother-in-law, Valentine Pritchard. Petitioner refers to the fact that the widow is now thinking up other schemes at the expense of himself and other members of William Cecil's family, and begs Cecil to take measures to counter them.—*Undated.*

1 p. (P. 1208.)

[See *H.M.C. Salisbury MSS*, Vol. VIII, pp. 83 and 165.]

GILBERT WAKERING (ex parte MARGARET VERNON) *versus* HENRY TOWNSHEND, DOROTHY HIS WIFE, JOHN MANNERS, JOHN VERNON AND OTHERS.

1598, June 6.—" A Certificate of the proceedings in the cause inter Wakeringe, gen : Mannors, Townsehend et al, defendants." —6 June, 1598.

1 p. (P. 2144.)

[See *H.M.C. Salisbury MSS*, Vol. VIII, p. 196.]

THE EASTLAND MERCHANTS to the PRIVY COUNCIL.

[After December, 1598].—They complain of injustices in the Sound where they are forced to pay customs duties on wraps, etc., and where errors in ships' entries lay them open to the confiscation of vessels and cargoes. A forfeiture of their goods occurred last year, as a consequence of which the Queen sent an ambassador to the King of Denmark. He attended the investigation of the case in the presence of many members of the Danish Privy Council and found their proceedings to be unjust, but his protests availed little. The King of Denmark offered to restore 30,000 dollars of confiscated goods, but the Queen decided to despatch another ambassador to demand justice, or alternatively, that the case be heard by the Princes and Kings, his neighbours. This proposal was rejected, but the King of Denmark's original offer was raised to 40,000 dollars. This was accepted by Dr Parkins. Since then, however, the King of Denmark has sent an envoy to England to resuscitate old unsettled businesses, and appears so unsatisfied with the results that petitioners fear a further seizure of their goods in the Sound. They ask that Cecil and the Queen take appropriate measures to find a remedy for this state of affairs.—*Undated*

On reverse : A summary of the principal points in the petition. ½ p. (P. 2102.)

[See *Acts of the Privy Council*, 1598–99, pp. 71–2, and *The Letters of John Chamberlain* (ed. McClure), Vol. 1, pp. 40, 57–8.]

LORD SANDYS.

[1598].—" The declaration of the Lord Sandys abilitie." 1 p. (P. 2148.)

[In its details this petition is a duplicate of CP. 186/139. [See *H.M.C. Salisbury MSS*, Vol. XIV, p. 94.]

THEOBALDS.

[1598 or before].—Plan of the porter's lodge at Theobalds, co. Herts.—*Undated*

Endorsed by Burghley : " The outward porters lodg." 1 *sheet.* (CPM *supplementary* 36a–s, General 12/29.)

[See *H.M.C. Salisbury MSS*, Vol. XIV, pp. 76–8.]

THOMAS FOVELL to SIR ROBERT CECIL.

[1598 or later].—Lord Burghley granted him the wardship of the daughter and heiress of David Morgan* on the condition that he could prove the Queen's title to it. This he has done and procured evidence to show that three acres were held of the Queen *in capite* within the honour of Brecknock, the remainder of Morgan's land being held in socage. Her Majesty is therefore entitled to the wardship of the daughter who is five years of age, and to the three acres worth five shillings annually. The ward's mother is to be endowed with the third part of the remaining patrimony which altogether is worth £6 a year. Petitioner is entitled only to the marriage of the ward, which is of little value. He requests that a reasonable rate be decided upon for the sale of the ward.—*Undated.*

On reverse: another copy. ½ p. (P. 120.)

PROCEEDINGS IN MADRID.

[1598–99] February 6.—Report on legal proceedings involving Diego Parcar *alias* Juan Borrer or John Bourrell, described as an " yngles que es un hombre de buen cuerpo " (" a well-shaped Englishman ").—Madrid, February 6.

Spanish 2 pp. (**205.** 64.)

[See *H.M.C. Salisbury MSS*, Vol. VIII, pp. 182–6, and Vol. XIV, p. 93, and *Cal. S.P. Dom.*, 1598–1601, p. 86. Also *Acts of the Privy Council*, 1598–99, p. 181.]

---

* Probate of his will granted in 1598. [See *Prerogative Court of Canterbury Wills*, Vol. IV, 1584–1604, p. 294.]

JOHN LITTLETON to [? SIR ROBERT CECIL].

[Before July, 1599].—The revenues of Gilbert Littleton issuing from certain manors, Prestwood House and its demesne, Frankley House and park, and the tithes of Wolverley and Hales Owen. A note on the debts of Gilbert Littleton and his eldest son John. Petitioner requests that after adequate portions of the estate have been assigned for the maintenance of Gilbert Littleton's wife and younger children, the estate may be assured to his father or to himself, as eldest son, on the condition that they give sureties for the payment of their debts. If this proposal is unacceptable, he asks that the estate may be taken over by, " some principall gent of blood and alliance to the children till such tyme as the debts of the father and the sonne may be discharged ".—*Undated.*

1 p. (P. 2448.)
[Warrant for *Inq. P.M.* on Gilbert Littleton was issued on July 2, 1599. See *PRO. Chancery* **142**, 257/71.]

ANDREW DE RYMA SECHEI to the PRIVY COUNCIL.

[Before September 17, 1599].—He is a Hungarian who was taken prisoner in Turkey some six or seven years ago. Although he mortgaged his estate he was unable to pay the ransom demanded by the Turks, and was forced two or three years ago to travel to England and other countries to raise money for that purpose. Queen Elizabeth gave him £20, the King and Queen of Poland donated 400 French crowns, and other sympathetic benefactors in England contributed sums which amounted in all to £220. During a visit to Devon he left £108 out of what had been gathered on his behalf in the safe-keeping of William Lowther, parson of Cadbury, John Taylor, a constable of Exeter and father-in-law to Lowther, and Peter Parkman, also of Cadbury. Since then he has often requested them for the money but has been refused every time, not without threats to his life. He is a foreigner, and is impotent to act without the support of the Council. He asks that letters be sent to J.P.s in Devon, directing them to summon Lowther, Taylor and Parkman before them, to examine the matter and to oblige them to satisfy petitioner or to explain the reasons for their refusal.—*Undated.*

1 p. (P. 1300.)
[See *Acts of the Privy Council*, 1598–99, p. 741.]

RICHARD TUNSTALL to [SIR ROBERT CECIL].

[c. September, 1599].—He is a prisoner in Bridewell where he has remained for three months. During this time he has had no allowance for his relief, and so has been obliged to sell what he and his wife have received from friends to assist him. His case is sufficiently known to Mr Wade who declares that he has no authority to release him. He asks to be allowed bail, and undertakes to be ready at any time to answer whatever charges are preferred against him.—*Undated*.

1 p.   (P. 138.)

[See *Catholic Record Society*, Vol. 53, p. 159, and *Cal. S.P. Dom*, 1598–1601, p. 226.]

—— to ——.

[? *c*. October, 1599].—Dispute over money matters with Corsini (details given).   The writer asks that his plea be brought before the Lord Chief Justice.—*Undated and unsigned*.

Holograph ?   Italian.   1 p.   (**186.**   121.)

[See *H.M.C. Salisbury MSS*, Vol. IX, p. 376.]

THE EARL OF WORCESTER to [? LORD MOUNTJOY].

[? 1599] November 31.—" I am requested by the bearer herof to recomend his service unto youer Lordship yf this burthen of Irishe imployment doe lyght uppon youe.* He hathe served there heartofore, and ys very desierouse to followe the wars. And the rather bycawse he may doe youer Lordship service ether in that or ayny other imployment that may seeme good to youe. His desier is to have the goverment of the sowldiers eyther of Monmothe or Breknoke sheer.   And he assurethe mee that by his dutyfyll respect towards youe and the well ordering of that charge, he wyll deserve youer Lordships good opynion for a better hearafter.   His name is Charles Herbert, sone to Mathewe Herbert, one of the deputie lyvtenants of Monmothe shere, and servant to mee this 5 or 6 yeres.   And yf the master for the man or the man for the master may obteyn youer favore herein, we wyll bothe endevor to acknowledg yt to the uttermost."— From Ragland, Nove. 31.

Holograph.   1 p.   (**113.**   39.)

AUGUSTINE NOVY to [SIR ROBERT CECIL].

[1599].—He refers to the business " whereon I have ymployed soe great chardge, travaill and indeavors to bring it fowrth ". He regrets that it may redound to Cecil's loss, but has heard that measures may be taken to meet that contingency and to place the business on a firmer footing.   He begs Cecil to bring about that desirable state of affairs, and " the prosperitie of the busines which nowe lyeth withering before it can take roote (except your honor bestowe a present wateringe ".—*Undated*.

⅓ p.   (P. 92.)

[See *H.M.C. Salisbury MSS*, Vol. IX, pp. 136, 401, 402.]

EDMUND GUNTER to SIR ROBERT CECIL.

[*c*. 1599].—He extols Cecil's virtues, in particular his interest in and patronage of scholarship, which transcend all temporal considerations and excite general admiration.   This has encour-

---

* Charles Blount, Lord Mountjoy, was appointed Lord Deputy of Ireland in December, 1599.

aged him to solicit Cecil's assistance in obtaining a place at Cambridge University,* a matter which he has discussed with the Dean of Westminster and secured his approval. If his wish is granted, he will remember Cecil's favour and benefaction throughout his life. He appends a poem in Greek.—*Undated.*

1 p. (**140.** 89.)

PETER PYTNEY to SIR ROBERT CECIL.

[Before March 29, 1600].—He is of Stourton, Wiltshire, and with his wife and six children is entirely dependent on five acres of meadow lying near Shaftesbury, co. Dorset, which he has held for 24 years and which were leased by John, late Lord Stourton, to Valentine Carter and Alice his daughter, who is now petitioner's wife. John Budden, of Shaftesbury, who is in Cecil's service, is trying by all means to obtain possession of four of the acres which adjoin his property. He has persuaded the present Lord Stourton to grant him a lease of them, he being Stourton's steward, and for the past three years he has been pestering petitioner with legal proceedings. During this time petitioner has not dared to make use of the acres in question, but allowed them to become waste to his great loss. Another tenant of the name of Kerley has likewise been harassed by Budden for his house and lands. Kerley has, however, chosen to defend his title by law, and petitioner decided to join forces with him for the same purpose. But when the case came to trial Budden abandoned all proceedings against Kerley " because he is a man hable to wage with him ", but prosecuted those against petitioner. Moreover, when the latter put a horse out to grass on part of the lands in dispute, Budden seized the animal and starved it to death. Petitioner asks Cecil to exercise restraint over Budden and to permit him to enjoy his acres in peace, or to invite certain disinterested Dorset gentlemen to examine and judge the case impartially.—*Undated.*

1 p. (P. 1295.)

[See *H.M.C. Salisbury MSS*, Vol. X, p. 85.]

RICHARD PERCEVAL to SIR ROBERT CECIL.

1600, April 17.—He has two daughters aged 16 and 17 respectively, but has not the means to arrange matches for them except by disposing of his property or being the recipient of Cecil's favour. He asks for the wardship of the heir of William Swan of Kent, which has been concealed during the past four years. Young Swan is now of age and married. 17 April, 1600.

Note by Cecil : " He may have a commission."

1 p. (P. 71.)

ELEANOR, JULIAN and ELIZABETH MAINWARING to SIR ROBERT CECIL.

[c. April 20, 1600].—Petition concerning the Croxton lands,

---

* Gunter entered Oxford University from Westminster School in 1599.

with a pedigree showing the intermarriage between the Croxton
and Mainwaring families and the direct and collateral descendants
thereof. Details are given of the descent of the property from
1584 to 1598. Three parties are involved in the suit which is
about the validity of inheritance by entail : (1) Mr Oldfield,
whose son has married the eldest of the three daughters of James
Mainwaring, the deceased owner, and who in return for an
advance of £2000 has the custody of the orphaned girls and of
the property : (2) the heirs male of the collateral branch of the
Mainwaring family, whose misdemeanours and violent entries
have forced Oldfield to bring a bill against them in the Star
Chamber : and (3) Sir John Egerton who supports the efforts of
the heirs male to nullify the conveyance of the lands to the
eldest daughter for life. Petitioners pray Cecil " that the cause
may receave a full hearinge in Court in presence of the two
Cheiff Justices, to yeld theire opinions in matters in lawe. And
hereuppon a direction to be geven to the Jurors what the Court
conceaveth fytt to be founde. Yf this may not be, the tytle of
the doughtors ys lyke to receave great prejudice, the said Sir
John beinge so great a man amonge the Jurors in the cuntrey."
—*Undated*.
2½ pp.   (P. 868.)
[See *H.M.C. Salisbury MSS*, Vol. X, p. 119, and *PRO. Star
Chamber Proceedings* 5, **O** 41/33.]

MARGERY WAYLETT to SIR ROBERT CECIL.

[After May, 1600].—Concerning the wardship of her son,
William Waylett.* She is unable to pay the £10 demanded of
her for it. Since the benefit accruing from the wardship is small,
she requests that it be given her as a free gift, or that she be
allowed the expenses defrayed by her in connection with the
wardship and the ward.—*Undated*.
½ p.   (P. 104.)

CHRISTOPHER PICKERING and WILLIAM HUTTON to [SIR ROBERT CECIL].

[*c.* August 11, 1600].—They are submitting the petition on
behalf of themselves and the other gentlemen of the east part
of the West Wardenry. They refer to the petition presented by
them last Sunday to the Privy Council, which has the support
of their Lord Warden and was subscribed by him. Two notes are
attached to it ; one is a breviate by the Justices of Assize of such
depositions as have been made before them ; the other a description of the worsening situation in Gillesland and the reasons for
its deterioration, together with an account of a recent misdemean-
our committed there against the land-sergeant and which calls
for immediate disciplinary action. They ask that the petition

---

* His father Robert Waylett died on November 4, 1599, and an *Inq. P.M.*
was held on May 15, 1600. [See *PRO.* **C.** 142.   Vol. 261, No. 42.]

and notes be perused or they themselves allowed to explain the position in person, and that their suit be furthered.—*Undated.* ½ p. (P. 2345.)

[See *The Border Papers (Scottish Record Publications)* ed. Joseph Bain, Vol. 11, pp. 677–8, 689 (No. 1241) and 689–90.]

ACCOUNTS.

1600, September.—Payment of an allowance of 6/8 to Cuthbert Stillingfleet, one of the messengers of the Queen's Chamber, " for riding in hast at the commandement of the right hon. Sir Robert Cescell, knight, her highnes principall secretary frome London with letters for her Ma^{ts} sarvis unto the right hon. the L. Cobham unto the Cort at Otlands ".—September, 1600.

Signed : Robert Cecyll. ½ p. (**223.** 22.)

SIR ROBERT CECIL to SIR THOMAS POSTHUMUS HOBY.

1600 [November 1].—" Uppon the receipt of your letter I was forced to deferr any answer becawse the counsaile mett not, and in this case above all others you know I must be curious to shew ether passion or affection. For the matter I find it a very fowle riot as it is sett downe, and dowbtless we shold have don our selfs wrong not to have censured it accordingly. But yet when I consider the nature of railings especially in that kind, I never found that any took less scandall then they cold after have wished they might have avoyded, and therfore I assure you I am very gladd that the matter is reconciled, not doubting but you have very good satisfaction for so great an injury."—1600.

Holograph. Endorsed : " 1 November, 1600. Receyved from Mr Secretary Cecil." *Fragment of seal.* 1 p. (**206.** 113.)

[For the background to this letter see *H.M.C. Salisbury MSS,* Vol. X, pp. 302–4.]

[? The EARL OF ESSEX] to [? MR PLONDEN].

[After November 29, 1600].—" Mr Broughton for the causes by me and Justice Owen hard and (as we thought) ended betwene you and Mr Blunden and others, he alledgeth that you not onelie refuze to agre to the settinge them downe accordinge to my ende and your then assent, but also refuze to performe anie of them and molest and troble his ffrinds in the meane tyme above measure. He at your beinge in towne did often ymportune me in those causes and wished an ende, you beinge here : or that he might procede with my favor in course of lawe which seemeth reasonable. I pray you therfore, eyther cum up your self in the begyninge of the next terme to ende those causes, or fully instruct Mr Bromley or some other of your councell and under your hand and seale suffycientlie authorise them to ende all matters betwene you and him and his ffrinds, or ells at your owne choyce and election lett the lawe take his course betwene you, for I will noe longer staye him, for other favor he requireth not."—*Undated and unsigned.*

Draft corrected. ½ p. (P. 2119.)

[See *H.M.C. Salisbury MSS,* Vol. XIV, p. 143.]

MATTHEW DAVIES to [SIR ROBERT CECIL].

[1600] December 2.—He is the servant of Mr Michael Hicks, and asks to be given the wardship of the two daughters of Agnes Larkes for the use of the mother.* The wardship has no greater value than £8 annually. 20 December.

½ p. (P. 789.)

THOMAS ADDISON to SIR ROBERT CECIL.

[? 1600] He is one of the messengers of the Queen's Chamber. Before his death the late Lord Burghley bestowed on him a ward named Goddard at Bury St. Edmunds, co. Suffolk. Petitioner has spent much money in establishing the Queen's title to the wardship, and he asks that the gift be confirmed by Cecil. *Undated.*

Note at bottom : " To bring a testimonie."

On reverse : A letter from Gilbert Wakering to Richard Perceval. " Thomas Addyson, one of the messengers of her Ma[ties] Chamber brought this petition to me and saide yt was the Mr. of the Wardes his pleasure that I shoulde certefie my knowledge and proceedinge in the wardshipp of Thomas Goddard which is as followeth. This petitioner obteyned a graunte thereof in my Lord Treasurer his tyme some two yeares since (the thinge beinge small and long concealed), and thereupon sued out a writt of *mandamus,* and I beinge then Escheator of the countyes of Norffolke and Suffolke yt came to my hande. Whereupon I charged a jury to enquire of the tenure at Bury St. Edmonds in the saide countie of Suffolke, and for that I coulde not sett forth any certaine tenure for the Queene, nor he that followed yt, and for that the parties that defended yt againste us there, havinge sufficient warninge thereof, coulde not proove the tenure on their partes nor by what services they helde the same, there was an *ignoramus* founde by the jury at that tyme, and the same was certefied and returned by me into the Chauncery. Then this petitioner, after that, obteyned Mr Atturney of the Wardes his warrante under his hand for a writt of *melius inquirendum,* the which writt was likewise delivered to me and was executed accordinglie, and thereupon a seconde *ignoramus* founde which breedes unto her Ma[tie] a tenure *in capite.* And all was at the charge and followinge of this petitioner." *Undated.*

½ p. (P. 1775.)

[*See PRO. Inq. P.M.,* C 142, **261**/29 and 58.]

JOHN ELLYSTON to SIR ROBERT CECIL.

[? 1600].—He is an innkeeper, and complains that last July he was persuaded by Henry Lok to become a surety to Francis Growte and Roger Dan in the Strand for two hackney horses, which two of John Killigrew's servants hired to go into the country on their master's business. Lok promised that petitioner

---

* .Agnes Larkes was granted the wardship of the elder daughter, Mary, on May 25, 1601. [See *PRO. Wards* **9**, Vol. 348.]

should not suffer from this transaction. The two servants, however, sold the horses without indemnifying the owners, whereupon petitioner was arrested and forced to pay £7 as compensation. Despite his appeals for relief, Lok has refused to help him, and he is now a prisoner in the Gatehouse following upon other people's legal proceedings against him. Petitioner requests that he be allowed to recover from Lok what he can by law, particularly as he lost money when serving Mr Danson. On that occasion Cecil favoured him with his letters whereby he was able to discover who had robbed him, but failed to obtain restitution of his money.—*Undated.*

¾ p. (P. 68.)

[See *Cal. S.P. Dom.*, 1598–1601, pp. 426, 509. See also *H.M.C. Salisbury MSS*, Vol. XI, p. 497.]

ISAAC LE MOYNE to [SIR ROBERT CECIL].

[1600 or before].—He informs him that after the latest destruction of his goods at Dieppe he retired to the Low Countries where he took up arms in the service of Count Maurice and Queen Elizabeth. Later on he served in the city and garrison of Dublin, as the passport issued by the Earl of Essex will show. He asks Cecil to take him into his service, inasmuch as in addition to his own language he is conversant with Latin, Flemish and English. As a testimonial to his competence and conduct, he mentions that he spent some time in the house of Mr Tufton, one of the gentlemen in Cecil's suite when he went to France, and that he had taught French to his eldest son.—*Undated.*

At bottom : two lines of verse in Latin.

French. ½ p. (P. 474.)

HUBERT FOX to SIR ROBERT CECIL.

[? 1600].—He requests the payment of the allowance of 7/8 a day granted to him and twenty kerns, so that he may discharge his debts and " attend and wayt uppon the L. Mountjoy to Irland, to be employed in hir Ma^{ts} service, otherwise he is not hable to depart ".—*Undated.*

¾ p. (P. 392.)

[See *H.M.C. Salisbury MSS*, Vol. XIV, p. 155.]

CLARE HALL, CAMBRIDGE.

[1600].—Opinions expressed by the heads of various college- at Cambridge on the meaning of the statute regulating the appointment of the Master of Clare Hall, and the requisite qualifications demanded of candidates for the post.

" I am in opinion that the meaninge of this statute and divers other braunches contayned in the statute is directly for a divine." *Signed:* John Duport.

"I am also of that opinion." *Signed* : Thomas Legg.

" I am of opinion that the meaning of this statute is to present a divine to the mastership." *Signed*: Richard Clayton.

" I am of the same opinion that the statute can not otherwyse be taken according to the grammaticall sense but only for a divine." *Signed :* Laurence Chaderton.

At bottom : " The heads of colledges above named, not having ether by custome or statut, any right to interprete our statuts, at the request of William Boyses,* competitor for the mastership of Clare Hall, gave their interpretation of the foresayde statut in manner above mentioned under their hands before the 31 of December last past which we whose names are underwritten will justifie upon our othes." *Signed ;* Richard Thomson, Edward Manistie, John Allerton, George Ruggle.

On reverse : " Memorandum that Mr Proctor before the delivery of the copies of theis laws made protestation that he did not deliver them any wayes to prejudice the Statuts of the Colledge or any good and honest proceedings which have bene in the said Colledge. In the presence of us." *Signed :* Ed. Manistie, John Brasbone.—*Undated.*

1¼ pp. **(136.** 202.)

CLARE HALL, CAMBRIDGE.

[1600].—Further opinions expressed on the meaning of the statute concerning the appointment of a Master of Clare Hall.

" *Quaeritur,* whether the persone to bee elected being a Master of Arts of sixteen yeares continuance, having competent knowledge in divinity and so approved him selfe by exercise in that kind, though not within ecclesiasticall orders, may bee elected Master of the Colledge aforesayd."

" I am of opinion that suche a master of art is eligible to the mastership of suche a college." *Signed :* John Cowell.

" I am of the same opinion." *Signed :* Martin Berye.

" I am of the same opinion." *Signed :* Robert Turner.

" I am of the same opinion." *Signed :* Charles Belassis.

" I am of the same opinion." *Signed :* Robert Nucome.

" I am likwise of opinion with oute doute that yt is not necessarie that the person to be elected ought by the statute to be within ecclesiasticall orders." *Signed :* Henry Stewarde.

" I can not conjecture what cawse there shoold be of question why the person elected or to be elected shoold be in orders, so far I am from supposing that statute required he shoold be in orders." *Signed :* John Hone.

On reverse : " Applieng my answer directlie to the question and everie parte of it, I am of opinion that a Master of Artes so qualified may bee elected to bee master of the said College, and that there is no worde in the Statute within laid downe that can necessarily evince that hee should be within ecclesiasticall orders." *Signed :* John Lloyd of tharches.—*Undated.*

1¼ pp. **(136.** 203.)

---

* His appointment as Master in December, 1599, led to much opposition and controversy within and outside the college, and eventually to his refusal of the post. [See *H.M.C. Salisbury MSS*, Vol. IX, p. 418 and Vol. X under *Boys.*]

[Sir Robert Cecil] to [Lord Willoughby].

[1600 or before] October 28.—" I have receaved a letter of yours whereby I am distracted in opinion what to doe because I see the particuler request which I made you may be occasion of question wherein, if the cause come to hearinge, my judgment may peradventure be thought unindifferent in respect I may be held a party. It is verie trew, my lord, that when I wrote unto your Lordshipe for Parker I knew nothinge more of the matter then that a roome was voyd and that himself was worthy of that place and a better, havinge seen the warrs abroad and receaved many hurtes in service. But now I doe perceave that by the demonstration of your desyre to gratify me, there is a question risen between your authority and that of the captens wherein I will playnly deliver your Lordshipe my opinion, not as that by which I will be concluded if your Lordshipe bringe it to argument, for then I will presume to receave from you reason sufficient to mayntayne what you require, for whom I doe assure I will engage my self in any question as farr as I will doe for any nobleman in England.

I doe fynd in the establishment that your Lordshipe hath the appoyntment of the captens of the ffoote, constables of the horse and other places of marke in the garrison, and I doe alsoe fynd a clause that noe capten may take or dismisse a souldyer without your privity, wherein I doe assure me that you have an absolute negative voyce. Soe as methinkes there is never a capten in that garrison that should be soe opiniastre as to think that Chattocke could be preferred without you ; but that on the other syde, that your Lordshipe should peremptorily impose uppon a capten his officers by other authority then by the interest of love and respect which everie wise capten ought to leane to soe moderate and judiciall a governor, I must confesse for my owne opinion I am not thereof perswaded for any thinge that I have yet heard; and therefore in this case I am thus resolved nether to pull uppon your Lordshipe for my sake the cumber to contend with the captens, nor to drive you to the indignity to be beholdinge to any of them for me, whoe for my owne part disdayne, now I see some of their humours, to have cause to give them thankes for the best curtesye which they could offer, not doubtinge but it may ether fall into your Lordshipes lott that *authoritate propria* to grace Parker with some other thinge, or unto myne to helpe him els where to as good a fortune as to be Capten Selbyes lieutenant."—*Undated.*

Draft corrected by Cecil. Endorsed : " Mynute to the L. Willoughby* from my Master. October 28." 4½ pp. (**197.** 78.)

Gregory Champante to Sir Robert Cecil.

[? 1600].—He has been ordered by Cecil to pay Hare £20 and to confirm the term of years yet to come in Conradus's leases of

---

* Lord Willoughby died on June 25, 1601.

the tenements in question. He is ready to do so, but Conradus opposes the implementation of Cecil's order. He begs Cecil to have compassion on his age, poverty and eight children, to allow him to leave London, and to accept his explanation for not being able to attend Cecil when he was first ordered to appear before him. At that time he was indisposed and unable to move about, as Mr Clerke of the Privy Council can testify.—*Undated*.

½ p. (P. 108.)

[See *H.M.C. Salisbury MSS*, Vol. XII, p. 579.]

MR JORDAN.

[Before 1601].—" The names of certaine gentlemen of the best accompte dwellinge neere to Mr Jordan." They are : Thomas Arrandell, John Thynne, Edwarde Hungerforde,* Jasper Moore, Henrie Willougbie and Edmonde Lambert.—*Undated*.

½ p. (P. 2213.)

HERCULES WYTHAN to SIR ROBERT CECIL.

[Before 1601].—He is the tenant of the inn called the *Black Lion* at Hoddesdon. It is now in such a ruinous condition that he " hath beene forced thereby to pull downe the signe for that there is neither chamber fitt to receive any person or stable for their horses ". Repairs are imperative this summer, and he requests a warrant to Mr Amyas, Cecil's surveyor, to allow him timber, bricks and tiles within the manor of Baas. He also asks that £20 be abated from his yearly rent of £25:13:4, which he will spend on the necessary repairs, and more if required.— *Undated*.

On reverse note signed by Cecil : " To be considered by Mr Amice and John Styleman."

½ p. (P. 1737.)

[See *H.M.C. Salisbury MSS*, Vol. XIII, p. 464. In 1601, the inn was held by John Wytham. See Tregelles *A History of Hoddesdon*, p. 129 and note, and Victoria County History, *Hertfordshire*, Vol. 11, p. 280, for a reference to Hercules Wytham.]

LADY BACON to the EARL OF ESSEX.

[Before 1601] December 23.—She remarked recently to a court friend of hers in a place of a preaching ministry in the City that she wished that Her Majesty herself heard such wholesome and fruitful doctrine as they did hear and enjoy under her. She mentioned one who in his youth remembers his Creator and goes beyond his elders in avoiding swearing and gaming, namely, the Earl of Essex. But she has been told by her friend that the Earl was a terrible swearer. She was so terrified by these words that she could not rest until she had committed it thus in scribbling to his Honour, her dear Lord. She adds several texts from the Scriptures proving the wickedness of swearing. As her state of body is, so is her scribbling weak and blurred, and unworthy

---

* Knighted in 1601.

of his Lordship's trouble to read it with so many cares and affairs on his mind. From the confines of ruinared [*sic*] Verulam.—23 December.

Unsigned. Endorsed: "The La. Bacon." 1 p. (**128.** 68.)

JOHN BOWYER to SIR ROBERT CECIL.

[? *c.* 1600–1].—Three years ago Sir John Poyntz decided to dispose of some of his lands in order to pay his debts, and petitioner, who is his brother-in-law (he and Poyntz having married two sisters and living in the same house) found a kinsman of his to purchase them. Petitioner also entered into a bond with Poyntz for the payment of £500 to certain creditors, but Sir John by underhand means has made him responsible for his debts, and left him to the discretion of the creditors. They have arrested him twice already, and for the past year he has not dared to venture outside his house for fear of being harassed by them. Despite his appeals, Sir John has refused to discharge his debts, and allowed judgments and outlawries to be issued against petitioner. He asks Cecil to order Poyntz to take measures for petitioner's discharge.—*Undated.*

¾ p. (P. 1352.)

[See *H.M.C. Salisbury MSS*, Vol. XIV, p. 222.]

SURVEY.

1600–1.—A survey of the estates of Sir Robert Cecil in 1600–1, with index of place names and with maps.

Signed: Israel Amyce. 216 pp. (**349.**)

MEMORIAL.

[Before February 17, 1600–1].

" Remember Michelborns woords to Smyth.

Dynsanys Letters.

Erl of Shrewsburys woords.

Speake to Mr Attorney for Wrights confession and Alablasters.

The Erls speeches to Alderman Martyn testefied by D—n.

The B. of Kerry being imploied by my L. Mountjoy heard those speeches of a letter written by the Erl which Owney McRoys man James Keeond doth certefy.

He told it his brother Crosby and M bad him ask Gerrald fitz Gerrald who dyd tell him those woords, and that he was bedfellow to Tiron who showed him the copy of a letter.

Examine Ewes.

D. Hawkins.

Bacon.

The L. Treasurer hath Leas* confession.

Meddle not with the Erls letter to Lea till he do disprouve Lea.

---

* Executed for his part in the Earl of Essex's conspiracy on February 17, 1601.

Let the things of Wright in any wise be delt in as casuall."
—*Undated.*

In Sir Robert Cecil's hand. Endorsed : " Memoriall." 1 p.
(**109.** 35.)

DANIEL LE NOMAGHE to ——.

[Before February 17, 1600–1].—" As I passed in Ffebruary
last from Dublin towards upper Ossory, John Eustace, nowe
sherife of the countie of Kildare, did meete me at the Nace, who
having enquired of such nywes as I had ffrom England did
quostion what was becom of Capten Lee. I told him that (as
I was enformed) he was arested for som matter which I did not
knowe, but, said I, he useth very bad speches of thearle of Ormod.
Well, said he, he is more to be spoken of him selfe, for he sent a
barrell of poulder with lead and mach to one Mr Rory to feught
against thearle of Essex when he went to Leix. It is hard, said
I, to prove it against him. By God, said he, if I were dryven
to it, I woold find good proof. Whether this be trywe or not,
I do not knowe."—*Undated.*

Signed only. 1 p. (**90.** 52.)

THE EARL OF KILDARE.

[*c.* March 16, 1600–1].—A note of certain lands granted by
Queen Mary to Gerald, late Earl of Kildare, and to his wife Lady
Mabel, which are to return to the Crown after Lady Mabel's death.
The Earl of Kildare is a suitor for the reversion of these lands
which are : the monastery of Down, co. Down, with property
called Lecale formerly leased by Gerald, late Earl of Kildare, to
Sir Henry Sidney and now in the possession of Tyrone's son-in-
law, McGenees ; the manor of Rathwyre, West Meath, and the
dissolved monastery of Ballybogan, West Meath, with certain
lands belonging to the dissolved monastery of Lesmolin, some
of this property having been leased in July, 1599, to Sir Edward
Fitzgerald.—*Undated.*

Endorsed : " A note of the contents of the Earl of Kildare his
suit." ⅓ p. (P. 2366.)
[See *Cal. S.P. Ireland*, 1600–1, pp. 229, 336–7.]

ROGER WYNFORD to [SIR ROBERT CECIL].

[Before June 22, 1601].–He requests that the custody of
Richard Wood *alias* Hull, a lunatic, be granted to his uncle
Robert Dichur and Thomas Pylborough, a kinsman, which may
be of benefit to petitioner.—*Undated.*

Note by Cecil : " Let a commission be granted for inquiry of
the lunaticks estate."
¾ p. (P. 887.)
[See *PRO. Wards* **9**/348.]

STEPHEN MICHELL to SIR ROBERT CECIL.

[After June 24, 1601].—Recently Cecil was informed that
petitioner had made " very uncivill and most dishonest speeches "

about him, and committed him to prison for the offence. Petitioner protests that he had had no intention of defaming Cecil in any way, and that he cannot remember doing so. He asks for his pardon, as well as his release from prison without paying the customary fees and charges.—*Undated.*

1 p. (P. 1094.)

[See *Acts of the Privy Council,* 1600–1, p. 457, and *H.M.C. Salisbury MSS,* Vol. XI, p. 267.]

LORD MOUNTJOY to the EARL OF SOUTHAMPTON.

[1601] July 14.—" I have given Fitzgarrett a protection allthough agaynst my determination, which is presently to call in all protections, and nott sortinge with the course I helde with the knave Udall in the same case. Iff I fynde him willinge to doo servis, I will nurishe him in the best sorte I can, and att my next meetynge with your Lordship conferr with you farther about him." 14 July.

Holograph. Endorsed : " To the Erle of Southampt. from the Lord Deputy." ½ p. (**106.** 1.)

[See *H.M.C. Salisbury MSS,* Vol. XV, p. 281.)

JOHN MEERE to SIR ROBERT CECIL.

[After October 23, 1601].—Because of his being committed to prison by Cecil from July 31 to October 23 last, he could not appear to defend himself in a suit brought against him for debt in the Court of Common Pleas by Thomas Anthony and his attorney, Robert Dolbery, when judgment was passed against him. Petitioner alleges that they took advantage of his detention, and he fears that his goods and lands may be seized as a result of this adverse verdict. He asks Cecil to send for Anthony and Dolbery, and to make some arrangement with them " agreeable to equitie ".—*Undated.*

At bottom in another hand : Counter arguments proving that Meere has deliberately prevaricated in the matter of the debt, *followed by answers to this charge by Meere.*

1⅓ pp. (P. 1798.)

[See *H.M.C. Salisbury MSS,* Vol. XI, p. 403.]

ROBERT WHINYARD to SIR ROBERT CECIL.

1601, November 23.—He is a yeoman of Chellaston, co. Derby. William Bradshaw, late of Derby, was seised of certain lands in Osmaston and other places to the value of £10 *per annum,* of which some portion is supposed to be held *in capite.* In his will, Bradshaw devised a part of these lands to Anne, his wife, sister of petitioner, to be sold for the payment of his debts. The remainder he left to her for the education of his younger children during the minority of his heir. Since her husband's death, which was some six years ago, Anne Bradshaw has remained a widow and has used the profits of both lands and goods for the education of the children and the liquidation of debts. But many of the latter still remain to be discharged, and since the children are still young, she is facing many difficulties. Petitioner requests that either he or she be given the wardship of the heir and property for a reasonable rate, particularly as no effort has been made to conceal it nor the lands assumed to be held by knight's service. Neither, during the past four years, has the Queen's title to the wardship been established.—23 No. 1601.

Note by Cecil : " If the mother proceed in fynding the office in any convenient tyme, shee shall be preferred."

1 p. (P. 608.)

RICHARD DRAKE to [SIR ROBERT CECIL].

[After December 14, 1601].—Petitioner's nephew has bought the wardship of young Rosewell from Harvey with the intention of marrying him to his daughter, and has offered Dr Davyes as much rent for the house and lands as any other person will give. Nevertheless, Dr Davyes has caused the ward's household stuff there to be valued at very low prices in order to benefit from it, to the great loss of the ward, and has ordered that petitioner's nephew is not to be allowed on the grounds. There is every indication that he intends to spoil the house as well as the land. Petitioner requests that his nephew be permitted to rent the land for as much as any other person would offer, and that Dr Davyes be forced to give security to answer for the goods in specie and not as they were valued at a fourth of what they were worth. He asks that this should be done before Sir John Davies obtains his pardon otherwise he doubts whether he would conform to the order.—*Undated.*

1 p. (P. 1437.)

[See *H.M.C. Salisbury MSS*, Vol. XI, pp. 409 and 520.]

THE EARL OF DERBY'S LANDS.

[? 1601].—A list of properties to be sold for the liquidation of the Earl of Derby's debts. They include : Kellet, Halliwell, Anglezarke, Alston, Thornley, Torrisholme, Oxcliffe, Bretby, Bolton, Bare, Wraysholme, Norres lands and Coppull in Lancashire ; Haughton, Claughton, Langley, Nantwich and Bradley in Cheshire ; Bradworthy (Derby) in Devonshire ; Sturminster Marshall in Dorsetshire ; Haselbury in Somersetshire ; Ardington in Berkshire ; lands in Shropshire ; Brackley in Northamptonshire ; Holborn in London ; Bassenthwaite, Whicham and Silecroft in Cumberland, and some tenements in Southwark, Surrey. The total amount of money involved is £478 : 19 : 1.—*Undated.*

Endorsed : " Lands of the Erle of Derby to be sold." 1 p. (P. 2380.)

[See *Victoria County History, Lancashire*, Vol. V, p. 12, where the sale of Halliwell is said to have taken place around 1601. See also *H.M.C. Salisbury MSS*, Vol. IX, p. 405.]

THOMAS CRAFORD to SIR ROBERT CECIL.

[1601].—He and other townsmen of Cambridge have been committed to the Gatehouse. Since his incarceration he has lived in utter misery without hope of relief. He fears that any prolongation of his detention will result in the ruin of his family, and begs to be released.—*Undated.*

1 p. (P. 367.)

[See *H.M.C. Salisbury MSS*, Vol. XIV, p. 199, and *Cal. S.P. Dom.*, 1601–3, pp. 51–3.]

THOMAS CRAFORD to SIR ROBERT CECIL.

[1601].—He is a prisoner in the Gatehouse with others from Cambridge, and has spent his estate to meet the charges of his lengthy imprisonment. He is so impoverished that he is now in danger of having to " forsake the company of his neighbors and betake him to the thole (? hole) unto the feardfull hazards of his health and lyffe ". He protests that he never " opposed himselfe, nor will, gainst the goverment nor governors of the university wilfully", and craves pardon if he has offended Cecil or wronged Dr. Jegon. He accepts his punishment with submission, and only asks that he may quietly enjoy his leases.— *Undated.*

Note by Cecil : " If this petitioner will find swerty to ask Mr Dean of Norwich forgivenes in some publick place at Cambridg he shalbe delivered."

1 p. (P. 1110.) *See P. 367. supra.*

ACCOUNTS.

[1601].—Two accounts :

(1) " Thaccompte of charges layd out by me Thomas Honyman upon the sugers receaved out of the *Lyonesse* prise called the *Whyte Grayhounde* brought out of the Straights by Capteyn Traughton."

These charges include expenses for Customs dues, Admiralty Court fees, warehouse charges, the " favours " of Customs officials, etc.

(2) " The accompte of all such sales as are made of your Honors (Sir Robert Cecil's) part and portion of sugers receaved out of the prise called the *Whyt Hart* [*sic*] for your Honors adventure of 743¹ in the settinge fforth of the honeste Capteyn John Traughton, and of all such sums of moneys as I have receaved for your Honors use tochinge this voyage."

The sum realised for Sir Robert Cecil from the sale of his part of the sugar to various London merchants and others was £7389 : 14:3.—*Undated.*

1½ pp. (Accounts **119**/12.)

[See *H.M.C. Salisbury MSS*, Vol. XI, pp. 171, 177, 539.]

WILLIAM CALDER and JOHN LEITCHE to the QUEEN and the PRIVY COUNCIL.

[1601].—For the redress of a wrong done to them at Dunkirk. —*Undated.*

On reverse : " This petition the Clark of the Counsell gave unto

me from them to advertise of and be meanes to my L. Admirall
for relief of the parties. I have thereon acquainted my L.
Secretary that it is so unreasonable for us to do as I can not move
it, seing my L. of Mar is at London the King's Ambassador,* and
that the parties may have recourse to them of Dunkirk for their
owne mony, and so redres be had where it ought knowing they
have her warranted there to them. Allwaies at my L. Secretaries request I foresend it to be considered of by my L. Admirall,
beseeching your L. to give it his L. as shall stand with your
pleasure."—*Unsigned.*

1 p. (P. 552.)

CAPTAIN ANTHONY CROMPTON to SIR ROBERT CECIL.

[1601].—The Queen's favour, the letters of the Privy Council
to the Lord Deputy of Ireland, Cecil's endorsement of his petition
and the recommendation of certain commanders of the Queen's
forces, have all encouraged him to ask Cecil for a company of 150
foot in the new troops which are to be sent to Ireland. Petitioner
was a Captain and a Sergeant-Major in one of the regiments
"passinge the blacke water with my L. Burghe", and since then
he has been a Lieutenant-Colonel in another. Apart from his
military experience and his loyalty, a further reason advanced
by him in his own favour is "because there are divers Captens
in that realme who hoolde companies of that number who were
but inferior officers and some private gentlemen when your
suppliant served her Ma^ty honestly and loyallie as a Capten in
that kingedome ".—*Undated.*

¾ p. (P. 369.)
[See *H.M.C. Salisbury MSS*, Vol. XIV, p. 192.]

LORD HENRY HOWARD to the LORD HIGH TREASURER OF
ENGLAND and SIR JOHN FORTESCUE, CHANCELLOR OF THE
EXCHEQUER.

[1601].—"May it please your honores to be advertised that
wheras sondrie slanderouse and detractive spechis have bene
secretlie given out against my honorable nephew the Lord Thomas
Howard in his absence as if he went about to seeke advantage
by a newe lease taken from hir Ma^ty to overthrowe the states of
certaine persones that eyther had a right or a possession before,
my nephewes meaninge is not to offer wronge or hinderance
to anie suche but to allowe, assiste and strengthen anie titele
whatsoever may be justified by lawe, which ought to decide all
questiones and litigious sutes amonge subjectes. Touchinge satisfaction to Morrisis demaunde in as ample forme and manner as
the late Dukes patent to his father in lawe can beare, two sufficient and honest gentilmen are readie at this instant to enter
bonde, which is the utter moste that he can aske, seekinge onlie

---

* John Erskine, 7th Earl of Mar, was sent as special envoy by James VI
of Scotland to Queen Elizabeth, and remained in London from March to May,
1601.

to revive the same right in himselfe which by the deathe of his agid father in lawe must otherwise have bene extinguished.

Touching Mr Sackviles clayme (though my Lord Thomas will marvell at the manner of this course all thinges considerid at his retourne), yet I will undertake that in the meane time suche warrantise shall be given in his behalfe that he shall hinder ore impugne no lawfull right by this lease from hir Majestye as your honores shall thinke meet agreably to the state of the matter. My Ladies humble sute unto your honores is that my Lord maie not be pressid by anie importunity to the creatinge of a newe right by this occasion that never was before, because that weare detractive from hir Ma^{ts} most princelie graunt, but onlie tied to allowance of all rightes and claymes that may justely stande by course of lawe, which is very consonante to his owne enclynacion ; otherwise, to countenance the defective assurancis of encrochinge officers against hir Ma^{ts} owne right wolde emboldene hungrie dispositiones to raise a titele out of anie sleight, discourage diligent endevores from bringinge matters of this qualitye to light, and let in a worlde of abusis to the greate hinderance and losse of hir Majesty. Beside, my Ladie hopes that his absence at this presente in the service of the state will move your honores more respectively and tenderlie to regarde the pointe in questione that very muche concernithe him. Herin he shall be bounde to praye daily for his graciouse soverayne as the onlie author of his good, and for your honores as most favorable helperes and assistantes to hir Royall enclynacion."—*Undated.*

Endorsed : "H. Ho: 1601." 1 p. (**124.** 80.)

—— to THE KING (JAMES VI OF SCOTLAND].

[1601].—He is grateful for the royal favour shown to the bearer who conveyed to him the last letter from his Majesty. As for affairs in general, he has no doubt that the Duke of Lennox, newly returned from France,* has advertised his Majesty of the French King's disposition. He himself finds it strange and disturbing, for it seems to take the form of a preoccupation with the accumulation of funds. These, it is said, are to be employed in the future with a view to enabling the House of Bourbon to eclipse the House of Valois in promoting its own aggrandisement and the honour of France, even to the detriment of the legitimate interests of his Majesty in the kingdom of England. As to friends, his Majesty has none except those of the House of Guise who, however, are slow to act if not constantly reminded of their honour and duty. The French King is in constant touch with England through the good offices of Biron and under the pretence of a hatred of Spain, and his motives are, in the opinion of the writer, hardly consonant with the best interests of his Majesty. He requests special consideration for the bearer whose life was in danger during his last visit to Scotland, and begs for his safe

---

* Lennox was sent on an embassy to France in July, 1601, and returned in November the same year, passing through London where he had an interview with Queen Elizabeth.

return. He has communicated the rest of the news to him while awaiting the result of the Italian business which at the moment is the only means of restraining the King of France.— *Undated.*

Endorsed : " To the King." *French.* ¾ p. **(109.** 91.)

SIR EDWARD CECIL to SIR ROBERT CECIL.

[1601].—" When I laste parted with you, I was resolved to have returned into the low countryes. But to excuse my selfe truly (as I am resolved ever to do soe to your Honor) I can confes nothing that hath hindered mee but beyng a nwe maryed mann. And littell occation I had to be any where this winter but where I mighte have the pleasantest garison considering I howlde my selvfe a commander of horse and not of foote. And now that it drawes nighe that my charge is to com in to the fealde, I woulde be loth that your Honor shoulde knowe that I missed an hower of beyng with them. For my dispositione of the wares was never so earneste as it is with hope, and as longe as it shall please your Honor to favoure my fortunes there in, which if eyther your blude, or a harte by all reasons to be honest and affectionatt to you, can deserve, then assure your Honor you ar not onely to looke for it of mee but challenge it by more reasons then you can from any man living. My wife, may it please your Honor, as drawing in the same yoake, is as desierus to drawe some of my lode, and not knowing in any thing how to showe her diutefullnes hath presumed to make use of slight sweat meates that your Honor might regard the more her diutefull miende. And with all she hath desiered mee that be cause the[y] ar suche tryfelles and that sweat meattes may very well be demineshed passing many handes, to lett your Honor know that there is 3 bockes and 12 porringers, which if the[y] may any waye like your Honor, she will reast a most happie womann."—*Undated.*

Holograph. Seal. Endorsed : " 1601. Sir Edward Cecyll to my Mr." 1½ pp. **(90.** 47.)

[Printed in Dalton's *Life and Times of General Sir Edward Cecil, Viscount Wimbledon,* Vol. 1, pp. 65–6.]

THOMAS RAYNTON to SIR ROBERT CECIL.

[1601 or before].—He was formerly in the service of Lord Burghley, and is now in attendance on Lady Susan Vere. He asks for the wardship of the son of John Cave of Chancery Lane,* and undertakes to establish the Queen's title to it at his own expense.—*Undated.*

¼ p. (P. 229.)

BERMONDSEY.

[? 1601].—Plan of land near the River Thames at Rotherhithe, co. Surrey. The names of property owners include that of

---

* Probate of his will was granted in 1601. [See *Prerogative Court of Canterbury Wills,* Vol. IV 1584–1604, p. 82.]

R. Trappes, which appears in an *Inquisition post mortem* dated 1601. *See* CP. Legal **29**/3.).—*Undated.*
Endorsed : " Bermondsey." 1 *Sheet.* (CPM *supplementary* 50)

HENRY DOBER to SIR ROBERT CECIL.

[After February, 1601–2].—He is a prisoner in the Fleet, and formerly held the lease of a tenement at Murston in Kent, which was the inheritance of John Croft, a lunatic committed to the care of Lucy Dynham, widow. From the time petitioner was committed to prison, she has made every effort to get the tenement into her hands, and the lunatic has since died.* With his demise petitioner's lease has terminated, but although he is in prison, he still owns implements and moveable goods worth £300 which the widow has seized and converted to her own use, although she has no right to do so except by warrant from Cecil or by the title of one Croft, one of the heirs of the deceased lunatic, who has married her daughter since his death, and thus claims a part of the lunatic's land. Petitioner can not pay his debts or redeem himself except through the sale of his goods. He therefore asks that he be granted possession of them and reasonable time to remove them for his own use ; and that Lucy Dynham be forbidden to meddle with them unless she can prove right of ownership, which petitioner denies she can do.—*Undated.*
1 p. (P. 1115.)

SIR WILLIAM BOWES to SIR ROBERT CECIL.

[*c.* July, 1602].—Lady Mallory was in possession of Aldwark by right of dowry from her late husband, Sir Godfrey Foljambe. She leased it to his son Godfrey who, when he died, conveyed the lease to his wife Isabel. At the request of Francis Foljambe, Isabel gave him permission to reside at Aldwark with an allowance of £20 annually. But he proved so refractory that petitioner, now husband of Isabel Foljambe, had to sue him at York, and obtained restitution of Aldwark. Foljambe ignored the decree and all succeeding legal processes and was therefore declared an outlaw. When he died petitioner renewed his suit against his widow, and would have regained possession but for a letter from Cecil which she produced to stay proceedings. The letter would seem to have been procured by Wortley, the widow's son, who informed Mr Francis Bacon that the eviction of his mother would prejudice his ward. Bacon therefore applied for and obtained the letter from Cecil. Petitioner adduces reasons why this state of affairs is prejudicial to the rights and interests of Lady Mallory as rightful owner of the property, and asks Cecil to discuss the matter with Bacon and to direct the court at York to proceed in it.—*Undated.*
1 p. (P. 473.)
[See *H.M.C. Salisbury MSS*, Vol. XII, pp. 259–60.]

---

* Letters of administration were granted to his sisters on February 5, 1601–2. [See *Archaeologia Cantiana*, Vol. XVIII, p. 39, and also Hasted *History of Kent*, Vol. VI, p. 148.]

GIORGIO LUNAUER to THOMAS WILSON.

1602, September 27.—He has received his letter of September 26 from Padua, and sends him Birone's writings [*la scrittura del Birone*]. He will send the account as instructed. He encloses the usual *foglio* [? receipt] and in future will send it as instructed with the news-sheet from Milan as soon as it comes. He refers to a conversation in an unnamed place where he [Wilson] was very freely spoken of, but he [Wilson] has a clear conscience and need not mind what is said. He will keep the letter for Mr Hugh Lloid until his arrival. He understands that Wilson was in Venice, but left as it was not to his taste. He asks whether he [Wilson] has had the agate—grey pill [*bolo griso d'agata*] which was in the box.—Venice, 27 of September, 1602.

Italian. 1½ pp. (**107.** 40.)

[See *PRO*, S.P. 99 (Venice), Bundle 2, p. 148.]

HERBERT CROFT *versus* the COUNTESS OF ESSEX.

[*c.* November, 1602].—A note that Mr Baskerville of Here fordshire, who died some 14 years ago,* held land of the Crown by knight service, besides other property of the late Earl of Essex. The Queen granted the wardship of his heir to the Earl of Essex. but the feodary of Herefordshire claimed that the tenures were held of the Crown not of the Earl of Essex. The matter was examined in the Court of Wards, and judgment given in favour of the Earl, who was confirmed in the grant of the wardship. Now Mr Crofts has obtained a *melius inquirendum*, and found the tenures to be of the Crown, and some to be *in capite*. The matter is to be heard, and the Countess of Essex who holds the tenures for term of life is to contest the claim. The manors held of her are Staunton, Eardisley, Over Letton and Chanston. —*Undated.*

1 p. (P. 2336.)

[See *H.M.C. Salisbury MSS*, Vol. XII, pp. 498–9, and Vol. VII, p. 532.]

PEMBROKE COLLEGE.

[1602].—Two of the statutes of Pembroke College, Cambridge. —*Undated.*

Latin. ½ p. (**136.** 140.)

SIR WILLIAM STRODE to ——.

[1602].—Sir George Southcott, then resident in London, did not leave for the country until within a fortnight of the execution of the commission, and did not disclose the *supersedeas* he had obtained to his adversaries until the present time. The undersheriff failed to return a jury until the day before the commission was to sit at Crediton, and claimed that he had been forced to pick most of them from that parish and the rest in the neighbourhood of the house of the Lord Chief Baron, who is father-in-law

---

* Died on January 8, 1588–89. [See *PRO, Inq. P.M. C.* 142. 221/107.]

to the sheriff.* Petitioner asks that no new commission be granted while the present sheriff holds office.—*Undated and unsigned*

Endorsed : " Sir W. Strowd." $\frac{1}{3}$ p. (P. 1951.) *See* P. 2394 *infra* p. 115.

BRIGSTOCK PARK.

1602.—Map of the Great and Little Parks of Brigstock, signed by R. Treswell and dated 1602.

Endorsed : " Brigstock 1602." 1 *sheet.* (CPM *supplementary* 40.)

BRIGSTOCK.

[? *c.* 1602].—Map of the Great and Little Parks at Brigstock, co. Northants. The writing in the two inset tables suggests that it may be the work of Israel Amyes, who prepared a survey of Sir Robert Cecil's lands in Hertfordshire in 1600. Cecil was granted the two parks by Queen Elizabeth in December, 1602.†
—*Undated.*

1 *sheet.* (CPM *supplementary* 39.)

POOLE.

[Before 1603].—Petitioner states that Henry Poole‡ holds the site and demesne land of the manor of Poole by a lease granted to one Twymo in Edward VI's reign, and that since the time of Henry VIII, Twymo, Poole and his father have had eight leases of the premises, none of them being granted as a reward for services, nor fines paid to the Crown for them. Petitioner declares that the leases were improperly granted and that his complaint can be substantiated by the records of the " Court of Dochy ". If any part of his charge is not true " I will now loose my lease, the grounde whereof was her Ma^{tyes} princelye rewarde to her servante ; bought by my honorable maister, and geven to me with as kinde and trewe heart as ever noble gentellman bestowed a rewarde upon his lovinge servante."—*Undated and unsigned.*

Endorsed : " Chambers." $\frac{1}{2}$ p. (P. 2294.)

LISLE CAVE to SIR ROBERT CECIL.

1602–3, March 23.—His cousin, Francis Cave, of Hugglescote Grange, has just died, and petitioner asks that he be given the wardship of his heir Brian Cave, who is 17 years of age. He refers to a previous request made at the wish of the father, who was his cousin-german and nearest neighbour, and to Cecil's

---

* Mary, the eldest daughter of Sir William Peryam, Lord Chief Baron of the Exchequer, was married to William Poole, of Colcombe, co. Devon, who was sheriff of that shire from December, 1601, to December, 1602. Peryam had a house called Little Fulford near Crediton, where he died in 1604. See *D.N.B.*, p. 44.

† See *Northants Records Society*, Vol. XXIII, p. 172.

‡ Knighted in 1603.

favourable response to it.—From Horsepool, the xxiii of Marche, 1602.

Holograph. 1 p. (P. 2464.)

WILLIAM HILL to SIR ROBERT CECIL.

[c. 1603].—He requests to be granted the wardship of the heir of Walter Smith, deceased, of Herefordshire, and also that of the heir of Robert Dupper,* deceased, of the same county, which have been concealed for three years or more. He undertakes to prove the Queen's title to these wardships at his own expense.— *Undated.*

Note by Cecil: " Let a warrant be made for a comission, and if the suggestion be treu I will consyder of his sute with favour." ¾ p. (P. 63.)

JOHN WARAHOUSE to SIR ROBERT CECIL.

[*temp.* Elizabeth].—He is a subject of the Duke of Saxony and sent 4½ lasts of wheat on board the Hamburg ship which were delivered to the Queen. He is in debt to various people and begs Cecil to expedite the payment for his corn, for which he has been waiting for some sixteen months.—*Undated.*

½ p. (P. 407.)

—— to [? SIR ROBERT CECIL].

[? *temp.* Elizabeth].—" The post who brought this packet from Yarmouth fell sick by the way, and at London hired me to ride post to the Court, and for lack of instructions I cannot mak any bill of particulars, but leave the allowance to your honorable pleasure to be rated and set down in this warrant annexed."— *Undated and unsigned.*

½ p. (P. 505.)

JOHN SHOEMAKER to SIR ROBERT CECIL.

[*temp.* Elizabeth].—He is a prisoner in the Counter in the Poultry. Recently a London citizen, Solomon Prowde, promised to obtain for him £500 worth of cloth on credit, upon condition that petitioner paid him £100. Petitioner was induced to enter into bonds for the payment of that sum, but Prowde never fulfilled his part of the bargain. He has, moreover, not only refused to return the bonds signed by Shoemaker, but has caused him to be committed to prison. Petitioner adds that during the past ten years he has redeemed many English captains from Spain and Portugal without receiving any compensation, a fact to which the Lord Admiral can attest. He has also some important and confidential information to impart to Cecil, which he will not reveal to any other person. He requests to be allowed to do so, and asks Cecil to consider his case.—*Undated.*

Endorsed: " The petition of one John Shoomaker, a straunger,

---

* Probate of his will granted in 1601. [See *Prerogative Court of Canterbury Wills*, Vol. IV, 1584–1604, p. 135.]

whoe hathe some important secrete to reveile unto your Honor, which he woold not willingly shewe to any other but to your selfe." ½ p. (P. 1207.)

YARMOUTH.

[*temp.* Elizabeth].—A description of the antiquity of Yarmouth, giving the main events in the history of the town from the reign of Canute to that of Henry IV. Another hand has added the names of the Stewards of Yarmouth, the last being Robert Devereux, 2nd Earl of Essex.—*Undated.*
Latin. Endorsed : "Yermouthe Antiquitye." 1 p. (**230. 12.**)
[See *H.M.C. Salisbury MSS*, Vol. XIII, p. 369.]

—— to his CATHOLIC MAJESTY.

[*temp.* Elizabeth].—Portugal being at present quiet, the writer urges that the army and ships now ready should be used against England. This action would both settle Flanders and restore England to the Catholic faith. There is every assurance of Papal approval and support.—*Undated.*
Holograph? Italian. ½ p. (**186.** 128.)

W. KING to ——.

[*temp.* Elizabeth].—He is preparing an expedition to the Indies and asks for favour and protection in prosecuting the same. He also furnishes the following details :
" A pinnesse to lie in the *passagio* one moneth for interceptinge such smale vessels as shall goe to St John de Porterico.
All which tyme my shipp shall be at the Sona for such shippinge as shalbe bounde for St Domingo.
Then shall the pynnesse goe on the north side of Hispaniola, and the shippe on the south side, and meete at St Antonia there to water.
Ffrom thence to the Hundoros and to rainge the bay alonge to the Cracols, and soe upp all the Bay of Messico to certeyne places, where and at what tymes in my knowledge shippes doe lade."
King would be pleased to hear whether the recipient of his letter would like to " adventure " something in the proposed expedition.—*Undated.*
Holograph. Endorsed : " W. Kings bill of adventure to the W. Indies." ¾ p. (**98.** 137.)

VALUATION.

[? *temp.* Elizabeth].—The particulars of corn and other tithes and of profits from certain lands at Thorpe, co. Northants. Kirkoswald, co. Cumberland, the manor of Ingoldsby, co. Notts, and Dodworth, Beadlam and Wombleton, co. Yorks.—*Undated.*
Endorsed : " My L. of Lincoln." ⅓ p. (P. 2367.)

M S—H

VALUATION.

[? *temp.* Elizabeth].—Annual value of the rectories of Abbots Ann and Haughton, co. Hants, and of the Deanery of Winchester.—*Undated.*

Endorsed : " Deane of Winchester." ½ p. (P. 2180.)

WILLIAM, LORD COBHAM.

[*temp.* Elizabeth].—Arrears owed by William Brooke, 10th Lord Cobham, for subsidies during various years in the reign of Queen Elizabeth.—*Undated.*

Endorsed : " The note of suche wrytts of debts as is cum fforth owtt of the exchequer for my lord." 1 p. (**145.** 108.)

SHIPPING.

[? *temp.* Elizabeth].—List of ships destroyed or captured by enemy action or lost at sea during the past three years. Their value is given as well as the names of the ports and towns to which they belonged. Two further items are added :

" Only one companie of marchants trading to the Eastlands from London, Ipswich, Hull and Newcastle in halfe this space of tyme have lost 100,000¹ taken by the enemie.

A great number of maryners alsoe proportionable to this losse of shipping have been taken and destroyed by the enemye and cast away throughe disorderly pressing and forceing uppon winter voyages, besides many more whoe by reason of those discouragements and want of pay have either rune away to the enemie or betaken themselves to forreine service or to any other trade rather then to a sea manns life, to the inestimable losse and danger of the kingdome."—*Undated.*

Endorsed : " A list of English ships lost and taken by the enemie within space of 3 years." 2 pp. (**141.** 343.)

ST. ALBANS.

[*temp.* Elizabeth].—A list of freeholders within the liberties of St. Albans, that is at Watford, Sarratt, Rickmansworth, Aldenham, Abbots Langley, East Barnet, Chipping Barnet, Northaw, Bolton, St. Michaels, St. Stephens, Sandridge, St. Peters, Redbourne, Ridge, Codicote, Bramfield, Shephall, Hexton, Newnham, Norton and St. Paul's Walden.—*Undated.*

14 pp. (**213.** 49.)

SIR JOHN FORTESCUE.

[? *temp.* Elizabeth].—" Out of Sir John Ffortescues booke of defence of the tytle of the Howse of Lancaster." The passage concerns the alleged title to the Crown of England of Edward IV, based on "the right of a woman called Dame Phillip, doughter as he saieth to Sir Lyonell of Andwerp, elder brother to Sir John of Gaunt, of whom is lyneallie discended the verie true Christian

Prince K. Henry the VI ", and sets out to prove the historical falsity of the claim.*—*Undated.*

½ p. (**230.** 4.)

EPITAPH.

[? *temp.* Elizabeth].—Epitaph on Edward Corton.—*Undated.* *Latin.* 1 p. (**140.** 92.)

ROBERT CECIL.

[*temp.* Elizabeth].—The commonplace book of Robert Cecil which contains *inter alia* copies of speeches in Parliament, addresses to Queen Elizabeth, letters to the Queen and others, reflections on the political problems of the day, in particular that of the Queen's survival, arguments for and against the execution of Mary, Queen of Scots. There are also copies of two poems, one by Fulke Greville.—*Undated.*

57 pp. (**286.**)

GENEALOGY.

[*temp.* Elizabeth].—Genealogy of the family of Cecil in Northamptonshire.—*Undated.*

1 *m.* (**213.** 125.)

FRANCE.

[? *temp.* Elizabeth].—Genealogical tables of the Kings of France, Aragon, Castille, Sicily and Naples, and of the ducal houses of Burgundy and Gelders, drawn from the *History* of Philippe de Commines.—*Undated.*

5 pp. (**230.** 5.)

BOOKS.

[? *temp.* Elizabeth].—A list of Latin books, with authors' names and dates, dealing with subjects of theological and historical interest.—*Undated.*

Latin. 20 pp. (**210.** 7.)

DIVINATION.

[? *temp.* Elizabeth].—" Whether that the cumming or staying of M may concerne the present or future good or evell of him self and of C and N. In the considering whereof 48 cases following doe result by the combination of them." There follows a series of permutations involving M, C and N.—*Undated.*

2 pp. (**135.** 105.)

LIVERY.

[? *temp.* Elizabeth].—Details of fees and charges incidental to the legal delivery of property and the grants of warrants for that

---

* The original has been printed in *The Works of Sir John Fortescue, Knight,* collected and edited by Thomas (Fortescue), Lord Clermont. See Part 2, pp. 517-18.

purpose. There are two lists of such payments—one for an ordinary, and the other for a special, livery.—*Undated.*

2 pp. (**130.** 154.)

EXCERPTS.

[? *temp.* Elizabeth].—Passages dealing with "de revocand : Donationibus " by Andreas Tiraquellus.—*Undated.*

Latin. 2¾ pp. (**140.** 247.)

[These passages appear (Nos. 166 to 171) in the preface to Volume VI of the *Opera Omnia* of Tiraquellus which was printed in Frankfurt in 1597.]

CHART.

[*temp.* Elizabeth].—Copy of a coloured chart by Gerard Mercator (1512-94).

1 *sheet.* (CPM *supplementary* 80.)

SKENFRITH.

[*temp.* Elizabeth].—Plan of lands at Skenfrith, co. Monmouth, now used as the cover of a terrier of Hoddesdon *post* 1581.— *Undated.*

1 *sheet.* (CPM *supplementary* 19.)

WESTMINSTER.

[*temp.* Elizabeth *or* James I].–Plan of the upper floor of the Strand block of old Somerset House.—*Undated.*

1 *sheet.* (CPM **11.** 56.)

EDMONTON.

[*temp.* Elizabeth].—Plan of the garret at Pymmes, Edmonton, co. Middlesex.—*Undated.*

Endorsed : " A plott. Pyms." 1 *sheet.* (CPM *supplementary* 35.)

EDMONTON.

[*temp.* Elizabeth].—Ground plan of Pymmes at Edmonton, co. Middlesex.—*Undated.*

Endorsed in Sir William Cecil's hand : " Pyms at Edmonton." *and in other hands :* " Plotte of Pyms Howse new built " and " Mr Sacretary Wyllsons plottes ffor Edmondton."—1 *sheet.* (CPM *supplementary* 31.)

SOUTH WEST ENGLAND and SOUTH WALES.

[*temp.* Elizabeth].—Map of Somerset, Devon, Cornwall, Monmouth and Glamorgan. The main towns are marked, three principal roads represented by dotted lines, and the localities where deposits of lead and copper are found or worked indicated by crosses.—*Undated.*

Endorsed in Sir William Cecil's hand : " Cornubia, Devonia et pars Walliae huis opposita." 1 *sheet.* (CPM *supplementary* 1.)

FENLAND.

[*temp*. Elizabeth].—Map of the Fenland between Peterborough and Wisbech drawn by John Hexham of Huntingdon.—*Undated*.
1 *sheet*. (CPM *supplementary* 29.)

CHESTER.

[*temp*. Elizabeth].—Plan of Chester and the River Dee, showing fishermen with conical salmon nets.—*Undated*.
1 *sheet*. (CPM *supplementary* 3.)

GOLLETA, TUNIS.

[*temp*. Elizabeth].—Plan of the citadel of Golleta, showing the enlargement of the fortress by the construction of additional bastions. The legends are in English.—*Undated*.
½ *sheet*. (CPM **1.** 53a.)

EXEGESIS.

[? *temp*. Elizabeth].—Interpretation of a scriptural theme with appropriate exhortations.—*Undated*.
Latin. 1 p. (**250.** 1.)

TREATISE.

[? *temp*. Elizabeth].—A critical dissertation on the subject of secret marriages.—*Undated*.
Endorsed : "p. clandestino matrimonio." *Latin*. 22 pp. (**210.** 9.)

SERMON.

[? *temp*. Elizabeth].—A religious discourse or sermon.—*Undated*.
Latin. 7½ pp. (**140.** 254–7.)

COMMONPLACE BOOK.

[? *temp*. Elizabeth].—Quotations, mostly in Latin but a few in English, from the Scriptures and classical writers on a number of moral and philosophical topics.—*Undated*.
255 pp. *mostly blank*. (**243.** 8.)

LADY UNTON to SIR ROBERT CECIL.

1603, April 24.—It is doubtful whether her brother-in-law, Mr Ralph Gibbs, of Warwickshire, will recover from his present illness. She therefore requests Cecil not to take away the wardship of the son from his mother, her sister, because of the smallness of the estate and the debts which burden it. Besides, it provides a jointure for herself who has to maintain eight young children. 24 April, 1603.
⅓p. (P. 1440.)

LORD DARCY to SIR ROBERT CECIL.

1603, April 26.—Concerning the dispute between him and Rie, he declares that he complied with the injunctions contained in

Cecil's letter to him, and allowed Rie to take possession of certain cattle and household stuff. When the late Queen Elizabeth died, Rie's wife, who insolently referred to her as "her greatest enimie", slanderously accused Darcy's people of stealing her goods. Darcy protested strongly to Rie about these allegations and informed him that in future any restitution of his goods would be done according to inventory, and that he would indemnify him for anything that was missing. Darcy gives his reasons for detaining Rie's property as follows : (1) that the late Queen and present King had an interest in them since Rie stood indicted for burglary and felony ; (2) that he himself had a good claim to them ; (3) Rie had, contrary to an order from the Court of Wards, detained lands from Darcy which were worth £140 annually. Darcy states that he did not receive Cecil's letters requesting him to answer certain charges preferred against him until the 20th of April. " I humblie praie that by reason of myne attendaunce, I maie be spared for puttinge myne answere untill the coronation of his Matie be paste." He asks that Rie be obliged to surrender to him the lands which he detains contrary to the injunction of the Court of Wards.—This xxvi of Aprill, 1603.

½ p. (P. 2337.)

[See H.M.C., Salisbury MSS, Vol. XII, pp. 4 and 581.]

John Bellott to Sir Robert Cecil.*

[Before May 13, 1603].—He has been Feodary of Denbighshire for twenty years by the gift of Lord Burghley, Cecil's father. Because of indisposition he can no longer perform the duties of that office, and therefore asks that it be granted to Roger Williams.†—Undated.

½ p. (P. 748.)

William Maddocks to Sir Robert Cecil.

[Before May 13, 1603.].—His late father, John Maddocks, died seised of the office of the Ushership of the Exchequer and Marshal of the Common Pleas, which are held of the King in chief by grand serjeantry. Petitioner is therefore a King's ward. Cecil has granted his wardship to his mother, Frances Maddocks, but inasmuch as his father died owing £700, leaving many children to be provided for, and that petitioner will receive only a small rent out of the said office during the remaining years of the lease, he asks that Cecil show consideration to him in the matter of composition of his wardship and livery, since he will hardly be in a position to pay the fine and fees arising from it.—Undated.

½ p. (P. 1366.)

---

* Sir Robert Cecil was created Baron Cecil of Essendon on May 13, 1603.

† Bellott was replaced as Feodary by Thomas Hughes in 1604. [See PRO. Wards 9, Vol. 471, under Denbighshire.]

JOAN WOOD to SIR ROBERT CECIL.

[Before May 13, 1603].—Ralph Wood, her late husband, and his ancestors have occupied for two hundred years a cottage formerly owned by one Langford and now in Cecil's possession. " By resonn that your poare oratrix husbande being olde and lying bedride fyve yeares, on Henri Rigby, a neyghbur of his, uncharitablie hathe tacken the same cottadg and land, in all but six acres, over our heades to the utter undoing of my selffe and six smalle children lefte me by my deceased husbande. " For the non-payment of rent during the past two years, Rigby has forfeited his lease which has come to Cecil's hands. Petitioner asks for a letter to Mr Bestonn directing him to lease the property to her and her children for the rent which Cecil would ask of any other lessee.—*Undated.*

Endorsed: " The humble petissionn of Joan Wood to the end that the righte honoorable Sir Robert Sissille wolde pleas to graunte to hir and hir poar childeren a further estat of a poar cottedge and six accars of lande the which hir latte husbande and his awnsestors hathe beenn tennant into theis 200 years and moare, and will geve for the same so mutche as any other man whatsoever. "

½ p. (P. 829.)

MARTIN ADYS to SIR ROBERT CECIL.

[Before May 13, 1603].—Since he submitted his petition he has been indisposed and prevented from following up his suit. Lord Cobham has now in his custody the books which were delivered to him by the searcher at Sandwich. Petitioner requests that he " maye have some consideration in this soe cheargeable a matter to me ".—*Undated.*

½ p. (P. 176.)

JOHN LEEKE to SIR ROBERT CECIL.

[Before May 13, 1603].—A certain Locksmith has procured from Cecil the promise of the wardship of Hutchinson, the grandson of petitioner's late wife, on the grounds that the ward's father was married to Locksmith's sister. This is untrue, neither is there any kinship or family alliance between Locksmith and the ward. Petitioner asks that he be granted the wardship, and is ready to pay Locksmith such compensation as Cecil thinks reasonable. —*Undated.*

⅓ p. (P. 132.)

The MAYOR and ALDERMEN of HULL to SIR ROBERT CECIL [*sic*].

1603, May 14.—They appeal to him once again on behalf of the unfortunate people of Hull who suffered a severe loss because of the action of the King of Denmark. The death of the late Queen Elizabeth deprived them of their hopes of restitution, and they can only turn to the King for their relief. " The town can no longer maintain the whole burden of alleviating their misery. " Hull this xiiiith of May, 1603.

PS. " Right honorable. By reason of the convenyency of this bearer, our solicitor Thomas Hartcastle for the losses of our inhabitants, we have sent your honor vi^l xiii^s iiii^d due to your honor from this place at the feast of St Michell last past for your honors ffee as Stewarde here. "

Signed: W. Barnard, Mayor *and eight other signatures.* Damaged. 1 p. (P. 2072.) *See* P. 2020 *infra* p. 219.

[See *H.M.C. Salisbury MSS*, Vol. XV, p. 208.]

BRIGSTOCK.

May, 1603.—A notebook, probably that of a bailiff, containing various memoranda and accounts relating to Brigstock, together with drafts of letters, mostly undated, presumably written to Lord Cecil. They include:

(1) A letter dealing with a survey by Sir Edward Watson and other commissioners appointed by the King. It refers to Lord Mordaunt's desire to become tenant of Brigstock Park, and his willingness to maintain 500 deer there. His house is within half a mile of the Park and his grounds are adjacent to it. " Your Lordships mony commythe in very slowly. I fynde the men of this contry very carelesse of their woords and promyses. "— *Undated.*

(2) A letter to the effect that the sheriff of Northamptonshire and Lord Mordaunt " have effectually performyd the tenure of the Kings Ma^ts pleasure concerninge Brigstock parcks, wherby I fynde all men nowe well satisfied of your Lordships right, and the unruly people of Brigstock are thereby made quiett ". Money is still slow in coming in because of its scarcity in the country. " But they nowe endevor to sell their wooll which beinge don, I doubt not but we shalbe satisfied. I understande that it wolde have ben a very pleasinge thinge unto the contrie if in case your Honour wold either have continuyd the Little Parck a parck still, or have forborne to lett the same unto Sir Thomas Tressam, a gentleman whom I finde most odiouse in this contrie, not only for his religion but also for his harde and extreme usage of his tenants and countrymen. The rebelliouse people of Brigstock and som others in this contry have not forborne to speake it openly that your Honour and we your Lordships officers are of Sir Thomas his religion. But I trust the wisest and honestest sorte are otherwise perswaded. " Other matters discussed deal with the deer in the parks, petitions against Cecil from certain inhabitants of Essendine concerning alleged concealed lands, and a movement to persuade Cecil to abate his rents out of Essendine by £20 or £30 annually.—*Undated.*

(3) A letter describing an incident on May 19, when Chany " a beggerly fellowe who hathe ben the follower of the dishonest cawse of the rebelliouse people of Brigstock against your Honour ", rode into the Great Park of Brigstock and with one, Mr Simon Montague of Brigstock, his brother-in-law, ordered all the labourers who were working there to leave the park in accordance

with the King's alleged wishes. He eventually confessed to Cecil's bailiff, when the latter met him, that he had no warrant to interfere with the workmen, and that the King had only spoken of the preservation of the deer and not of the park's timber. Chany also told him that it was the King's pleasure that his brother-in-law should have charge of the deer. " But I answeryd that unlesse he cowlde showe a better warrant then his owne reporte Mr Mowntagewe, whom I know to be your Lordships enemy, shuld have nothinge to doe there unlesse I sawe your Lordships warrant for it." Chany's activities may be calculated to hinder many people from paying money for the wood they have bought out of the parks. " The badd people of Brigstock made a collection of mony amountinge unto the som of 5¹, as I understande, to beare Chanys charges in the soliciting of this dishonest cawse unto his Matie."—*Undated.*

(4) Another incident at Brigstock. " Uppon Chany his last badd usage of hym selfe here, a troope of lewde women of Brigstock assemblyd them selves toguither uppon Friday last in the Greate Parck and behavd them selves very disorderly there, forbiddinge and commandinge in his Maties name suche as were workinge to deciste from fellinge any more trees or bushes there (beinge suche as we had sowlde at our furst comminge there), straightly charginge them not to come thether any more for that purpose." Chany has departed for the Court, and has been given a horse and some money by Simon Montague. His reason for going was the bailiff's refusal to allow Montague to assume charge of the deer. Cecil is urged to acquaint the King with these misdemeanours. " Also notwithstandinge your Lordships most honorable bountie lately publishyd here in the Markett Townes nerest adjoyninge unto the Greate Parck, I fynde that the rebelliouse people of Brigstock doe accepte most unthanckfully therof, accomptinge your Honours right in these parcks to be nothinge worthe, and verely belevinge that his Highnes will shortly take them from your Honour and converte them unto their former usage." He would like to see Cecil appoint a commission to inquire into these late disorders, and their authors made an example of. Otherwise there is a danger that they will increase.—Ketteringe, May, 1603.

(5) A letter dealing with the treatment of deer in the parks and other matters. " I understand that Chany still followithe the corte with a wickyed purpose to wrook [*sic* ? wreak] against your Lordship what myschiefe he may, beinge incoreged therunto by his brother in law, Mr Si. Mountegue, who hathe furnishyd hym both with horse and mony for the purpose."—*Undated.*

(6) The King's directive for an inquiry to be held into the slaughter of deer in the Great Park. Cecil's enemies have averred that no deer were turned out into the forest ; the truth is that many deer from the Great and Little Parks were turned out to the number of about 3 or 400. Two hundred of them were turned out of the Little Park into a walk in Rockingham Forest called Farmynge Woods, of which walk Simon Montague is

keeper under Lord Burghley. Despite a request to take charge
of these deer, Montague refused to do so, with the result that the
greatest number of them " doe ronn straggelinge in the contrie
and permittyd to be killyd by any base companion ". A good
number of deer in the Great Park were also turned out into the
walk called Geddington Woods. But the keeper there refused
to allow them to remain in the place where they had been put,
a large coppice called Lotaftes, where there was suitable pasture.
These deer, too, are now scattered over the countryside. There
remain 500 deer in the Great Park and some 100 in the Little
Park.—*Undated.*

(7) Cecil is informed that if Sir Thomas Tresham succeeds in
persuading him to place the keeping of the Little Park in his
son's charge, " it will fall out to be a matter most displeasinge
unto the contrie if either he or any of his shall have any thinge
to doe there. Uppon the former communycateon of a lease to be
grantyd unto Mr F. Tressam, Sir Thomas cawsyd one of his ser-
vaunts namyd Thomas Walker (a notable recusaunt) to be placyd
in the Lodge in the Little Parck whoe (as yet) is there still remayninge. This Walker, as I am credebly informyd, hathe had once
or twyse masse sayde there sithence his comminge thether, and
divers men and women hereabouts of that religion have congre-
gatyd them selves thether in the night tyme to be partakers of
his idolletry." Cecil is urged not to allow any lease or farm to be
awarded to Tresham or his family, for this and other reasons.
—*Undated.*

130 pp. (CP. Deeds **137**/6.)

[See *The Royal Forests of Northamptonshire,* 1558–1714, by
Philip A. J. Petit (Northants Record Society, Vol. XXIII),
pp. 172–4.)

JOHN STANLEY to LORD CECIL.

1603, June 4.—He encloses details of the annual value of
certain manors now in the King's hands for Cecil's information.
He will provide further particulars of leases, etc., if they are
required.—iiii Junii, 1603.

Endorsed : " 1603. Auditor Stanley to my lord with a note of
certayne mannors now in his Ma^{ts} hands." *Holograph.* ⅓ p.
(P. 2452.)

The Enclosure

Annual value of the manors of Patrington, Bishop Wilton,
Cloughton, Wetwang, Cottingham, Hemingbrough and Nunning-
ton in Yorkshire, Dent in the county of Richmond, and the
rectory and part of the college of Staindrop in the Bishopric of
Durham.

1½ pp.

RICHARD FRANCKE to LORD CECIL.

1603, June 5.—Rance,* stepfather to Henry Burle, and the executors of the will of Burle's father, have petitioned Cecil for the wardship of Burle. Cecil has postponed his decision until he has been informed by their neighbours of their respective qualities and fitness to be entrusted with the wardship. Petitioner is closely acquainted with the claimants and their estates, and is of the opinion that it should be bestowed upon the executors of the child's father, together with the person who has been made responsible for the administration of the minor's goods. This ffyfte of June, 1603.

Holograph. Endorsed : " June, 1603. Certificat concerning Burles wardship." ½ p. (P. 2379.)

The INHABITANTS OF PENZANCE to the KING.

[1603, June 19].—From time immemorial a market has been held every week on Saturday in the town, as well as three yearly fairs. The inhabitants have also enjoyed the issues of anchorage and quayage, and the use of certain curtilages, greens and other grounds for which they have paid a farm to the Crown. Nine years ago, however, Penzance was raided and burnt by the Spaniards and the inhabitants can not, by the laws of the realm, buy or sell victuals nor keep markets and fairs for the maintenance of themselves and their families and the port without a special dispensation from the King to confirm the same. If this grant is not awarded, the port faces extinction and the repercussions would be felt by neighbouring towns such as (St.) Buryan, Madron, Paul, (St.) Levan, St. Just, Sennen, Sancreed, Morvah, Zennor and Gulvall, whose inhabitants have always obtained what they needed from Penzance market. Petitioners request that the King grant by charter the incorporation and liberties above mentioned, and the authority to hold pleas in actions under £20, for which they will pay the customary farm, besides continuing to maintain the town and port and paying their rents.—*Undated.*

Note by Sir Julius Caesar : 1603, June 19. The King has referred the petition to the consideration of the Lord Treasurer, Lord Admiral and the Chancellor of the Exchequer who, if they think it fit, are to give order for the legal formulation of petitioners' requests, to which the King will append his signature.

Note by Lord Buckhurst, the Earl of Nottingham and Sir George Home : 1603, July 29. Before the petitioners can be granted their requests, a writ of *ad quod damnum* and a commission of inquiry are both necessary to satisfy and determine certain aspects of the case. When these prerequisites have been completed, the King may grant his charter to Penzance.

Note by the Earl of Nottingham : That care must be exercised

---

* Edward Rance married Alice, widow of Henry Burle, senior, and the mother of the ward. [See *PRO. Wards* **9**, Vol. 348, fol. 137b.]

to preserve the rights of the Admiralty in the matter of anchorage and quayage.

Note by Lord Buckhurst and Sir George Home : A writ of *ad quod damnum* has been granted by the Lords.

Note by Lord Buckhurst : The names of the commissioners for anchorage and quayage are—Steward of the manor, Surveyor of the county, Sir John Parker, Sir William Lower, John Hender, Thomas Cheverton, William Stalling.

Note by Lord Buckhurst : 1603, November 27. The commission of *ad quod damnum* has not been executed, and is to be renewed to the former commissioners. *Addressed to the Counsellor of the Chancery of Cornwall.*

3 pp. (P. 2034.)

RICHARD GEORGE to THOMAS HESKETH.

1603, June 27.—In conformity with the instructions contained in Hesketh's letter of May 19, he summoned William Hanikcorn and Anthony Webb *alias* Woolworth, the King's ward, with a view to arranging a composition for Webb's marriage. During the discussion that followed, he found that the total value of the land was less than £4 a year, out of which the King's rent of 23/4 was to be deducted. In the light of this estimate the marriage could not have been worth more than the £30 composition which he would have offered to Hanikcorn. But the latter and Webb were not able to reach an agreement, and he therefore informs Hesketh of what he has done in the matter, leaving it to him to bring it to a satisfactory conclusion.—Cicester, this xxviith of June, 1603.

Holograph. Endorsed : " Oct. 1603. Mr George his certificat."
¾ p. (P. 2391.)

JOHN ARUNDEL to the PRIVY COUNCIL.

[1603, ? June].—He fears that the congregating of so many Londoners at Highgate, where he has been confined for recusancy, may endanger his family and himself. He has found accommodation there in too small a house, and can neither procure a more convenient house nearer to London nor friends who would be willing to receive him and his dependents into their homes. He therefore requests permission to move to his own house at Chideock in Dorsetshire, and is prepared to comply with any conditions imposed on him by the Council.—*Undated.*

½ p. (P. 785.)
[See *H.M.C. Salisbury MSS*, Vol. XV, pp. 124, 178-9.]

The COUNTESS OF WARWICK and SIR WILLIAM RUSSELL to ——.

[June, 1603].—They request that the case of the Countess of Cumberland be brought to the attention of the King. Differences of opinion have long alienated her from her husband, and attempts to reconcile them have failed. As far back as 1601 the matter was entrusted to Sir Drue Drury, Sir John Peyton and

Mr Beale, who induced the Earl of Cumberland to agree to certain financial arrangements for the maintenance of his wife, daughter and household. However he did not observe them, and the matter was then taken up by Lord Cecil, who persuaded the Earl to conclude a similar agreement whereby he granted allowances to his family and discharged their debts. Again he did not honour this undertaking, despite appeals and requests from Lord Cecil and the Countess of Cumberland who " can have no answer nor gett any thinge to furnishe her selfe as is fitt to attend on her Matie nowe comeinge* or for other solempnyties of the tyme present ". Since all other means have proved ineffectual, there is no alternative but to solicit the King's intervention.—*Undated.*

Signed only. Seal. Endorsed : " 1603. Countesse of Warwick. Sir William Russell. Concerning the Countesse of Cumbreland." 1 p. **(115.** 6.)

[? Henry, Lord Cobham] to Sir Roger Ashton.

[Before July, 1603].—" I unterstande you have compounded to procur a pardon for Thomas Lucas, the murderer of my brother Sir William Brooke, whose memory is every day dearer to me then other. I will not be so unjust as to beleeve it before your self confesse it, nor so idle as to describe unto you the nature and degree of so notorious an injurie. Only I will remember you that I know (and you should know it better) that wee live under a kinge who will bothe maintaine the right of his subjects and the peace of his kingdome, and that by so hainous a wronge you shalle throw your self upon a whole family wherof I dare assure you there be some that will lose there lives with there honor. I pray you, Sir, let me receave your answear."— Chanon Row, this ——†.—*Undated.*

½ p. **(206.** 91.)

Thomas Eviseed to Lord Cecil.

[Before July, 1603].—In November two years ago the late Queen Elizabeth ordered Alderman Holmeden and Alderman Anderson‡ through the Earl of Nottingham, the Lord Admiral, to find accommodation for 24 Turks and Moors at 6d a day until shipping could be found to convey them to their own country. Petitioner was appointed to provide them with lodging and succeeded in doing so. But the owner of the house where they were accommodated has lately arrested him for the sum of £23:2:0, which he claims to be due to him, and which was not paid, as promised by the late Queen. He is held responsible for the debt simply for having brought the Turks and Moors to that house, and he asks Cecil to arrange for its payment without delay.—*Undated.*

½ p. (P. 795.)

---

* Queen Anne left Scotland at the beginning of June, 1603, to join King James in London.
† Lord Cobham was arrested in July, 1603 and committed to the Tower of London.   ‡ Knighted on July 26, 1603.

Thomas Bramston to Lord Cecil.

[1603] July 7.—He is writing from Newgate where he has been confined since his voluntary return from banishment. He assures Cecil that he had no sinister or disloyal motive in entering England clandestinely, but had done so for reasons of ill health, since he is still suffering from the infirmities which he acquired during twenty years of imprisonment. He was advised by physicians abroad that a visit to Bath might have a restorative effect upon him. He asks Cecil to mediate with the King for permission to go to Bath, particularly as there is an outbreak of infection at Newgate which is endangering him and the other prisoners there. He will provide as many sureties to answer for his appearance as the Privy Council thinks fit.—From Newgate, 7 July.

Endorsed : " 1603. The humble petition of Tho. Bramston, for his goinge to the Bathe."

½ p. (P. 785.)

[See *H.M.C. Salisbury MSS*, Vol. XV, pp. 101, 102.]

Roger Houghton to Lord Cecil.

1603, July 15.—Regarding the steps taken by Mr Dackeres and Mr Ames to deal with plague infected houses at " Walltom Crose ". " The[y] have caused the dores to be shutte up, and them selves deow give them relyife untill the controbution determined, and then the[y] are to be repayide againe, which wilbe one Sunday after service." He does not doubt but that his Lordship will bear the greatest burden. " The[y] have apoynted a wattch to continue day and night to abridge such Lonndoneres as wolde come thither, and to see that the[y] keape good order and tarye in there howses which are infected. There is two apoynted to watch att the lawne ende which comes from the hyie waye to your Lordships howse, only to keape away rogges which we are very muche trowbled with. There deoth not resorte so fewe as twentie in a day moste commenly. There is one howse more infectted since Humfrey Fflynte was with your Lordship, and theere [three] there in sicke att this instaunt. The Lord be mersyfull to them. Out of those other foure howses hath dyed 1111." He hopes that the measures already taken will help to prevent the plague from intensifying. All the members of his Lordship's household are in good health. He has received £408 brought by Mr Ames from Brigstock. " Theoballes, this xvth of Julii, 1603."

Holograph. Endorsed : " 1603, Roger Houghton to my Lord from Theobalds." 1 p. (General 27/17.)

Edward Geaste, William Geaste and Edward Geaste, junior, to ——.

[After July 16, 1603].—They have become sureties for other men's debts, and have recently been harassed by one creditor, who is a recusant. They presume that the reason for this is the fact that, upon the King's proclamation of high treason against Clerke and Watson, the two priests,* they arrested Clerke in Worcestershire and brought him to Sir John Pakington, Lieutenant of that shire. They are now unable to prosecute their debtors for recovery of the debts in order to pay their own creditors, and ask to be granted the King's protection for three years. —*Undated.*

1 p. (P. 745.)

JOHN WATKIS to LORD CECIL.

1603, July 29.—In the 43rd year of the late Queen Elizabeth's reign, he was able to establish by examining authentic documents that the lands held by the late Henry Clifford, of Brackenborough, were subject to the conditions governing tenure *in capite*. He requests that Cecil " of your honourable accustomed bountie towardes such as travell in this kinde for the benefitt of the Kinges Matie " bestow upon him the wardship of Clifford's heir. —June 29, 1603.

Note signed by Cecil : " Let him resort to any two of the Counsayle of the Court whereof the Surveyor or Atturney to be one, and if he can show pregnant matter and procure an order, he shall have my warrant."

1 p. (P. 235.)

MARGARET VALYNE and MARGARET SVINMISTER *alias* VALYNE to the KING.

[Before August, 1603].—They are resident in Brussels with eleven orphan children. Their brother Nicholas Valyne, who died in England, bequeathed half his goods to their children, and appointed John Poiteau and John Johnson to act as his executors. The latter survived Poiteau and arranged a marriage between Valyne's widow† and one Gerrad Gosin, a close friend of his, which was contrary to the testator's will. He then conspired with them to ignore the stipulations of the will regarding the legacy to Valyne's nephews and nieces, and to convey the whole estate to their own use. Petitioners are too poor to proceed against them by law, and request that a Master of the Court of Requests be appointed to hear and determine the case.—*Undated.*

1 p. (P. 764.)

THOMAS SCUDAMORE to LORD CECIL.

[After August 3, 1603].—He refers to a petition to the King which has been handed over to Lord Kinloss for perusal, and which concerns the offences committed by his son John Scudamore, whom petitioner was able to have released from the Tower by an appeal to Cecil through the good offices of Sir William

---

* The King's proclamation for the arrest of Clerke and Watson was published on July 16, 1603.

† Buried on August 2, 1603, and her husband Gerrard Gosin on September 4 in the same year. [See *The Registry of St. Olave, Hart Street, London,* 1563–1700, pp. 134, 136.]

Waad. John Scudamore has been informed against by Copley as being accessory to Watson's conspiracy, and is now bound over in the sum of £500 for his appearance upon summons. Petitioner resides near Altyrynys and was formerly well known to Lord Burghley. He asks that his son be summoned to appear with little delay, since he is capable of fraudulent dealing and malicious behaviour towards petitioner. So is his wife Amy, who was the means of bringing him into contact with Copley and Watson, and continues to commend Watson's activities.— *Undated.*

1 p. (P. 603.)

[See *Cal. S.P. Dom.*, 1603–10, p. 27, and *H.M.C. Salisbury MSS*, Vol. XV, pp. 210, 213–14.]

SIR EUSTACE HART to LORD CECIL.

1603, August.—He complains on behalf of himself and his wife, Lady Mary Willoughby, widow of Peregrine, Lord Willoughby, that an injunction has been awarded against them by the Court of Wards prohibiting them from felling any woods on the lands of Robert, Lord Willoughby, son of Lady Mary. The injunction seems to have been issued because of information given that they had committed spoil within these woods, which they emphatically deny. Only such trees as were granted as her dower to Lady Mary by the Court have been cut down, which as a tenant in dower she was at liberty to fell. Inasmuch as these woods belong to petitioners, and that they are contented with the property assigned to them during the minority of Lord Willoughby, they ask that the injunction by withdrawn and that they be permitted to enjoy the benefits accruing from their lands.— August, 1603.

¾ p. (P. 1621.)

SIR THOMAS BOURKE to the KING.

[Before September 11, 1603].—He refers to his services to the late Queen Elizabeth and to him, and mentions the £2000 due to him from the Crown in the right of his wife, the widow of Anthony Brabazon. Petitioner has refrained from being too troublesome in this matter of debt, but he now asks for a grant of so much escheated land and attainted estates in Ireland as the King thinks fit ; for a pension out of the English or Irish Exchequer ; and for the remission of all arrears of rent due from him for the lands he holds of the Crown, and which have been ruined by the late rebellion in Ireland.—*Undated.*

½ p. (P. 547.)

[See *Cal. S.P. Ireland*, 1603–6, p. 86.]

NEVILLE BLIGH.

[1603, October 1].—Particulars of the lands held by Neville Bligh by knight service and other tenures, and now descended to his heir who is a year and three months old and a King's ward.

Details are given of the annual rental of the property, what portion is due to the King, the money allowed to Bligh's mother as her jointure and to his widow as her dower, and what remains for the maintenance of the heir.—*Undated.*

Endorsed : " 1 October, 1605. D. Sharp for Blighs here (heir)." 1 p. (P. 2282.)

MATTHEW WOODWARD to LORD CECIL.

[1603, October 1].—Upon receipt of letters from the Mayor and Aldermen of Windsor, Cecil ordered that petitioner should have the disposal of the person and estate of James Gallis, a lunatic. At the same time Richard Gallis, one of James's brothers, had a joint estate with him for the term of their two lives in a certain inn in New Windsor called the *Garter.* It was rented at £12 *per annum,* and half of this sum was all that James Gallis had for his maintenance. Upon the expiration of the current lease, and contrary to Cecil's order, Richard Gallis made another in his own name only to one Nicholas Woods. Gallis died recently, and now Woods continues to occupy the property without paying rent. Moreover he threatens to procure a revocation of the order issued by Cecil on behalf of petitioner. Petitioner has provided James Gallis for the past nine years with food, clothing, lodging and medical care, for which he has received only £6 annually. Since all others interested in this affair are concerned solely with their own material benefits, petitioner requests that the first order, for the disposal of Gallis's person and estate by him, be confirmed.—*Undated.*

Endorsed : " 1 Oct. 1603. The state of the case with the humble petition of Mathewe Woodwarde of Windsore." 1 p. (P. 772.) *See* P. 2392 *infra* p. 119.

WILLIAM ERBURY to LORD CECIL.

1603, October 12.—He is the King's farmer of one third of the manor of Elsham, co. Lincoln, which is in his Majesty's hand. Since the death of the late Queen Elizabeth the tenants have refused to pay their rents until they are assured that the manor is in the King's possession, and that they may safely pay them to him as farmer. Requests letters that the tenants be given every assurance on this point, so that in this way litigation may be avoided.—12 Oct. 1603.

½ p. (P. 1198.)

SIR GEORGE SOUTHCOTT to LORD CECIL.

1603, October 15.—He has been informed that his adversary, Poole, has complained to Cecil about his behaviour when delivering a *supersedeas,* which he had received from the Court of Wards. He protests that he executed it with rigid observance of the law, and that he has done so with all court orders during the three years taken up by his case. He accuses his opponents of conducting themselves with impropriety and in a derogatory manner towards the orders of that court, and has protested about it in a petition to the King. He proposes to prefer a bill in the Court of Wards on this point and wishes to answer any charges brought against him. He requests that this and his opponents' bill may proceed together.—From Buckland Toutsaincts, the 15th of October, 1603.

Holograph. Seal. ½ p. (P. 2394.) *See* P. 1951 *supra* p. 97.

SIR WILLIAM STRODE to LORD CECIL.

1603, October 15.—At the request of John Woolcombe, of Plymton Mary, when he was on his death bed (he having been Strode's servant for 20 years) and that of his wife, he asks for the wardship and marriage of the deceased's son, William Woolcombe, who is seven years old and who has only inherited ten pounds in rents. Of this sum two parts are allocated to the use of four sisters for their maintenance and education during their brother's minority, so that all he has is £3:6:8 every year until he comes of age. Strode offers to pay a reasonable composition for the wardship " which I seek not to make the lest profytt unto my self but for the good of the sonne, whose fathers faithfull service doth require noe lesse at my hands then to be soe provident for him as his father was carefull of my occasions ".—From Meavie, the 15th of October, 1603.

Holograph. Seal. Endorsed : " 1603, October 15. Sir William Strode to my Lord for the wardship of the heyre of Jhon Woulcombe, decessed." ½ p. (P. 2395.)

JOHN BROWNE to LORD CECIL.

1603, October 17.—Recently Cecil bestowed on him the wardship of the heir of one of petitioner's brothers-in-law. But the father being restored to health, he has received no benefit from it. He now asks for the wardship of the son of his eldest brother, who has just died.—From Burleigh, the xviith of October, 1603.

Endorsed : " 17 Oct. 1603. Mr John Browne to my Lord." ½ p. (P. 1962.)

RICHARD ASHTON and OTHERS to LORD CECIL.

1603, October 22.—They have received a commission from Sir Richard Molyneux to hold an inquiry after the death of Thomas Barton, which was directed to Thomas Bold and others. They and Sir Richard met at Wigan on two occasions, but inasmuch as the commission was directed to Bold under the designation of Escheator of Lancashire, whereas he is only Deputy-Escheator, the proceedings were postponed on the grounds that he was not properly warranted to proceed with them. They ask that the commission be renewed but the name of Escheator removed.—Wygan, this xxiith of October, 1603.

Signed : Richard Asheton, Thomas Bold, Roger Downes, Feodary, Thomas Asheton. 1 p. (P. 2199.)

SIR RICHARD MOLYNEUX to LORD CECIL.

1603, October 24.—He thanks him for his favour concerning the wardship of the heir of Thomas Barton, of Barton, co. Lancs. He requests the renewal of Cecil's warrant for a new commission for the finding of the wardship " for that the Eschetor beinge wronglie named in the last commission made, all the proceedings therein voide ".—The xxiiiith of October, 1603.

Endorsed : " 24 Oct. 1603. Sir Richard Molineux for a new commission." ½ p. (P. 1933.)

[LORD CECIL] to the SHERIFFS and FEODARIES of various shires.

1603, October 28.—Since the accession of the King there has been an unparalleled negligence in collecting debts due to the Court of Wards and accounting for them to the receipt of that court. This may be partly due to the prevalence of the plague, which is wide-spread throughout the kingdom, but the fact that " allmost no one penny hath ben brought in this halfe year " can only be attributed to the perversion of the collectors " whoe seeme by this course to be agreed amongst themselves to keep the Kings Maties moneys in there hands, and to make their particular gayne under this pretext of the generall contagion ". By the command of the King, the High Sheriff is to order the under-sheriff to pay over immediately all moneys levied by him to the receipt of the Court of Wards at Richmond. He is also to return personally any process directed to him, to the Court of Wards when it is held in Winchester, and not to depart until the process has been duly examined by the counsel of the Court. The feodaries are hereby enjoined to surrender all sums of money received by them to the same receipt without delay, and to warn those lessees who withhold their rents that if they continue to do so, Cecil will be regretfully obliged to grant new leases to other people in their place. " I must plainly lett you know, the ffeodary, that if you bringe not in such moneys as you have already receaved, I must not only displace and appoint others in your roome but allso take such course with you and your sureties for the arrierages as the law doth provide in that behalfe." He assumes that henceforth they will perform their duties properly out of respect to the King " particularly at this time when the very ordinary assignations out of the Receipt cannot bee satisfied, the discredyt wherof doth light upon me and the reste of the officers of the Courte ".—From the Court at Wilton, this 28 of Octobr. 1603.

Endorsed : " 28, 29 Octobr. 1603. To the sheriffs and feodaries of divers shires." 1¼ pp. (P. 2377.) *Two other copies.*

EVAN AP EVAN, THOMAS AP EVAN and ELIZABETH MORRIS to the KING.

[1603, October 29].—Elizabeth Morris inherited certain lands after the death of her father and married the petitioner Thomas ap Evan. Some six years ago, Edward Whittingham and Margaret Whittingham *alias* Bethell brought an action against them in the Courts of Star Chamber, Exchequer and Common Pleas, claiming a title to the lands. Petitioners obtained an order from the Court of the Welsh Marches to stop proceedings and to have the title to the premises tried at the common law in Montgomeryshire where the property lies. However Edward Whittingham went to London and entered the service of Sir Edward Herbert, and was thus able to circumvent the order on the grounds that he was no longer resident in the Welsh Marches. He proceeded to prosecute his suit in the Court of Requests, but finding that he was likely to have an adverse verdict there, he transferred it to the Court of Wards. By these proceedings and by the exaction of £9 from petitioners for so-called arrears, he has reduced them to penury ; he now threatens a further attachment for alleged arrears of £19:10, which would result in imprisonment for petitioners who cannot pay. They therefore ask the King to stay the payment of that sum until the title to the lands in question be determined either by the Lord President and Council of Wales, or in Montgomeryshire where Whittingham is again resident.—*Undated.*

Note signed by Sir Julius Caesar : " At the Court at Wilton, the xxixth of October, 1603. These suppliants are to attend upon the Court of Wards for order in this cause without further trouble to his Matie."

Endorsed : " The humble request of your poore subjects is to have the xix^l 10^s within mentioned forborne the payment untill the title of the premisses alsoe herein specified be tried either before your Highnes Counsell in your Marches of Wales or ells in the county of Mountgomery where the landes doe lye. And that it will please your Highnes to prefixe a tyme for tryall of the same with expedition, and that the sute may beginne att the comissions whereupon witnesses are already examined. And also that the ix^l within mentioned which were wrongfully levied on your subjects may be repayed unto them." 1 p. (P. 561.)

[For this case see *PRO. Star Chamber Proceedings* **5,** W 4/13.]

Thomas Hesketh to Lord Cecil.

1603, October 30.—It has been reported that the term is to begin on November 12th in Winchester and to end on the 14th, but no proclamation has been published to this effect. He is at a loss what to do to attend since the journey is long and dangerous " in the tyme of this generall infection and in the depe of wynter ". If Cecil has special need of his services, he will " nether spare labor nor ffeare annie daunger ffor (as I thincke) I can be in no greatter then yow are continuallie whose lyffe is ten thousand tymes of more value then myne for mannie respects ". But since the business of the term cannot be heavy or important inasmuch the court is only to be held for two days, he asks that Cecil inform him through Myles Whitaker or Brereton whether his attendance is necessary, particularly as he surmises that the counsel of the court will be present. Concerning the letters which have been distributed throughout the English shires about the sale of wardships, the return of the certificates having been fixed before the 10th of December, he proposes to leave on November 7th and make his way towards Cecil, unless he will have heard from him in the mean time, " which will hardlie be except the posts be more speedie then ordinarie ".—Heslington, nere the citie of Yorke, October the 30th, 1603.

PS. " The letters for the sale of wards do take smale effect in these parts as yett, ffor men generallie cannot ffynd in their harts to part with monnie allthoughe it be for their good."

Holograph. Seal. 1 p. (P. 2397.)

The MAYOR and ALDERMEN of NEW WINDSOR to LORD CECIL.

[October, 1603].—In previous letters Cecil had ordered that Matthew Woodward should be given the custody of the person and estate of James Gallis, a lunatic, and that the Mayor and Aldermen should deal with any person who attempted to meddle with this arrangement and disturb Woodward in his possession of the lunatic and his estate. In the case of any refractoriness and contempt of this order, the guilty party was to be reported to Cecil. In accordance with that instruction, they now certify that Richard Gallis, brother of James, who had a joint estate with the latter in an inn called the *Garter* in New Windsor, has leased the inn to Nicholas Woods and reserved the whole of the rent of £16 yearly to himself, with intent to defraud James Gallis and Matthew Woodward, thereby depriving his brother of the sole source of maintenance that he possesses. Moreover, both Woods and Richard Gallis refuse to apportion any part of this rent towards his upkeep except on the condition that they be entrusted exclusively with the custody of the lunatic and the disposal of his estate. They are reporting this state of affairs so that Cecil may take appropriate measures to deal with it.—*Undated.*

Signed : Humphrey Fawcet, Mayor *and nine other signatures.*
Endorsed : " The seconde certificat. 1603. The humble certificat of the Mayor and Aldermen of the Towne of Newe Windsor."
In another hand : " Oct. 1603." 1 p. (P. 2392.) *See P. 772 supra* p. 115.

EDMUND RILEY to LORD CECIL.

[Before November, 1603].—He refers to a previous disclosure by him of the conspiracy of Warbara Riley, widow of John Riley, deceased, and others to hinder the claims and titles of other people to her late husband's property. Petitioner had asked that the wardship of the son should not be granted to the mother, and that all papers and evidences should be produced before the Court of Wards for the purpose of an inquisition. Despite Cecil's order to this effect, Warbara Riley had not arranged such an inquisition, and petitioner adds that some of the commissioners nominated on her behalf are partial to her. He requests that

Cecil again issue his former instructions so as to prevent any injustice being committced against his mother and sisters who are claimants, and that he demand an explanation why the other party has not proceeded in the matter according to his injunctions.*—*Undated.*

Endorsed : " The humble petition of Edmond Riley, who most humbly beseecheth your Lordship commaunde the due procedinge in a cause betweene your suppliant, Warbara Riley and others." ½ p. (P. 844.)

WILLIAM SCRUTTON to LORD CECIL.

[? *c.* November, 1603].—He is the Bailiff of the King's manor of Walton cum Trimley and Felixstowe, co. Suffolk, and has held the office by letters patent from the late Queen Elizabeth and the King. Owing to his being heavily engaged in his duties, he did not find the time to get the King's patent passed by the Great Seal. The manor has been conveyed recently to the Queen as part of her jointure, and one Thomas Rowe, with the assistance of Mr Hitcham, the Queen's Attorney, has procured a grant of the bailiwick from Cecil. Petitioner assures Cecil that " had it not beene for this infectious tyme (the sicknes beinge in those partes) he would have bene heretofore an humble suitor to your honor for the same ". He asks to be allowed to retain his office as bailiff, and names Sir Michael Stanhope and Mr Wentworth, Steward of the manor, as persons who could testify to his worth and character.—*Undated.*

1 p. (P. 1625.)
[See *Cal. S.P. Dom.*, 1603–10, pp. 48 and 52.]

PAUL BAYNING to the PRIVY COUNCIL.

[Before December 5, 1603].—In January 1602, upon the earnest entreaty of Henry, late Lord Cobham, and George Brooke his brother,† he lent them £1980 in ready money and took their bond of £4000 for its repayment within one year. Lord Cobham and his brother are now condemned for high treason ; neither have they discharged their due debt to petitioner. He asks to be assisted in obtaining the money from them.—*Undated.*

½ p. (P. 1036.)

WILLIAM BISPHAME to ——.

[After December 5, 1603].—He and Thomas Waile, at the earnest request of George Brooke, late executed, and his wife became sureties on his behalf to one Adams in the sum of £200. Since the time of Brooke's arrest for treason, Adams has sued petitioner and he has been obliged to pay the money. He asks that the sum paid by him as well as other debts owed by Brooks

---

* An *Inquisition Post Mortem* was held on November 8, 1603. [See *PRO, Wards* 7, 38/175.]

† Executed at Winchester on December 5, 1603.

to him be restored out of the latter's lands which are due to be sold.—*Undated.*

1 p.   (P. 32.)

EDWARD PAYNE to LORD CECIL.

[Before December 6, 1603].—The King has bestowed the manor of St. Neots, co. Huntingdon, upon the Queen as part of her jointure. Certain fairs are held annually within the manor, one of them on St. Nicholas's Day* which will be in three weeks' time. But the King's proclamation issued three months ago prohibiting fairs within 50 miles of London " in respect of resort of Londoners thether " makes him apprehensive of keeping the fair without Cecil's approval, since St. Neots lies within 42 miles of London. Petitioner requests that approval, since the Queen can expect to derive some benefit from the fair which, in turn, " dependeth upon resort of cuntry people thether ".

¾ p.   (P. 1626.)

JANE FITZGERALD to SIR ROBERT CECIL, BARON OF ESSENDON

[1603].—She feels ashamed of having to importune him, but the destitution of her sister and herself forces her to do so, particularly as they can only depend upon him for some relief. " I need not to your Honor agravate our miserie, who for want ly pawned in our lodginge at Greenewiche, being debarred of the smale meanes formerly allowed us, so that we are not able to followe the court to be suitors." She begs that, being orphans, they be allowed adequate means of livelihood, thereby freeing him from further solicitations on their part.—*Undated.*

Holograph. Seal. Endorsed : " 1603. One of the ladyes of Desmond to my lord." ⅓ p. **(113.** 163.)

[See *H.M.C. Salisbury MSS*, Vol. XV, p. 373.]

KIRKSTALL ABBEY.

[1603].—" The fee farm of so many of the abbay landes of Cristall *alias* Kirkstall Abbay in the county of York, as be not yet sold away to Justice Walmesley, reserving his Maties rent.'— *Undated.*

Endorsed : " 1603. Cristale Abbay." ¼ p. (P. 2286.)

ELLEN McCARTHY to LORD CECIL.

[1603].-Following upon her last interview with him, she entreated Sir Thomas Lake to deliver a letter from her to the King concerning her petition for an increase in her pension. The King replied that he would be willing to grant it if he obtained the concurrence of both Cecil and the Privy Council, to whom he referred her suit. Her petition is to be discussed by the Council tomorrow, and petitioner reposes her complete confidence in Cecil and the Vice-Chamberlain that it will be granted

---

* December 6th.

and her position assured, so that she need no longer be troublesome to the King and the Council.—*Undated.*

Seal. Endorsed: "1603. M^rs McCarty to my Lord." ⅓ p.
(P. 1947.)

[See *H.M.C. Salisbury MSS*, Vol. XV, pp. 142 and 154.]

Sir William Bowyer to the King.

[1603].—He served the late Queen Elizabeth as a captain for
30 years, and has since then been engaged in suppressing the
insurrections on the borders. He was "the first captayne that
tooke armes and daunted the proud insolensies of those rebells
whoe otherwise were likelie to have overrun and oppressed the
whole borders". He now asks to be granted £20 yearly in
fee farm in return for these services.—*Undated.*

½ p. (P. 970.)

[See *H.M.C. Salisbury MSS*, Vol. XV, pp. 354–5.]

John Correll, Sieur de Meautis, to the Privy Council.

[1603 or after].—In March, 1601, petitioner's ship was captured
and pillaged at sea by Sir Richard Cowper. He obtained judgment against him and his two sureties, Sir Robert Bassett and
John Young, in 1603 in the High Court of Admiralty. He was
granted letters by the Council to execute the order for reparations
to be given him for his losses, and delivered it to Peter Woodall,
one of the messengers of the Chamber, who proceeded to arrest
Young. But because of the latter's obstinacy and Woodall's
duplicity, petitioner still remains without compensation. Sir
Richard Cowper and his sureties are in the service of the Earl of
Nottingham and are greatly favoured by the King's messengers.
Petitioner requests a warrant for the arrest of the three men, and
that Woodall be summoned before the Council to answer for his
fraudulent dealings.—*Undated.*

½ p. (P. 1824.)

Sir John Fitzedmund Gerald to the Privy Council.

[1603].—Petitioner's ancestors have always remained loyal to
the Crown, and he himself opposed the rebels in the last four
revolts in Munster, which cost him all his goods. In consideration of his services and past letters of appreciation and promises
of remuneration, he asks to be elevated to the status of Baron.
The late Queen Elizabeth granted him 100 marks a year of
attainted and escheated lands which he did not prosecute because
of his military commitments and in order not to hinder the
undertakers of the plantation which had begun in Munster. He
asks for the renewal of the grant, and also for the King's letters
to the Lord Deputy to accept the surrender of his lands and the
regranting of them to him, in compliance with the general directive
that all the King's subjects in Ireland should yield up their lands
and receive them back again from the Crown. He wishes the
regranting to be done in as absolute and favourable a manner

as that awarded to the Lord of Up Ossory and Sir Richard Boyle. —*Undated.*

1 p. (P. 1823.)

[See *Cal. S.P. Ireland*, 1603–6, p. 71.]

SIR JAMES SANDILAND'S suit.

[? 1603].—It has been reduced by the Lord Treasurer " into these 3 heades which are things verie casuall and harde to be recovered." First, all moneys which were due to the late Queen Elizabeth from the recusancy of James Braybrook, Francis Morris and William Fitton, and which were concealed from the Queen. Secondly, all moneys due as rents, arrears of rents, issues and profits of recusants' lands seized in the reign of Queen Elizabeth, and which were received or are to be answered for by any sheriffs or officers before March 24 in the first year of the King's reign, and which have not been paid. Thirdly, all recusants' goods which have been seized by any officer or person and which were due to the late Queen before the said March 24th. The suit is valued by the officers of the Exchequer at £5000. But since they estimate that £1000 will be spent, and much time taken, in recovering the money, there is not likely to be more than £3000 for Sir James Sandilands when the whole business is ended.

½ p. (P. 978.)

[See *Cal. S.P. Dom.*, 1603–10, p. 61, and *H.M.C. Salisbury MSS*, Vol. XIX, p. 285.]

SIR ROBERT WROTH to the KING.

[1603].—He is the King's tenant for 40 years yet to come of the manor of Loughton, parcel of the Duchy of Lancaster and situated within the King's Forest of Waltham, co. Essex. The manor house, " whereof, as your Ma. well knowes, is of old low buildings, in great decay, the roomes very smale and unfitt to receve your Ma. at your repaire to the said Forest ". He asks to be granted a lease in reversion of the manor for 41 years, paying annually the ancient rent of £48 without provision, as well as a lease of the perquisites and profits of the manor in paying the old rent without provision. In return he will pay a four years' fine and spend £500 in six years on buildings within the manor.—*Undated.*

Endorsed : " 1603. Sir Robert Wroth." ¾ p. (P. 778.)

TURLAGH McHENRY to LORD CECIL.

[1603].—He is of the Fews and petitioned the King to be allowed to surrender the Fews, the vicarage of the Kregan with Twoaghue, to the Crown and to be regranted the same on condition that he was to be free from all impositions, etc, claimed by the Earl of Tyrone, by reason of the attainder of Shane O'Neill in the 11th year of the late Queen Elizabeth's reign, and the patent of the county of Tyrone made for the Earl in the 29th year of her reign. According to the attainder the chieftains in Ulster were to be exempt from O'Neill's taxations. Besides, the Fews were never part of Tyrone or under the Earl of Tyrone's jurisdiction. In respect of these considerations petitioner requests the region to be discharged from impositions or the latter reduced, and that he and his tenants be rendered safe from " the feare and danger of soe greate a neighbour ".—*Undated.*

½ p. (P. 1662.)

[See *Cal. S.P. Ireland*, 1603–6, p. 14.]

ELIZABETH WOODROVE to LORD CECIL.

[1603].—It was her misfortune to submit a petition to the Privy Council when Cecil happened to be absent. She requests his help, " for the good report of your honorable and pittifull disposition towards the distressed hath perswaded me chiefly to depend upon your Lordship ". She regards herself as the poorest petitioner who ever applied to him for assistance, for she is not " only voyd of maintenance butt allso of limmes and all other worldly comforts ".—*Undated.*

Holograph. Seal. Endorsed : " 1603. Mrs Woodroof to my lord." ⅓ p. (P. 2477.)

RALPH RIVELEY to the KING.

[1603 or after].—He served Robert Bowes, deceased, former ambassador of the late Queen Elizabeth in Scotland, for nine years in that country. He was promised promotion but Bowes's death destroyed his hopes and left him in poor circumstances. He asks that he be granted the next soldier's pay of 8d a day that shall become available in the garrison at Berwick.—*Undated.*

Note by Cecil : " His Matie proposeth to continew the payes of that garrison no longer then those do live that have served in it,* and for his services to the Ambassador hath no purpose to give rewards, and therefore thinks it a vaine motion."

1 p. (P. 1895.)

DEPOSITION.

[Before January 13, 1603–4].—" Deposition de Maistre Claude Giraudet, Advocat en Parlement a Paris, sur ce qui cest passe en la mort de Francois Faure tue par un gentilhomme Anglois nomme Wiseman, ledit Sr Giraudet ayant este present.

Le jour des Roys dernier, ledit Wiseman et Faure jouant ensemble aux tables tomberent en different de sorte que ledit de Faure donna un desmentir audit Wiseman qui se contenta de luy en voir un autre en eschange.

Depuis ce temps la ils ont tousjours beu et mange ensemble sans se dire rien l'un a l'autre jusques a samady vintquatrieme jour de janvier quayant soupe ensemble ledit Wiseman se leva le premier de table et prenant une chair de natte la rangea a un coing de la cheminee et sassit dedans pour se chaufer.

A l'instant mesme se leva ledit de Faure lequel s'estant aussi

---

* This decision was taken by James I in 1603. [See *H.M.C. Salisbury MSS.* Vol. XV, under Berwick.]

approche du feu print ledit Wiseman par derriere et luy dit 'Levez-
vous de la, vous estes sur ma chaire.' Auquel ledit Wiseman
respondit ' Cest la raison ', et se levant la luy ceda. Faure luy
repliqua quil la luy devoit ceder d'autant quil estoit le premier en
la maison. Ce entendant ledit Wiseman luy demanda comme il
avoit entendu le faire lever de sa place, sur quoy sans autre propos
ledit Faure luy donna un coup de poing en la face de telle force que
le sang luy sortit en grand abondance par le nez et par la bouche.

Ledit Wiseman se promenant par la salle estanchant son sang,
murmurant et menaceant ledit de Faure de tirer raison de
loutrage quil avoit receu de luy, de Faure luy dit quil ne le
craignoit point pourveu quil le print en homme de bien. A quoy
ledit Wiseman respondit quil se souvint de quelle facon il le
lavoit prins, et ainsi ledit de Faure se meist a regarder les joueurs.
Et comme ledit Wiseman se fust adresse a son hoste et luy eust
demande si la chaire estoit pas a luy, et luy eust dit quil eust a se
resouvenir de loutrage quil avoit receu en sa maison, ledit de
Faure print la parolle et luy dit que de ce qui sestoit passe il
ne s'en fallait prendre a l'hoste, et quil estoit la beste qui avoit
fait le dommage. Et ainsi pres d'un cart d'heure apres le coup
de poing donne ledit Wiseman print une espee qui estoit sur un
buffet et en donna un coup dans le coste droit dudit de Faure
dont il mourut environ deux heures apres."—*Undated.*

Endorsed : " An abstract of the proces agaynst Mr Wiseman."
2 pp. (**130.** 186.)
[See *PRO, State Papers France*, Vol. 51, pp. 25b–27, 85, 164b.]

GRANT BY THE CITY OF GLOUCESTER.

1603–4, January 20.—Declaration by the Mayor and burgesses
of the city of Gloucester that " as well for and in consideration
that the right honorable Robert, Lorde Cecill, Barron of Essing-
den, wilbee pleased to vouchsafe his ho: freindshippe and favourable countenance towardes the saide Cittie of Gloucester, the
which the saide Maior and Burgesses doe very humblie praye
and intreate, as also for divers other good causes and considerations them moveinge " : they hereby grant to Lord Cecil an
annuity of five pounds for the term of his life.—January 20,
1 Jac 1.
1 *m.* *Seal.* (Deeds **119**/9.)

MR RAINSFORD'S ESTATE.

[1603–4, January 24].—" A true abstract of Mr Raynsfords
estate at the tyme of his death with such money as Mrs Raynsford
hath receved since for wards by your Lordships favour granted
unto her husband in his lyff tyme."

Details of the debts, valuation of goods and property, and
money allocated for the education and portions of his children
and for his mother's jointure. Persons named include Mr
Houghton, Mr Henry Rainsford, Mr Miles Whitaker and Mrs
Anne Rainsford.—*Undated.*

Endorsed : "Mr Raynsford decesed, 1603, 24th January, his estate." ½ p. (P. 2461.)
[See *H.M.C. Salisbury MSS*, Vol. XVI, p. 12.]

FRANCIS HEYBORN to LORD CECIL.

[1603–4] January 29.—It is only the desperate situation in which he finds himself that forces him to be troublesome to Cecil, since it concerns the office which he has held for 24 years under the Earl of Derby and his predecessors. Immediately after hearing that the Earl was to be Chamberlain,* he obtained his promise that he would continue his favour to petitioner. Upon writing to Cecil he was advised to attend upon the Countess at Manchester, which he did and secured a promise from her likewise that she would write to her husband on his behalf. But in the course of time he received a word from her that the office had been promised to others ; but almost simultaneously he was reassured by the Earl that he would not be deprived of it. Thereupon petitioner communicated this information to the King. He protests that he has not been over-presumptuous in his suit, and begs Cecil to entertain a better opinion of him than others would have him do. The loss of his office would be a severe blow to him " and the greefe to me wilbe the more to be thought worthy to receyve such loss and disgrace at those hands wher I had made profession of my services ".—29 January.
1 p. (P. 1954.)

FRANCIS RAINE to LORD CECIL.

1603–4, January.—Sir Anthony Cooke enjoys for the term of his life the stewardship of the Queen's manor of Havering-at-Bow, co. Essex. He is now reported to be gravely ill, and petitioner, who has occupied the post of understeward for forty years since the days of Sir Anthony's grandfather, requests that should he die, he be allowed to continue in that office under Cecil or whoever shall be appointed to take Sir Anthony Cooke's place.—January, 1603.
1 p. (P. 1318.)

THOMAS RAWSON to LORD CECIL.

1603–4, February 12.—He requests the grant of the concealed wardship of the heir of Robert Moor, co. Yorks, petitioner undertaking to prove the King's title to it at his own expense.—12 February, 1603–4.
Note at bottom signed by Cecil : " Let him resort to any two of the Counsayle of the Court, whereof Mr Surveyor or Mr Atturny to be one, and if he can shewe sufficient matter and procure an order he shall have my warrant."
1 p. (P. 1617.)

---

* William Stanley, 6th Earl of Derby, was made Chamberlain of the county Palatine of Chester on October 30, 1603.

The BAILIFFS of SPALDING to LORD CECIL.

[? After February 19, 1603–4].—Nicholas Perry, John Old-field, Nicholas Brymston, Thomas Greaves, William Ederich, Isaac Elwood and Thomas Bennett, Bailiffs of the late Queen Elizabeth in the manors of Spalding and Paulets in Godney, Lincolnshire. These manors have lately been assigned to the Queen as part of her jointure. Petitioners declare that they, their parents and friends have performed the duties of bailiffs for forty years. After the death of the late Queen they renewed their patents and became bound to the King for the execution of their duties, at their own charges. They have now been deprived of their offices, and request that Cecil should award them some reasonable composition to be paid by those who have been granted their bailiwicks.—*Undated.*

½ p. (P. 1320.)

[See *Cal. S.P. Dom.,* 1603–10, p. 78.]

EDWARD FIELD to LORD CECIL.

[Before February 21, 1603–4].—He is a yeoman of the King's Chamber. After serving the late Queen Elizabeth for 20 years he was granted the stewardship of the manor of King's Norton in Worcestershire for life. Last September he was ordered by Cecil and the Lord Treasurer not to hold any more courts there until he had received further warrant, because the manor had been conveyed to the Queen as part of her jointure. He complied with the order and has been expecting a warrant ever since. However the suspension of the court has caused inconvenience to the tenants and proved prejudicial to the interests of the Queen. He therefore asks that he be authorized by warrant to keep the court which is held every three weeks.—*Undated.*

Note by Cecil: " Lett this petitioner make it appeare to the Queenes Counsayle that he hath this office by letters patent for life, and he shall have warrant for keeping of the Court."

Note by Robert Hitcham: " May it please your Lordship, I have seene a patent wherby the stewardship of Kinges Norton was lawfully graunted by the late Queene to Edward Feilde for his life, butt ther are many complaints made against him for mis-demenors in his office."

1¼ pp. (P. 1627.)

[See *Cal. S.P. Dom.,* 1603–10, pp. 68 and 72.]

STEVEN HARISTEGIN and JOHN HARRANEDER to the KING.

[Before March 13, 1603–4].—The French Ambassador has already presented petitions on their behalf concerning the damage inflicted on their ship and cargo by Captain Thomasin and his company, for whom Sir Robert Bassett became surety. After it had been decided to compensate them to the amount of £1500, Lady Bassett was summoned to make satisfaction to them. She, however, endeavoured to avoid that obligation by falsely stating that her husband's lands had been seized for debt by

Lord Buckhurst,* Lord Treasurer, Mr Drake, the High Sheriff of Devon, and Mr Poole. Petitioners request that Lady Bassett be forced to pay the £1500 out of Sir Robert's lands or that, in view of his absence abroad, his property be distrained for that purpose.—*Undated*.

1 p. (P. 9.)

[See *H.M.C. Salisbury MSS*, Vol. XVI, p. 438.]

JOHN GEYNKYN and OTHERS to the PRIVY COUNCIL

[? After March 15, 1603–4].—The Lord Chancellor, the Lord Admiral, the Lord Treasurer, Sir John Stanhope and others of the Privy Council issued an order to the inhabitants between Temple Bar and Charing Cross to arrange a pageant to receive the King joyfully and loyally as he passed through London to Westminster. Petitioner and many other poor people and artisans have contributed liberally towards the same, but some of the better sort have refused to do so. They should be commanded to donate money or be summoned before the Council for contempt. —*Undated*.

1 p. (P. 732.)

[See Nichols *Progresses of King James the First*, Vol. 1, p. 375.]

SIR RICHARD BULKELEY to LORD CECIL.

[After March 16, 1603–4].—In answer to the petition of Jane Owen, he acknowledges that she inherited, as a child, the lands which were in the possession of Richard Owen, deceased, mentioned in her petition. Moreover Lewis Owen, Sergeant of the King's Larder, was granted the wardship of Jane Owen, and sued forth a commission to Bulkeley, to the Feodary and the Escheator of Anglesey, and to Henry Lloyd, esquire, who found that the King had a title to her wardship. After the bestowal of the wardship on Lewis Owen, Griffith ap John Griffith, " beinge a turbulent and clamarous person and a common solicitor of suts, having spent all his tyme in suts and brabells ", exhibited a bill in the Star Chamber against the commissioners,† charging them with underhand actions. Petitioner has answered his allegations, but Griffith has now addressed a petition to Cecil in the hope of tarnishing Bulkeley's good name. Lastly, petitioner declares that he never claimed any interest in the wardship, and asks that Griffith be punished for his insinuations against him, " that thereby the Kings officers and commissioners hereafter maie not be discouraged to doe the Kings Matie any service. Otherwise the gentlemen in that contrie will absent them selves from executing any of the Kings commissions, and the tenurs that are due to the King there will hardely be founde."—*Undated*.

1 p. (P. 1554.)

---

* Created Earl of Dorset on March 13, 1603–4.

† Griffith ap John Griffith exhibited his bill in the Star Chamber on March 16, 1603–4. [See Edwards *Star Chamber Cases relating to Wales*, James 1, Anglesey, 157/13.

WILLIAM CARRIER to LORD CECIL.

[Before March 17, 1603–4].—He is the Bailiff of the King's manor of Yaxley, and held the office for a long time under the late Queen Elizabeth. When the King came to the throne he renewed his patent at his own expense, but recently the King granted the manor to the Queen as part of her jointure. Petitioner understands that he has to renew his patent again from Cecil. In consideration of his lengthy service and his charges, he requests that he be granted the bailiwick.

In a different handwriting: Since he drew up his petition, petitioner has been given to understand that a Mr Proby, to whom he had entrusted his case and its presentation to Cecil, has procured a patent of the bailiwick in his own name. But since Proby is resident in London, he has to find a deputy to perform the duties of the office. Petitioner explains that he had sent up his old patent and the assignment which he had obtained from the King, to London with a Mr Tuck, one of Cecil's employees, inasmuch as he was afraid to come himself last Christmas because of the plague. Tuck appears to have been slack about the whole business, and petitioner asks that Proby surrender his patent to him, he himself undertaking to defray Proby's expenses in the matter.—*Undated.*

1 p. (P. 1518.)

[See *Cal. S.P. Dom.*, 1603–10, p. 88.]

SIR JOHN CROKE to the KING.

[After March 19, 1603–4].—Before being elected Speaker in the last Parliament and during the sessions of the present one,* he was unable to attend to his legal duties as much as he could have desired. He asks that he be awarded some fee farm so that he may enjoy a better estate, and thus be enabled to fulfil his duties with greater freedom and efficiency.—*Undated.*

½ p. (P. 639.)

JAMES ANNESLEY to LORD CECIL.

[1603–4, March 21].—He is one of the officers of the King's Cellar. Thirty years ago Robert Stokes died seised of certain lands in Newport Pagnell. For lack of lawful heir, the land is either to escheat to the King or a fine is due for alienation. He is brother-in-law to the deceased Stokes, and since the land forms part of the Queen's jointure, he asks that at the next court held in the manor an heir be presented or the property seized for the Queen's use. If an escheat is declared, petitioner requests that he be made tenant before any other.—*Undated.*

Note by Cecil: "I desire to be enformed of this by her Ma^ts Chancelour."

Note by Sir Roger Wilbraham: "I think it meete your Lordship write to the Stuard to enquire of the Q's title, which founde he semes for his discoverie to deserve a lease for 21 yeres for such

---

* The first Parliament of James I was summoned on March 19, 1603–4.

fyne as the stuard and dep. surveior shall advise." 21 Marcii, 1603.
1½ pp. (P. 1680.)

PARLIAMENTARY DEBATES.

1603–4, March 23.—Die Veneris xxiii Martis, 1603. Sir
Robert Wroth (one of the knights of the shire returned for the
countie of Essex) moved that matters of most ymportance might
first bee handled, and to that purpose hee offered to the consideration of the Howse : the Wardship of mens children as a burden
and servitude to the subjects of this kingdome, etc.

Die Lune, 26 Martii

Sir Ffrancis Bacon (one of his Ma^{ts} Councell learned) maketh
report of the meeting of the Committees touching the matters
formerly propounded by Sir Robert Wroth, and of the first
endevoures and travell in the poynt of Wardship of mens children,
relating breifly what was said *Pro et Con,* viz :

That it was a thing never petitioned, never wonne of any King.

But having his ground from the tenure of Scutagium, voyage
royall in Esclose, that nowe determins by his Ma^{ts} possessinge of
the Crowne.

This no newe thing, for K.H.8, K.E.6 and Q.M. had a power
graunted them by Parlyament to dissolve the Court of Wards.

That the intention of the Howse was that both the Kinge and
meane Lords should bee comprehended.

The first resolution was for the matter, that petition should bee
made to the King ; then for the maner, it was debated : (1)
whether first to agree upon the plott and to offer to the King the
matter plotted, (2) or first to aske leave to treate, then, whether
first to pray a conference with the Lords touching a petition to
bee offered to his Matie for libertie to treate, which last was
thought the best course, and so resolved by the house.

Agreed by the Committees and delivered into the House at the
same tyme.

Concerning the Wardship of mens children, yt was agreed that
the House should bee moved this day touching a conference to
bee had with the Lords for joyning in a Petition to the Kings
Matie, that hee would bee pleased to give them leave to enter into
consideration of some project of recompence to bee given to his
Highnes for easing the subjects in the wardship of their children
for their bodies and lands.

Sir Henry Nevill offereth a motion touching two important
causes to bee considered by the House, viz : (1) a declaration of
all kinds of treasons, (2) an explanation of certaine maximes of
the Common lawe touching the K. graunts : which he prayed
(together with the matter of Wardship) might bee considered of
and remembred by such Committees as should bee named for
the conference to bee had with the Lords touching the matter of
Wardship. But yt was thought fitt that the matter of Wardship
onely and nothing els should bee handled in that conference :

and xxiiii were presently named to bee sent to the Lords to pray a conference, viz :

> All the privie councell of the House
> Sir George Carew, vicechamberlaine to the Queene
> Sir Ffrauncis Bacon
> Sir Edwyn Sandys
> Sir John Hollis
> Mr Ffrauncis Moore
> Sir Jerome Bowes
> Sir Ffrauncis Hastinge
> Mr Serjant Dodridge
> Sir John Scott
> Sir Richard Leveson
> Sir Edward Hobby
> Sir Maurice Berkley
> Sir Edward Mountague
> Mr Serjeant Tanfeild
> Sir George Moore
> Sir Arthur Atye
> Sir Robert Wroth
> Sir Henry Mountague
> Sir John Thynne
> Mr Ffuller
> Sir Henry Nevill
> Sir Thomas Lake
> Mr Ffr. Clifford
> Sir Robert Wingfeild
> Sir Edward Hobby [sic]
> Sir Maurice Berkley [sic]

The maner of proceeding in the matter of Wardship was further questioned, and being (by generall opinion) thought fittest to proceed by way of petition to the King, viz, that his Matie would bee pleased to give leave to treate, etc ;

It was first propounded as necessarie that the Lords, being part of the Bodie and sensible of the same burden, should joyne in petition : and for that purpose the House presently to pray a conference with their Lordships : which upon the question being resolved, Sir John Stanhope, kt, vicechamb. to his Matie accompaned with the xxiiii Committees formerly named by speciall commission and message delivered to their Lordships the desire and pleasure of the House accordingly, and upon his returne reported for aunswere from their Lordships that they lyked and well approved the care and respect of the House in the course they tooke to pray such a conference, and that they would willingly and readily joyne with them in that or any other thing which might so much concerne the common good. And for their numb[er] tyme and place of meeting, send aunswere by messengers of their owne.

Sir John Popham, knight, Lo : Chief Justice of England, Sir Christopher Yelverton, knight, one of the Judges of the Common

M S—K

Pleas, Sir John Crook, knight, deputie Chancellor of his Ma^ts
Court of Exchequor and one of the Ks Serjannts at Lawe, and Sir
Richard Swale, knight, Doctor of the Lawes and one of the
Masters of his Ma^ts Court of Chauncery, came downe in message
from the Lords and delivered : That whereas yt pleased the
House to pray conference touching their Lordships joyning with
them in petition to his Matie for leave to treat of matter of Wardship, etc, that they were comannded to make knowne unto them
howe well they lyked and how willingly they enterteyned their
carefull consideration and motion in that matter as in all other
matters of lyke importance. But desiered that some things els
of the same kind, and of as great waight and moment, might bee
drawne in to consultation together with the other at the same
conference, as namely Respit of Homage, Licence of Alienation,
etc, as also the generall abuse (so much complaynd of) of Purveyors
and Cartakers of which greevance (they sayd) the Lords themselves
had as much feeling as any whosoever, and wished that therein
such an order, proportion and certainty might bee established as
his Matie might bee better served, his Prerogative preserved and
the country eased : and this they desiered might bee debated in
the intended conference.

And that their Lordships had named thirty of that House to
meete with such number of this House at the said conference as
should bee thought fitt : the place and tyme to bee in the painted
Chamber at two a clock in the afternoone.

To this the House assented and gave aunswere by Mr Speaker,
that they would meet for conference with their Lordships with
the number of six score at the tyme and place desiered. And to
joyne with the xxiiii Committees formerly named and sent up
to the Lords, were presently added for the said conference :

Sir Henry Hubbard	Sir Robert Needham
Sir William Killigrew	Sir Edmond Bowyer
Sir Thomas Somersett	Sir Thomas Jermin
Sir William Herbert	Mr George Smyth
Sir Edward Herbert	Mr Martin
Sir William Harvey	Sir Anthony Rowse
Sir Philip Herbert	Sir Maurice Berkley [sic]
Sir Thomas Ridgway	Sir Henry Carey
Sir Robert Oxenbridge	Mr Robert Askwith
Sir Valentine Knightley	Mr Lawrence Hyde
Sir Ffrauncis Goodwin	Sir Edward Grevill
Sir Ffrauncis Barrington	Mr Ffrauncis Moore [sic]
Sir Roger Aston	Sir Thomas Monnson
Sir Edward Stafford	Sir John Savill
Sir Robert Cotton	Mr Nathaniel Bacon
Mr Allen Persie	Sir Nicholas Saunders
Sir William Woodhouse	Sir Rowland Litton
Sir Roger Wilbraham	Sir Charles Cornwallis
Sir John Townesend	Sir John Leveson
Sir Oliver St John	Sir John Thynn [sic]

And these Committees (besides the matter of Petition to the King touching Wardship) had warrant and authoritie from the House to treat and debate of whatsoever should bee accidentally propounded or arise by occasion in the said conference.

xxviii Martii 1604

Sir Ffrancis Bacon maketh report of the conference yesterday betweene the Lords and this House wherein (he sayd) he was meerely a relator, no actor.

And sayd further that the Lords upon their first meeting desired the Committees of this house to make the proposition : whereupon yt was thought fitt by the said Committees not to mention any objections but onely to shew their dutifull respect in the handling of the matter, and, secondly, to open the greif adding some cautions and considerations to prevent mistakinge.

The grief was that every mans eldest sonne or heire (the dearest thinge he hath in the world) was by Prerogatyve warranted by the lawes of the land to bee in ward to the King for his bodie and lands, then which (they conceyved) to a free nation nothing to bee more greyvous. But they esteemed it onely a greif, no wrong, sythence yt hath beene patiently endured by our auncestors and by our selves, and therefore they did presse to offer yt to the Kings grace and not to his justice.

They knewe yt concerned the King in two sorts, (1) in his revenewe, (2) and in reward to his well deserving servants and officers of the wards.

That the discharge of the wardship of meane Lords was also to bee thought on. And concluded that their desire and resolution was not to proceed by way of Bill but by way of Petition to his Matie for licence to treat, etc.

Of the Lords, first one aunswered that they had as much feeling as any of the burden, and that with a double respect, because their families were planted in honor.

That there was one other great greevance complayned of in the matter of respect of Homage, wherein though the King were interressed in honor and profit, yet their desire was that yt might bee coupled in the Petition with the matter of Wardship, as growing upon that roote.

It was affirmed by another Lord that in the matter of respit of homage, present order was to bee taken by speciall direction from his Matie. And that for the greevance of Purveyors, etc.

Sir Ffrauncis Bacon continued the report of another Lords speach (which he said) he did but onely report not deliver as a message. It contayned 3 points, (1) his affection to the House of the Commons, (2) his good wishes unto yt, (3) the great benefit the King bringeth with him, as the peace wee have by him and the latitude and prospect of that peace. That the King was borne for us. That a people may bee without a King : a King cannot bee without a people. A perswasion that the House would aunswere him in all good correspondence, (1) in modestie, that our desires bee lymitted, (2) in plainnes, that wee lay our selves open in the naked truth of our hearts, (3) in order and comelynes of proceeding, which is the band and ornament of all societies.

Sir Edward Cooke, his Ma^{tyes} Atturney generall and Mr Doctor Hone bring a message from the Lords expressing with what acceptation their Lordships entertayned their motion yesterday, not onely for the matter, being of very great waight and consequence, but especially for the manner, namely that touching wardship they would not petition for ease in yt as matter of wrong but of greif, and pray to bee releyved by grace and not by justice. And their Lordships for aunswere were desierous and moved at that tyme to couple in the same Petition the matter of greyvance of respyt of Homage, which his Ma^{ty} out of his gratious favour and love to his people had him selfe taken knowledge of. And as they conceyve yt to bee lykely that the conference may contynue betweene the two houses touching the said matters, as they are very zealous of the furtherannce of their purpose, so are they jealous of any impediment that may breed let or hinderannce therein. Therefore they desire for a more cleare proceeding and removing of all stumbling blocks that the former Committees may in a second conference to bee had, have authoritie to treat touching the case of Sir Ffrauncis Goodwyn, the knight for Buckinghamshire, before any other matter were further proceeded in.

The aunswere to this message was :

That they would returne aunswere by messengers of their owne.

Aunswere to this message by Mr Secretary Herbert :

That they did conceive yt did not stand with the honor and order of the house to give account of any their proceedings or doyngs. But yf their Lordships have any purpose to conferre, for the residue, that then they wilbee ready at such tyme and place, and with such number as their Lordships shall thinke meete.

Die Mercurii xvi⁰ Maii 1604

Moved and perswaded, by long contynewed speach, that the matter of composition for Wardship, etc, might goe hand in hand with that of Purveyors.

In our message to the Lords to desire their Lordships to joyne in petition to his Matie for leave to treat, etc.

Others that the matter of Wardship may goe single.

These motions induced 3 questions, to bee agreed and made :

(1) Whether to desire the Lords to joyne with this House in a Petition for composition for Wardship.

Resolved.

(2) Whether composition for Wardship shall goe hand in hand with that of Purveyors.

Resolved to goe single.

(3) Whether to desire a conference touching the framing of a Petition for leave to treat, etc.

Resolved.

A Committee for conference with the Lords touching matters of Wardship moved and named.

All the privie Councell being members of the house

The Lo : Clinton	Sir Thomas Ridgeway
The Lo : Buckhurst	Sir John Savill
Sir Robert Wroth	All the Serjants at Lawe
Sir Henry Nevill	Sir Robert Oxenbridge
Sir Ffrancis Bacon	Sir William Strowd
Mr Sollicitor	Sir Thomas Ffreak
Sir George Moore	Sir Thomas Hesketh
Mr Ffrauncis Moore	Mr Pulliston
Sir Edward Hobby	Sir Jerome Horsey
Sir Nath. Bacon	Sir John Harper
Sir Edward Stafford	Sir Thomas Beamount
Sir Herbert Crofte	Sir Edward Tyrrell
Sir John Hollis	Sir Ffrancis Knollys
Sir Hugh Beeston	Sir Ffrancis Popham
Sir Ffranc. Hastinge	Sir Richard Verney
Mr Wentworth	Sir William Wray
Sir Thomas Crompton	Sir Richard Leveson
Sir Edward Mountague	Mr Ffuller
Mr Recorder of London	Mr Serjant Tanfeild
Sir Thomas Holcroft	Mr Lawrence Hyde
Sir Daniel Dun	Sir Edw. Lewkenor
Mr Doctor James	Sir Peter Manwood
Sir Edward Herbert	Sir Nicholas Saunders
Sir Robert Wingfeild	Sir Roger Aston
Mr Fferiam Dodridge	Sir Edwyn Sandys
Sir Henry Billingsley	Mr John Hare
Sir John Thynne	Sir Jerome Bowes
Sir Edmond Bowyer	Sir Henry Bromley
Sir Thomas Dunton	Sir John Scott
Sir William Burlacy	Sir Edward Herbert [sic]
Mr Sam. Bacchus	Sir Edward Grevill
Sir Maurice Berkley	Sir John Leveson
	Sir Henry Beamount

These Committees are appointed to conferre with the Lords on Ffryday next at two aclock in the afternoone in Camera Picta, touching matters of Wardship, respytt of homage, Licence of Alienation, primer seisin, and other the incidents, as also touching their Lordships joyning with the House in Petition to his Matie for leave to treat, etc.

And are first to meete this afternoone in the Parliament house, there to prepare furnish and arme themselves with such reasons and arguments as may induce the proceeding in the said Petition and give some instruction in the framinge of the same.

xxiiii° Maii 1604

Mr Doctor Swale and Mr Doctor Hone come in message from the Lords saying that their Lordships had considered of their dooble motion for conference.

Touching thact of the union, they desire the meeting may bee this afternoone.

Ffor ecclesiasticall matters, this day fortnight in the afternoone.

Ffor the matter of wards, where yt is already appointed on Ffryday, they desire yt may bee deferred till Saterday.

xxv Maii 1604

Sir Edwyn Sandys produceth in writing the heads of such course as was thought meet to bee proceeded in by the Committee, touching the matter of Wardship, etc, at their last meeting, readeth yt and offereth yt to the consideration of the House. but nothing then done upon it.

xxvi Maii 1604

Sir Edwyn Sandys moveth that the House would bee pleased to consider of some directions for the proceeding of the Committee appointed to conferre with the Lords touching the matter of Wardship, etc, and offered to the House such as were set downe in writing and read yesterday by himself, which were presently read by the Clerk and approved by the House, to the effect following :

In the conference with the Lords touching a Petition to bee made to the King to have leave to treat with his Matie of a composition for tenures and wardships, etc, these things to bee propounded,

(1) Ffirst what wee desire.

(2) Secondly the reasons for our desire.

(3) Thirdly the removing of impediments which may bee objected.

(4) Ffourthly what course to bee taken for the levying and assessing of our composition, if it please his Matie to assent to it.

(1) Our desire is the taking away the tenures *in capite*, and knights service, and the burdens depending on them, as Wardship of lands and body, marriage of wards, liveries, respit of homage, licence of Alienation, primer seisin, relief, etc.

(2) The reasons for our desire may bee reduced into three heads :

    (1) Ffirst why wee desire it.

    (2) Then why wee desire it more of his Matie then our auncestors did of his progenitors.

    (3) Lastly what reasons on his Maties behalf may induce him to graunt our desire.

Why wee desire it the reasons are many :

(1) It is but a restitution unto the originall right of all men by the lawe of God and nature, which is that children should bee

brought up by their parents and next of kin, and by them bee directed in their marriages.

(2) The greevance and damage of the subject in his estate to the great hinderance and decay of mens houses and posterity, and to the disabling of them to serve their Prince and country.

(3) The great mischeif by occasion of forced and ill suited marriage.

(4) The contempt and reproach of our nation in forreyne countries, which doth also consequently redound upon our Kings.

Why wee desire it more of his Matie then our auncestors of his progenitors (although it have bene in former princes tymes desiered), there are some reasons which wee will expresse, and other some wee will leave to their Lordships provident considerations.

(1) The originall of these tenures, which draw Wardships, was serving of the King in his warres against Scotland which cause is now ceased.

(2) The generall hope that at his Maties entrie the whole land embraced, that they should bee eased of this burthen, which hope hath bene increased by his Maties benigne offer made the last summer, that men might before hand compound for their childrens marriages.

The reasons which on his Maties behalfe may induce him to graunt our desire are two :

(1) One reason moves from his Matie, viz, his owne most gratious and most noble disposition in so accepting our chearefull love and loyalty towards him, at his entry into this kingdome, as to promise withall that this our duty should bee returned unto us not in words but royall deeds, to the easing of those oppressions and burdens under which wee groaned.

(2) An other reason must move from us : wee will offer unto his Matie the raysing of a perpetuall and certaine revenew out of our lands, not onely proportionable to the uttmost benefit that any of his progenitors ever reaped hereby, but also with such an overplus and larg addition as in great parte to supply his Maties other necessities.

(3) The impediments which may bee objected are these two principall :

(1) Ffirst, what to bee done touching the wards of subjects. They must bee also compounded for at such reasonable rate either of money in grosse or of yearely rent, as may give satisfaction and content to the severall lords.

(2) Secondly, what regard to bee had of his Maties officers. An honourable yearely pension to bee graunted unto them during their lives at the charge of the whole state and the same either to come to the Crowne after their decease, or else to bee extinguished to that rate, whereat wee shall make composition with his Matie.

(4) If his Matie bee pleased to compound with us, what course may bee taken for the levying and assessing of that which wee shall compound for, may then bee considered of when his Matie shall have assented to composition; howbeit because some thinke

it a matter of impossibility or great difficulty to bee overcome, if their Lordships desire any project thereof, this may be proposed by way of overture to occasion their Lordships to thinke of a better and more exquisite.

This Session onely his Ma^ty to bee agreed with for the generall somme of the yearely revenew to bee raysed, and commissioners to be chosen out of all the shires in England for the assessing of this revenewe.

The Commissioners first to informe themselves what land there is in knight service and capite, holden of his Matie, in every shire in England.

To set downe a proportionable rate what shalbee raysed of their lands and what of soccage land, if it bee thought fitt to taxe it also.

To consider then the proportion of the quantitie of ward land in every shire, and conferring the same with the whole quantitie of the severall shires (if soccage land bee also taxed) to allott what shalbee raysed out [of] every particular shire.

Afterward to devide themselves into the severall shires and agreeably to the proportion to proceed (as occasion shall require) to subdivide every shire, and so finally to the taxing of every perticular mans lande.

Their doeings to bee returned (as in way of proposition only) to the next Session of Parliament, which may proceede to a finall conclusion of this busines.

Moved by Mr Parkinson that some course bee taken to prevent that no newe tenures bee created hereafter.

Sir Robert Wroth. Impossible that any good should come of this course in the matter of Wardship, etc : hee foresawe it, hee knewe yt. Moved therefore that every man by his last will and testament might dispose of his child, paying the like fine, etc. And that some Bill to that purpose might bee thought on.

Primo Junii 1604

Sir Edwyn Sandys entreth into a report of the conference with the Lords touching matter of wardship, etc.

Hee related his owne speach to the Lords.

By the way, hee sayd : If the King did graunt yt, yt was great grace ; yf deny yt, no wronge.

Hee recyted the direction for the conference formerly read in the house xxvi May which (hee sayd) the Committee pursued.

The reply by the Lords was three folde :

(1) Expostulation or freindly reprehension.
(2) Aunswere to the reasons.
(3) Admonition.

They put us in mynde what wee were.

In what state wee were the XII of March was twelvemoneth. That wee would have given halfe that we had to have that wee now enjoy. Under what kinge wee lyved, with what habilitie.

How wee had spent our tyme in matters of privilegde, purveyors, ecclesiastic, etc.

Tenures onely in this land ;

Franck-almoigne. Copie. Soccage.

Wardship not proper to England alone. Scotland and some parts of France subject to yt.

The last comission for compounding but satisfactorie to the people brought in not above 4000^l.

The revenewe of the wards 31000^l

Respytt of homage, licences of Alienation, etc, 10000^l

What the conceyte of forreine ambassadors would bee of the King in selling his prerogative.

Ffyve Lords did concurre in one sense.

Sensi ex composto rem geri

Replyed by one. Marriage of children, no prerogatyve, no dishonour to take yt away.

Much dispute followed this report by sundry members of the house.

Amongst others, moved by Sir T.R. that a Committee might bee named to take a survey of the proceeding of the House and to sett downe something in wryting for his Ma^{ts} satisfaction and to exhibite yt unto him.

Mr Speaker propounded a petition to bee framed with reasons of satisfaction for the proceeding in matters of wardships, etc.

These both resolved upon the quest, and the former Committee named xx Maii for conference with the Lords touchinge Wardship, etc, appointed to meete with this authority, viz :

To take a survey of all the acts and proceedings of the House (which have bene excepted unto, or whereof any misinformation hath bene given unto his Matie,) from the beginning of this Session, and to advise of such a forme of satisfaction to bee offered to his Matie (eyther by writing or otherwise) as may informe him in the truth and clearenes of their proceeding, thereby to free them from the scandall of levitie and precipitation, so often imputed unto them. And particularly to consider of some satisfaction touching the proceeding in matter of wardship, etc. This being done to make report to the House, and from thence to receyve further direction.

To the former Committee were added upon this occasion ;

Sir Robert Mannsell

Mr Yelverton

Mr Martin

Mr Hare

Sir Rowland Litton

Sir Ffrauncis Barrington

Uppon the whole matter this order following was conceived by the Clerk, being so directed.

This daye, Sir Edwyn Sandys making report of the late conference had with the Lords, according to a former commission of this house, touching the matter of Wardship and other the incidents thereunto, in steede of acceptation and assent to joyne in

petition to his Matie, delivered from their Lordships no other then
matter of expostulation, opposition of reason to reason : admonition or precise caution in proceeding, which suitinge with the
groundes of his Maties speache subsequent, advisedly and of
purpose made upon that occasion, to the whole House assembled
by his Maties direction at Whitehall on Munday last (wherein
many perticular actions and passages of the house were objected
unto them with taxation and blame), summoned the dutie and
judgement of the House to consider what were fittest to bee done.
And amongst other, the motion of Sir Thomas Ridgeway, one of
the knights for Devonshire, induced the House to this consideration, that synce yt appeared his Matie had made such an impression
of myslike of the proceedings of the house in generall, as also that
the groundes conceyved touching wardship and matters of that
nature seemed to bee so weakened and impugned, yt were
necessarie and safe for the House, and dutyfull and convenient in
respect of his Matie, instantly to advise of such a forme of satisfaction, either by wrytinge or otherwise, as might in all humility
informe his Matie in the truth and clearenes of the actions and
intentions of the house from the beginning, thereby to free yt
from the scandall of levity and precipitation, as also of the
proceeding in particular touching the said matter of wardship,
with this speciall care that a matter so advisedly and gravely
undertaken and proceeded in might not die or bee buried in the
hands of those that first bred yt.

v Junii 1604

His Ma^{ts} message by Mr Speaker touching the matter of
satisfaction.

xx Junii

The forme of an Apologie and satisfaction to bee presented to
his Matie penned and agreed on by a former select Committee, was
now reported and delivered into the House by Sir Thomas
Ridgeway, one of the Committees, twice read, debated and agreed
pro et con. Whether the matter and the manner fitt, or what was
fytt to bee done in yt.

The Apologie directed to the Kings most excellent Matie
from the House of the Commons assembled in Parliament

Most gratious Sovereigne, wee cannot but with much joye and
thankfullnes of minde acknowledg your Ma^{ts} great graciousnes in
declaring lately unto us by the mouth of our Speaker, that you
rested now satisfyed with our doings : which satisfaction notwithstanding, thoughe most desired and deare unto us, yet
proceeding meerely from your Ma^{ts} most gracious disposition, and
not from any justification, which on our behalfe hath beene made,
wee found this our joye intermingled with no small greife and
could not (dread Soveraine) in our dutifull love to your Matie,
and in our ardent desire of the continewance of your favour

towards us, but tender in humble sort this farther satisfaction, being carefull to stand right not onely in the eye of your Ma^{ts} grace, but also and that much more in the ballance of your princely judgement, on which all assurednes of love and grace is founded. Into which course of proceeding wee have not bene rashly carryed by vaine humour of curiosity, of contradiction, of presumption, or of love of our owne devises and doings (unworthy affections in a counsell of Parliament, and more unworthy in subjects towards their Lord and Soveraine, but as the searcher and judge of all harts doth knowe, for these and for no other undew endes in the world :

(1) Ffirst, to encrease and nourish your Ma^{ts} gratious affection towards your loyall and most loving people.

(2) Secondly, to assure and knit all your subjects harts most firmely to your Matie.

(3) Thirdly, to take away all cause of jealousie on either parte and difference for tymes ensuing.

(4) Ffourthly and lastly, to prevent and controwle all sinister reports which might bee unseasonably spread, either at home or abroade, with prejudice to your Matie or the good estate of your kingdome.

With these minds (dread Soveraigne) your whole Commons of England, represented now in us, their knights, cittizens and burgesses, doe come with this humble declaration to your highnes, affiance of your most gratious disposition, that your Matie with benignity of minde, correspondent to our dutifullnes, wilbee pleased to peruse yt.

Wee know, and with great thanckfullnes to God acknowledge, that hee hath given us a kinge of such understanding and wisdome as is rare to finde in any Prince in the world : howbeit seeing no humane wisdome, how great soever, can peirce into the particularities of the rights and customes of people, or of the sayings and doeings of perticular persons, but by tract of experience and faithfull report of such as knowe them (which it hath pleased your Ma^{ts} princely mouth to deliver), what greif, what anguish of mind hath yt bene unto us, at sometimes in presence to heare and see, in other things to finde and feele by effect, your gratious Matie (to the extreame prejudice of all your subjects of England and in particular to this House of the Commons thereof) so greatly wronged by misinformation as well touching the state of the one as the priviledges of the other, and their severall proceedings during this Parlyament, which misinformations, though apparent in themselves and to your subjects most injurious, yet have wee in some humble and dutifull respect rather hitherto complayned of amongst ourselves, then presumed to discover and oppose against your Matie.

But now no other helpe or redresse appearing, and findinge those misinformations to have beene the first, yea the cheife and almost sole cause, of all the discontentfull and troublesome proceedings, so much blamed in this Parlyament, and that they might bee againe the cause of like or greater discontents and troubles hereafter (which the Allmighty Lord forbid) wee have bene constrayned as well in duety to your royall Matie, whome with faithfull harts wee serve, as to our deare native country, for which wee serve in this Parlyament, to breake our silence and freely to disclose unto your Matie the truth of such matters concerning your subjects the Commons, as hitherto by misinformation hath bene suppressed or perverted.   Wherein, that wee may more plainely proceede (which next unto truth wee affect in this discourse) wee shall reduce these misinformations to three principall heades :

(1) Ffirst, touching the cause of the joyfull receiving of your Matie into this your kingdome.

(2) Secondly, concerning the liberties and rights of your subjects of England and the priviledges of this House.

(3) Thirdly, touching the severall actions and speaches passed in the House.

(1) It hath bene tould us to our faces by some of no small place (and the same spoken also in presence of your Matie) that on the 24th of March was twelve moneth, wee stood in so great feare that wee would have given halfe wee were worth for the security wherein now wee stand, whereby some misunderstanders of things might perhaps conjecture that feare of our owne misery had more prevailed with us in the duty which on that day was performed than love of your Maties vertue and hope of your goodnes towards us. Wee contrarywise most truly protest the contrary that we stood not at that tyme, nor of many a day before, in any doubt or feare at all ; wee all professing true religion by lawe established (being by manifold degrees the greater, the stronger and more respective part of this your Ma^{ts} realme), standing cleare in our consciences touching your Maties right, were both resolute with our lives and all other our habilities to have mainteyned the same against all the world.   And vigilant also in all parts to have suppressed such tumults, as but regard of our power, united minds and readines, by the malecontented and turbulent might have bene attempted.   But the true cause of our extraordinary great chearefullnes and joye, in perfourming that days duety, was the great and extraordinary love which wee bare towards your Maties most royall and renowned person, and a longing thirst to enjoye the happy fruities of your Maties most wise, religious, just, vertuous and gratious hart, whereof not rumour but your Maties owne writings had geven us a strong and undoubted assurance. Ffor from hence (dread Soveraine) a generall hope was raysed in the minds of all your people that under your Matie religion, peace, justice and all vertue should renew againe and flourish, that the better sort should bee cherished, the bad reformed or repressed and some moderate ease should bee given us of those burdens and sore oppressions under which the whole land did groane. This hope being so generall and so firmely setled in the mindes of all your most loyall and most loving people, recounting what great alienation of mens harts the defeating of great hopes doth usually breede, wee could not in duty as well

unto your Matie as to our countries, citties and boroughes, who have sent us hither, not ignorant or uninstructed of their griefes, of their desires and hopes, but according to the auncient use and liberty of Parlyament present our severall humble petitions to your Matie of different nature, some for right and some for grace, to the easing and releeving us of some just burdens and of other some unjust oppressions. Wherein what due care, what respect wee have had that your Maties honor and profit should bee conjoyned with the content and satisfaction of your people shall afterward in their severall due places appeare.

(2) Now concerninge the auncient rights of the subjects of this realme, cheifly consisting in the priviledges of this House of Parlyament, the misinformation openly delivered to your Matie hath bene in three things :

(1) Ffirst, that wee hould not our priviledges of right but of grace onely, renewed every Parlyament by way of donative upon petition and so to bee limitted.

(2) Secondly, that wee are no Court of Record ne yet a Court that can commaund view of Records, but that our proceedings here are onely to acts and memorialls, and that the attendance with the Records is curtesie not duety.

(3) Lastly, that the examination of the returne of writts for knights and burgesses is without our compasse and due to the Chauncery.

(1) Against which assertions (most gratious Soveraine) tending directly and apparantly to the utter overthrowe of the very fundamentall priviledges of our House, and therein of the rights and liberties of the whole Commons of your realme of England, which they and their auncestors from tyme immemoriall have undoubtedly enjoyed under your Maties most noble progenitors : wee the knights, cittizens and burgesses of the House of Commons assembled in Parlyament and in the name of the whole Commons of the realme of England, with uniforme consent, for our selves and our posterities, doe expressely protest as being derogatory in the highest degree to the true dignitie, libertie and authority of your Maties highe Court of Parlyament, and consequently to the right of all your Maties said subjects and the whole body of this your kingdome, and desire that this our protestation may bee recorded to all posterity. And contrarywise with all humble and due respect to your Matie, our Soveraine Lord and head, against those misinformations wee most truely avouch that our priviledges and liberties are our right and due inheritance, no lesse then our very lands and goods, that they cannot bee witheld from us, denyed or ympayred but with apparannt wrong to the whole state of the realme. And that our makinge request in the entrannce of Parlyament to enjoye our priviledges is an act onely of manners and doth weaken our right no more then our sewing the King for our lands by petition which forme, thoughe new and more decent then the old by Precipe, yet the subjects right is no lesse now then of ould.

(2) We avouch also that our House is a Court of Record and so

ever esteemed, and that there is not the highest standing Court in this land that ought to enter into competency either for dignity or authority with these high Courts of Parliament which with your Maties royall assent give lawes to other Courts ; but from other Courts receive neither lawes nor orders.

(3) And lastly wee avouch that the House of Commons is the sole proper judge of the returne of all such writts and of the election of all such members as belong unto it, (without which the freedome of election were not entire) and that the Chauncery, though as a standing Court under your Matie bee to send out those writts and to receive the returnes and to preserve them, yet the same is done onely for the use of the Parlyament, over which neither the Chauncery nor any other Court ever had or ought to have any manner of jurisdiction. Ffrom these misinformed positions (most gratious Soveraine) the greatest parte of our troubles, distrusts and jealousies have arysen, having apparently found that in this first Parliament of the happy reigne of your Matie the priviledges of our House, and therein the liberties and stability of the whole kingdome, have bene more universally and daungerously impugned then ever, as wee suppose, since the beginning of Parlyaments. Ffor although yt may bee true that in the later tymes of Queene Elizabeth some one priviledg now and then were by some particuler act, attempted against yt, not obscurely injured, yet was not the same ever by so publique speach nor by positions in generall denounced against our priviledges. Besides that in regard of her sexe and age, which wee had great cause to tender and much more upon care to avoyde all trouble which by wicked practize might have bene drawne to impeach the quiett of your Maties right in the succession, those actions were then past over which wee hoped in succeeding tymes of freer accesse to your highnes so renowned grace and justice to redresse, restore and rectifie. Whereas contrarywise in this Parlyament (which your Matie in great grace, as wee nothing doubt, intended to bee a President for all Parlyaments that should succeede) cleane contrary to your Maties so gratious desire by reason of those misinformations, not one priviledge but the whole freedome of the Parlyament and realme hath from tyme to tyme upon all occasions beene mainely hewed at ; as the freedome of our persons in election hath beene impeached, the freedome of our speech prejudiced by often reproofe, perticular persons noted with taunte and disgrace, who have spoken their consciences in matters proposed to the House, but with all due respect and reverence to your Matie, whereby wee have in the end bene subject to so extreame contempt as a jaylour obstinately to withstand the decrees of our House, some of the higher clergie to write a booke against us even sitting in the Parlyament, the inferiour clergy to inveighe against us in pulpitt, yea to publishe their protestations tending to the impeachement of our most auncient and undoubted rights in treating of matters for the peace and good order of the church. What cause wee your poore Commons have to watch over our priviledges is manifest in itself to all men. The preroga-

tives of Princes may easily and doe daily growe. The priviledges of subjects are for the most parte at an everlasting stand. They may bee by good providence and care preferred, but being once lost are not recovered but with much disquiett. If good kings were immortall as well as kingdomes, to stryve so for priviledges were vanity perhapps and folly. But seeing the same God, who in his great mercy hath given us a wise kinge and religious, doth also sometymes permit hypocrites and tyrants in his displeasure and for sinnes of people, ffrom hence hath the desire of rightes, liberties and priviledges both for nobles and Commons had his just originall, by which an harmonicall and stable state is framed, each member under the head enjoying that right and perfourming that duty which for the honor of the head and happines of the whole is requisite. Thus much touching the wrong done to your Matie by misinformation touching our priviledges.

(3) The last kinde of misinformations made to your Matie hath bene touching the actions and speeches of perticular persons used in the House, which imputation notwithstanding, seeing it toucheth the whole House in generall who neither ought neither have at any tyme suffered any speach touching your Matie other then respective, dutifull and as became loyall subjects of a King so gratious. And for as much as yt ys very cleare unto us by the effect that dyvers things spoken in the House have bene perverted and very untruly reported to your Matie, yf it might so seeme fitt in your Maties wisdome and were seemely for us to crave, wee should bee most glad if for our better justification and for your further satisfaction, which wee principally desire, the accusers and accused might bee confronted.

And now (most gratious soveraigne) these necessary grounds of our cause and defence being truely layde and syncerely presented to your Ma^{ts} grace and wisedome, the justification of such particulers, wherein your highnes seemed doubtfull of our dutifull carryage (though not so much for the matter as for the manner of our proceeding), wee trust wilbee plaine and expedite : which particulers wee find to have beene of three different natures :

(1) The first sort concerned the dignity and priviledges of our House.

(2) The second the good estate of the Realme and Church.

(3) The third was for the ease of certaine greevances and oppressions.

(1) In the first rank there were five particulers:

(1) The matter of the Gentleman Usher.
(2) Of the Yeoman of the Guard.*
(3) Of the election of the kt of Buckinghamshire.
(4) Of Sir Thomas Sherleyes deliverance.
(5) Of the Bishopp of Bristowes pamphlett.

(2) The second rancke had two particulers :

(1) The Union.

---

* For this incident see *Parliamentary History of England,* Vol. V, 1603–23, p. 53.

(2) The matter of religion.
(3) The third had three :
    (1) The Bill of Asserte.
    (2) Matter of Purveyors.
    (3) The Petition for Wardship.

Of each of these wee must say somewhat to give your Matie satisfaction, and that with all brevitie to shunne tediousnes and trouble.

(1) The Gentleman Ushers faulte in depriving by his unaccustomed neglect a great parte of our House from hearing your Ma^{ts} speach the first day of Parliament, wee could not, in the greife of being frustrate of our so loving and just desire to heare your Maties voice and renowned wisdome, but complaine of in decent sort amongst our selves. And further wee proceeded not, your Ma^{ts} extraordinary great grace and favour in rehearsing the day ensueing your former admirable speach did give us content with aboundant increase of joye.

(2) The Yeoman of the Guards words were very opprobrious, and howsoever they might have beene not unfitly applyed to the pezants of Ffrannce and bores of Germany, yet could they not bee other then very reproachfull and injurious to the great dignity and honour of the Commons of this realme, who conteyne not onely the cittizens, burgesses and yeomanry but also the whole inferior nobilitie of the kingdome, knights, esquiors and gentlemen, many of which are come ymediately out of the most noble families, and some others for their worth advannced to the high honor of your Ma^{ts} privy Counsell, and otherwise have bene imployed in very honourable service. In summe, the sole persons of the higher nobility excepted, they conteyne the whole flower and power of your kingdome, with their bodies your warres, with their purses your treasures are upheld and supplied. Their harts are the strength and stability of your royall seate. All these amounting to many millions of people are representatively present in us of the House of Commons. The wrong done to us doth redound upon the whole land and will so bee construed. Wee could not therefore doe lesse in our duty to the realme then to advertise such a delinquent of the unseemelynes of his fault, neither yet could wee doe more in duty to your Matie then uppon his acknowledgment thereof freely to remitt yt.

The right of the liberties of the Commons of England in Parlyament consisteth cheifly in three things :

(1) Ffirst, that the shyres, citties and boroughes of England, by representation to bee present, have free choyce of such persons as they shall put in trust to represent them.

(2) Secondly, that the persons chosen, during the tyme of the Parlyament as also of their accesse and recesse, bee free from restraint, arrest and imprisonment.

(3) Thirdly, that in Parliament they may speake freely their consciences without check and controllment, doing the same with due reverence to the Soveraigne Court of

Parlyament, that is to your Matie and both the houses, who all in this case make but one politique body, whereof your highnes is the head.

Theise three severall braunches of the auncient inheritance of our libertie were in the three matters ensueing apparently injured :

(1) The freedome of election in the case of Sir Ffranncis Goodwyn.
(2) The freedome of the persons elected in Sir Thomas Sherleyes imprisonment.
(3) The freedome of our speach, as by dyvers other reproofes, so also in some sort by the Bishop of Bristowes invective.

(3) For the matter of Sir Fra. Goodwyn, the knight chosen for Buckinghamshire, wee were, and still are, of cleare opinion that the freedome of election was in that action extreamely injured : that by the same right it might bee at all tymes in a Lord Chauncellors power to reverse defeate, to reject and substitute all the elections and persons elected over all the realme. Neither thought wee that the judges opinion (which yet in due place wee greatly reverence) being delivered what the Common law was, which extends onely to inferior and standing courts, ought to bring any prejudice to these high courts of Parlyament, whose power being above the lawe is not founded on the Common lawes but have their rights and priviledges peculiar unto themselves.

Ffor the manner of our proceeding which your Matie seemed to blame, in that the second writ going out in your Maties name, wee presumed to censure it, without first craving accesse to acquaint your highnes with our reasons, therein wee trust our defence shall appeare just and reasonable. It is the forme of the Court of Channcery, as of dyvers other Courts, that writts going out in your Ma^ts name are returned also as to your Matie in that Court from whence they issue ; howbeit no man therefore ever repayreth to your Ma^ts person, but proceeds according to lawe, notwithstanding the writt. This being the universall custome of this kingdome, yt was not nor could bee admitted into our conceits that the difference was betweene your Matie and us (for God forbid that betweene so gracious a Sovereign and so dutiful and loving subjects any difference should arise). But it alwayes was and still is conceived that the controversy was betweene the Court of Channcery and our Court (an usuall controversy betweene Courts about preheminences and priviledges), and that the question was whether the Channcery or our house of the Commons were judge of the members returned for yt. Wherein, though wee supposed the wronge done us to bee most apparant and extreemely prejudiciall to the rights and liberties of this realme, yet such and so great was our willingnes to please your Matie as to yeld to a middle course proposed by your highnes, preserving onely our priviledges, by voluntary cession of the lawfull knight. And this course as it

M S—L

were of deceiving our selves and yelding in our apparant right, whensoever wee could but invent such wayes of escape, as that the President might not bee hurtfull, wee have held (dread Sovereigne) more then once in this Parliament, upon desire to avoyde that which your Matie by misinformation (whereof wee have had cause to stand alwaies in doubt) might bee distastfull or nor approvable. So deere hath your Ma^ts gracious favour bene unto us.

(4) In the delivery of Sir Thomas Sherley our proceedings were long, our defence of them shalbee breif. We had to doe with a man (the warden of the ffleete) so untractable, and of so resolved o[b]stinacy as that nothing wee could doe, no nor your Maties royall word for confirmation thereof, could satisfy him for his owne security. This was the cause of the lengthe of that busines. Our priviledges were so shaken before and so extreamely vilified as that wee held it not fitt in so unseasonable a tyme and against so meane a subject, to seeke our right by any other course then by course of lawe or by any other strength then by our owne.

(5) The Bishop of Bristowes booke was injurious and greevous to us, being written expressely with contempt of the Parliament and of both the houses in the highest degree ; undertaking to refute reasons proposed by the Commons, approved by the Lords, confirmed by the judges and finally by your royall Matie not disassented to. And to increase the wrong with strannge untruth, hee had perverted those reasons in their mayne drifte and scope, pretending that they were devised to impugne the union ytself, whereas by their title and by themselves it was cleere and evident that they were onely used against alteration of name and that not simply but before the union of both realmes in substance were perfected. This booke being thus written and published to the world, conteyning moreover sundry slannderous passages and tending to murmure, distraction and sedition, wee could not doe lesse against the writer thereof then to complaine of this injury to the Lords of the higher house, whereof hee had now attained to bee a member. These wronges were to the dignity of our house and priviledge.

(1) Touching the causes apperteininge to the State and Church : true it is wee were long in treating and debating the matter of union. The proposition was new, the importance great, the consequence farre reaching and not discovered but by long dispute. Our number also is larg, and each hath liberty to speake. But the doubts and difficulties once cleered or removed, how farre wee were from opposing to the just desires of your Matie (as some evill disposed minds would perhapps insinuate who live by division and prosper by the disgrace of other men) the great expedition, alacrity and unanimity which was used and shewed in passing of the Bill may sufficiently testify.

(2) For matter of Religion it will appeare by examination of truth and right that your Matie should be misinformed if any man should deliver that the Kings of England have any absolute power in themselves either to alter religion (which God defend should bee

in the power of any mortall man whatsoever) or to make any lawes concerning the same, otherwise then, as in temporall causes, by consent of Parliament. Wee have and shall at all tymes by our oathes acknowledg that your Matie is soveraine Lord and supreame Governour in both. Touching our owne desires and proceedings herein they have bene not a litle misconceived and misreported. Wee have not come in any puritane or Brownish spirit to introduce their party or to worke the subversion of the State Ecclesiasticall as now yt stanndeth : things so farre and so cleerely from our meaning as that with uniforme consent in the beginning of this Parliament wee committed to the Tower a man who, out of that humour in a petition exhibited to our house, had slanndered the Bishops. But according to the tenor of your Maties writts of summons, directed to the counties from which wee come, and according to the auncient and long continued use of Parliaments, as by many records from tyme to tyme appeareth, wee came with another spiritt, even the spirit of peace. Wee disputed, not of matters of faith and doctrine ; our desire was peace only and our devise of unitie, how this lamentable and long lasting dissention amongst the ministers (from which both atheisme, sects and ill life have received such encouragement and so daungerous encrease) might at length before help come to late bee extinguished. And for the wayes of this peace wee are not addicted at all to our owne inventions but ready to imbrace any fitt way that may bee offered, neither desier wee so much that any man in regard of weaknes of conscience may bee exempted after Parlyament from ob[e]dyence to lawes established, as that in this Parliament such lawes may bee enacted as by relinquishment of some few ceremonies of small importance, or by any way better, a perpetuall uniformity may bee enjoyed and observed. Our desire hath also bene to reforme certen abuses crept into the Ecclesiasticall State even as into the temporall. And lastly that the land might bee furnished with a learned, religious and godly ministery, for the mayntenance of whome wee would have granted no small contribution, if in these (as wee trust) just and religious desires we had found that correspondence from other, which was expected. These myndes and harts wee in secrett present to that Soveraigne Lord who gave them, and in publique professe to your gracious Matie who wee trust will so esteeme them.

(1) There remaynes the matters of oppression and greevance. In the Byll of Asserts your Ma^ts Counsell was heard, namely your Sollicitor and Sir Ffranncis Bacon. It was also desiered by the house that other of your Counsell would have bene present. Wee knew that our passing the Bill could not bynde your Matie ; howbeit for sundry equitable considerations, as to us they seemed, wee thought fitt to give so much passage to the Bill in hope that your Matie might either bee pleased to remitt in some sort unto this equity that right which the rigour of law had given, or otherwise bee entreated by this kind of sollicitation to let them fall into your Ma^ts hands, full of piety and mercy, and not into the jawes of devouring promoters. And this doe wee understand to

bee your gratious intent, wherewith wee rest joyfully content and satisfied.

(2) This greevance was not unjust in rigour of law and was perticular. But a generall extreeme unjust crying oppression is in Cartetakers and Purveyors, who have ravaged and ransacked, since your Maties coming in, farre more then under any of your royall progenitors. There hath bene no prince since Henry the third (except Queene Elizabeth) who hath not made some one law or other to represse or lymitt them. They have no prescription, no custome to plead, ffor there hath not bene any Parliament wherein complaynt hath not bene made and clayme of our right, which doth interrupt prescription. Wee have not in this Parlyament sought any thing against them but execution of those lawes which are in force already. Wee demaund but that justice which our Princes are sworne neither to deny, delay nor sell. That wee sought into the accompts of your Ma^ts expence was not our presumption but upon motion from the Lords of your Ma^ts Counsell and offer from the officers of your highness houshould, and that upon demannd of a perpetuall yerely revenew in leiwe of the taking away of these oppressors, unto which composition neither know wee well how to yeld, being only for justice and due right which is unsaleable. Neither yet durst wee ympose it by lawe upon the people without first acquainting them and havinge their consent unto it. But if your Matie might bee pleased in your gracious favour to treate of composition with us for some greevance which is by lawe and just, how ready wee should bee to take that occasion and colour to supply your Ma^ts desire concerning these also, which wee hold for unjust, should appeare, wee nothinge doubt of your Maties full satisfaction.

(3) And therefore wee come lastly to the matter of Wardes and such other just burthens (for so wee acknowledg them) as to the tenures of *capite* and knights servyce are incident. We cannot forgett (for how were it possible) how your Matie in a former most gracious speach in your Gallery at Whitehall advised us, for unjust burthens, to proceede against them by Bill, but for such as were just, if wee desiered any ease, that wee should come to yourselfe by way of Petition, with tender of such countervayleable composition in proffit as for the supporting of your royall estate was requisite. According to which your Ma^ts most favourable graunt and direction wee prepared a petition to your most excellent Matie for leave to treate with your highnes touchinge a perpetuall composition to bee raysed by yeerely revenewe out of the lands of your subjects for Wardshipps and other burdens depending on them or springing with them, wherein wee first entered into this duetifull consideration that this prerogative of the Crowne, which wee desiered to compound for, was a matter of meere proffit and not of any honor at all or princely dignity, ffor yt could not then neither yet can by any meanes sincke into our understandinge that these aeconomicall matters of education and marriage of children (which are common also to subjects) should bring any renowne or reputation to a potent monarch

whose honour is setled on a higher and stronger foundation: ffaithfull and loving subjects, valiannt souldiers, an honourable nobility, wise councellors, a learned and religious clergie, a contented and happy people, are the true honour of a king. And contrariwise, that it would bee an exceeding great honour and of memorable renowne to your Matie with all posterity, and in present an assured bond of the harts of all your people, to remitt unto us this burden under which our children are borne. This prerogative then appearing to bee a meere matter of proffit, wee entred into a second degree of consideration, with how great greevance and domage of the subject, to the decay of many houses and disabling of them to serve prince and country, with how great mischeife also by occasion of many forced and ill suited marriages, and lastly, with how great contempt and reproach of our nation in all forreine countries, how small a commodity was now raised to the Crowne in respect of that which, with great love, joy and thanckfullnes for restitution of this originall right in disposing of our children, wee would bee content and glad to assure unto your Matie. We fell also from hence into a third degree of consideration, that it might bee that in regard that the originall of these wardships was serving of the kinge in his warres against Scotland, which cause wee hope now to bee at an everlasting end ; and in regard moreover of that generall hope which at your Maties first entrie the whole land embraced (a thinge knowne unto all men) that they should now forever bee eased of this burthen, your Matie out of your most noble and most gracious disposition and desire to overcome our expectation with your goodnes might be pleased to accept an offer of our perpetuall and certaine revenewe, not onely proporcionable to the uttmost benefit that any of your progenitors ever reaped thereby, but also with such an overplus and large addition as in great parte to supply your Maties other occasions, that our ease might breede your plenty. With these humble minds, with these dutifull respects wee entended to crave accesse unto your Matie. But that ever it was said in our House by any man that this was a slavery under your Matie more then under our former Princes, hath come from an untrue and calumnious reporte. Our sayings have always bene, that this burthen was just, that the remitting thereof must come from your Maties grace, and that the denying of our suite were noe wrong unto us. And thus most gracious soveraigne, with dutifull minds and syncere harts towards your Ma^ty, have wee truly both disclosed our secreat intents and delivered our outward actions in all these so much traduced and blamed matters. And from henceforward shall remayne in great affiannce that your Matie rests satisfyed both in your grace and in your judgment, which above all thinges worldly wee must desire to effect before the dissolvinge of t is Parliament, where in so long tyme, with so much paines and endurance of so great sorrowe scarce any thinge hath bene done for their good and content who sent us hither, and whome wee left full of hope and joyfull expectation.

There remayneth (dread Soveraigne) yet one part more of our

dutie at this present which faithfullnes of hart, no presumption, doth presse upon us. We stand not in place to speake or to doe things pleasing : our care is and must bee to confirme the love and to tye the harts of your subjects the Commons most firmely to your Matie. Herein lyeth the meanes of our well deserving of both. There was never Prince entered with greater love, with greater joy and applause of all his people. This love, this joy, let it nowe flourish in their harts for ever. Let no suspition have accesse to their fearefull thoughts, that their priviledges, which they thinck by your Matie should bee protected, should now by sinister information or counsell bee violate or impaired, or that those which with dutifull respect to your Ma^{ty} speake freely for the right and good of their country, shalbee oppressed or disgraced. Let your Matie bee pleased to refuse publique information from your Commons in Parlyament as in the civill estate and government, ffor private informations passe often by practize. The voyce of the people in thinges of their knowledge is said to bee as the voyce of God. And if your Matie shall vouchsafe at your best pleasure and leasure to enter into gracious consideration of our petitions for ease of these burthens, under which your whole people have of longe tyme mourned, hopeing for releife by your Matie : then may you bee assured to bee possessor of their harts for ever ; and if of their harts, then of all they can doe or have. And so wee your Ma^{tyes} most humble and loyall subjects, whose auncestors have with loyalty, readynes and joyfullnes served your famous progenitors, Kings and Queenes of this Realme, shall with like loyalty and joye, both wee and our posteritie, serve your Matie and your most royall issue for ever with our lives, lands, goods and all other our habilityes, and by all meanes endevour to procure your Maties honour with all plenty, tranquillity, content, joy and felicity.

Moved by Sir William Strowde that the forme of satisfaction touching the proceedings of the House penned by the Committee and by them reported and read in this House might bee recommitted and some more Committees added, and such of the first Committee or others as found any cause of exception or were not present at the former severall meetings might bee commaunded to attend that they might receive satisfaction from the rest, or otherwise yeild their reasons of difference, so as upon report to the House some resolution may bee taken for further proceeding or surceasing in the said busines. And according to the motion ordered and the Committees appointed to meete on Munday next in the Court of Wards.

30 pp. (**367.**)

[See *H.M.C. Salisbury MSS*, Vol. XVI, pp. 42-3, 141-4.]

The DUKE OF LENNOX to LORD CECIL.

[1604] April 14.—" I have moved the Kinge for Mr Sydney Mountague, that it woulde please his Matie to place him secretarie to the Prince, which his Matie hath granted. I understande by

Mr Mountagu that he hathe a desyer to travell the better to fitt himselfe for that place againste suche tyme as his service shalbe requisyte aboute the Prynce. And for his further assurance of this place at his returne, hee is desyrous to procure a bill under his Maties signature of the grante therof, wherein I desyer your Lordship woulde give him your favoure and furtherance, and cause Sir Thomas Lake to present the same unto his Matie, and I shall rest ready to requyte your Lordship with any lyke kyndnesse that is in mee."—Courte, this 14 of Aprill.

Holograph. Endorsed : " Duke of Lenox to my lord concerning Sydney Montacut his being secretary to the Prince, 1606 [*sic*]." ⅓ p. (**116.** 5.)

[See *H.M.C. Salisbury MSS.*, Vol. XVI, pp. 99–100.]

—— to ——

[After April, 1604].—Jasper Hellam purchased from one of Sir George Harvey's servants the office of registrar or clerk of a three weeks' court held for the liberty of the Tower of London, for which he paid £20. He was admitted to the office by Sir George and Mr John Astell, Steward of the court, in whom the authority to award the office is invested by law. Hellam has been associated with the court for seven years and has first hand experience of its proceedings. Moreover, he was trained as clerk to the late Francis Tilney, attorney and gentleman.* " The said Jasper had att his admission all the records of the same court delievered unto him, which he still hath and detayneth in his owne hands." He now demands " either the place or his xx^l."—*Undated.*

¾ p. (P. 2338.)

EDWARD SMITH to the PRIVY COUNCIL.

[After May 27, 1604].—He is a soldier and is now prisoner in the Gatehouse, where he has no means of relief whatsoever. His imprisonment was " imposed upon him by your Honors for a certayne ballade or dyttie upon the dyssolution of Barwyck, the which your poor suppliant penetentlie confesseth he made at idle howers out of an humorous conceyte onlie for his owne pryvate exercyse, and for no evill intention against his Matie, Cownsell, state or country ". He expresses his regret for such indiscretion, and begs to be released from a detention which has already lasted fifteen weeks.—*Undated.*

1 p. (P. 1313.)

[See *Cal. S.P. Dom.*, 1603–10, p. 114.]

MAILLIART RICQUART to the GOVERNMENT of the SPANISH NETHERLANDS at Brussels (?).

1604, May 31.—He hopes that his preceding letters have been safely received. He thinks that the rate of 30% is being vigor-

---

* He was buried on April 9, 1604. [See *Harleian Society* Vol. LXXII, *Register of St. Michael Bassishaw*, 1538–1625, p. 170.]

ously enforced and maintained, but to the detriment of the local merchants, and with little benefit to the King.

This can be attributed, in the first place, to the fact that no French ships come to the port. Moreover the German vessels which arrived in spring with grain and other merchandise have left laden with salt and ballast, so that the port is empty of foreign ships, with the exception of a few small English vessels with cargoes of grain and fish, and two with cloth. The English expect to be treated in the same manner as the natives, but this is an error on their part : because since they are desirous of obtaining return cargoes of sugar and oil, the French here have six months to arrange such transports, and the English are obliged to pay cash down, which they find harmful and unreasonable, and so are in favour of a resumption of war. The question asked here is whether the English Parliament is about to chose between peace and war, but there are doubts about this since, if war broke out, trade would become more difficult than it is already.

Some twenty days ago five caracks left this place for the East Indies. It is feared that the Dutch fleet of 14 ships may meet them, but in the absence of bad news it is thought that the convoy may be making its way towards the Cape of Good Hope, where it is said forts are being built.

About twelve days ago two caracks arrived from V, where they had been blown by contrary winds twelve months ago. At the same time there arrived 6 galleons and 4 German ships which are in the King's service.

It is not possible to depend upon all these ships, apart from those which have already been made ready here, because some are damaged and things proceed slowly, since no money is sent from the court. Altogether there are 18 galleons here, and 12 more are expected from Calais, but how soon one cannot know, and they will not leave this year with the fleet.

Four days ago a caravel set out to see whether any ship of the Dutch fleet was in the vicinity of the coast. There is much business done here with the so-called Austrians who are in fact Dutchmen in receipt of passports from Don Albert.

Apart from that there is little to report here. The end of the Parliamentary session in England will show the best way to proceed. The merchants hope that there will be no peace between this country and England before the suppression of the 30%, and that if it be good for a nation, it will be useful to everybody.

A gentleman from the court has brought the news that it was the King's wish to withdraw the 30%, but that the council opposed him on the grounds that it was below the dignity of the King to do so, that other sovereigns would say that he had done so out of fear, that the King of France had lost the affection of his people, that if he did not agree to certain points in the peace plan it would be because of his fear of the English King : so that everything is in a state of suspense while one is waiting to see how the English Parliament will decide and what reply the ambassadors here will receive. But reports tend to confirm that the advantages gained will certainly not be withdrawn.

He protests his fidelity to Their Excellencies, and requests an allowance since life is very expensive where he is.—Lix, 31 May, 1604.

Holograph. Flemish. 1½ pp. (**105.** 66.)

Sir Robert Vernon to [? Lord Cecil].

[1604, May].—Lord Powis obtained from Henry VIII the site and lands of the Abbey of Buildwas, Salop, in exchange for property in Yorkshire. He died without heirs, and the lands came to the Vernons, descended from the daughter of Richard, Lord Powis, nearest cousin to the last Lord Powis. It is now claimed on behalf of one Grey, regarded as the illegitimate son of Edward, Lord Powis, that the latter made a feoffment in fee to the use of Grey, but this cannot be proved. Fox, a purchaser from Grey of part of the Abbey brought a suit in defence of Grey's title, but it was dismissed. Fox now is trying to establish the Crown's title to the property, announcing himself to be tenant in possession and so competent to compound with the King. The Vernons are hereby wronged. If the King has any title, they assume that they are the persons to whom the King should grant the property. Petitioner on their behalf asks that Fox and Tipper be called in and the whole question examined. If the King has a title, then the Vernons will pay him his fine and defray Fox's charges.—*Undated.*

⅓ p. (P. 1956.)

[See *H.M.C., Salisbury MSS.,* Vol. XVI, p. 114.]

Sir William Leighton to Lord Cecil.

[After May, 1604].—He is the next heir to Thomas Onslowe, deceased,* of Baschurch, Salop, and has obtained a commission to inquire into what lands Onslowe held of the King *in capite.* He requests that letters be directed to Onslowe's widow that some of petitioner's legal advisers, in the presence of the commissioners appointed to conduct the inquiry, may be allowed to consult the documents relating to his inheritance which are in her custody ; and also that she guard such evidences very carefully and produce whichever his legal advisers think most relevant when called upon to do so by the commissioners.—*Undated.*

½ p. (P. 1544.)

Dispute between Penzance and Marazion over markets.

1604, June 8.—Decree of Court. Refers to the intransigence of the inhabitants of Penzance in ignoring former injunctions not to keep markets to the prejudice of Marazion. The Court, willing to favour Penzance in view of the losses it sustained by the late occupation and spoliation of the town by Spaniards, referred the

---

* Died on May 30, 1604. [See *PRO. Inq. post mortem, Chancery* **2,** 289/88.]

matter to the Attorney and Solicitor General. The latter had listened to the arguments advanced by both parties, and had concluded that the former verdicts should not be rescinded. But with the consent of both towns they have recommended that any butcher of Penzance may sell flesh victuals to be spent within the said town and not otherwise, and that the inhabitants are not to keep a market on Saturdays. This is now made a decree of the Court.—Veneris octavo die Junii, 2 Jac.

6 pp. (Legal **39**/8.)

Thomas clarke to Lord Cecil.

1604, June 9.—The wardship of the heir of Clement Weare *alias* Browne, of Marlborough, co. Wilts., has been concealed for many years, and the King's title rejected. He asks for a grant of the wardship, undertaking to produce incontrovertible evidence that the property was held of the King.—9 June, 1604.

Note at bottom signed by Cecil : " Let him resort to any two of the Counsayle of the Court whereof Mr Surveyor or Mr Atturny to be one ; and if he can shewe pregnant matter and procure an order, I will have consideration of him in the composition."

1 p. (P. 1619.)

John Lisley to Lord Cecil.

[1604, June 13].—He is of Moxhull, co. Warwick, and is brother and heir of Francis Lisley, whose wardship was granted by the Court of Wards to Anthony Dyott, with an exhibition of £4 annually during his minority, and so from heir to heir. But Francis Lisley died before the grant passed the Great Seal, and petitioner became ward and compounded with Dyott for his wardship. He paid a fine to the late Queen Elizabeth for this but has been allowed none of the exhibition formerly given to Dyott, although he has submitted a claim to it. It has been denied him on the grounds that his brother died before the grant of the wardship to Dyott had been procured under the Great Seal. He now requests that Cecil consider his case favourably and issue a warrant that he be granted the exhibition.—*Undated.*

On reverse : Another and more legal version of the petition.

Endorsed : " 13 June, 1604. The humble petition of John Lisley, gent." ½ p. (P. 1608.)

Osbaldo Nonhaufer to Guillermo Sluderpach.

1604, June 14.—He begs him to remember a girl whom he baptised. She has been seriously ill and can only walk with great difficulty. She is now five years of age, and he requests that she be given a dress.—Valladolid, June 14, 1604.

Spanish. 1 p. (**105.** 90.)

Anthony Forrest to Richard Perceval.

1604, June 15.—He requests his favour in a personal matter, the marriage of a near relation of his to the son of Sir Edward

Denny, who is ward of his mother, Lady Denny. " This yonge gentellman cominge to my house in my absence, my selfe beinge a widdower and haveinge my sister my poore houskeeper, he fell in love with my sister and is maryed unto hir, I protest before God, contrarye to my knowledge, I beinge, as I sayde, with Sir Oliver Cromwell by the space of 3 weekes. Hir portion is £300. What is [*sic*] livinge is I knowe nott, butt his mother, I heare, is discontented and meaneth to draw hym into the Court of Wards." If Perceval hears anything of the matter, Forrest entreats him to inform Lord Cecil that she is his sister. Forrest fears that Lady Denny " wilbe trobelsome to my Lord in this matter ". From my house Morbom this 15 of Ju. 1604.

Holograph. 1 p. (P. 2172.)

ELIZABETH WOODROVE to LORD CECIL.

[Before June 19, 1604].—She has been a suitor to the King since he came to Hampton Court, for some relief to maintain herself and her children who are destitute, and has submitted a number of petitions to him and the Privy Council. She has received no answer, and her lack of means preclude her further attendance. She asks him to subscribe to the enclosed petition which she is sending to the King. If he does, she is assured that the King will grant her request. " If the Court should remove, I have no means to followe."—*Undated.*

Holograph. Seal. Endorsed : " 1604. Elizabeth Woodrove to my lord to subscribe a petition." $\frac{1}{4}$ p. (P. 2480)

ELIZABETH WOODROVE to LORD CECIL.

[Before June 19, 1604].—She apologises for troubling him so often, but she is apprehensive that because of the King's departure her suit will fail, since she is unable to follow the Court. Cecil has promised to intervene on her behalf, but she is aware of two difficulties. " The one that his Majesty doth hold no land of our house, the other is he hath beene so bountifull to divers as I feare I come to late." She begs Cecil to assist her, and if she receives word that he is willing to do so, " it will do me more good then if I were dead to restore my life. Why I make choyce thus espetially to rely upon your Lordships favor is the great reliefe I have received from your house."—*Undated.*

Holograph. Seal. Endorsed : " Mrs Eliz. Woodrove to my Lord." 1 p. (P. 2479.)

[See *Cal. S.P. Dom.*, 1603–10, p. 121.]

PHILIP STANHOPE to LORD CECIL.

[1604, June 19].—He is the son and heir of Sir John Stanhope, and one of the co-heirs of Jane Allington, deceased. In her lifetime, the latter conveyed her lands to certain feoffees until her will and that of Sir William Cordell were carried into effect ; and then to Sir George Carey, Lord Deputy of Ireland, till he had levied 2000 marks. Thereafter the feoffees should stand seised of one half of her lands during the lifetime of Sir John Savage and Dame Mary, his wife, one of the daughters and co-heirs of Jane Allington, and afterwards to the use of Sir Thomas Savage, son and heir of Sir John Savage, with remainders to the other children. In the absence of such issue, the lands were to descend to petitioner. The feoffees should also stand seised of the other half of Jane Allington's lands to the use of petitioner until he was 21 years of age, and should account to him for all issues and profits, when he inherited the property. Jane Allington died last Christmas, petitioner being then under age, but had appointed Sir George Carey, now absent in Ireland, and Sir Thomas Savage her executors, both to occupy her lands until all debts were paid and her will performed. In Carey's absence, Sir Thomas Savage had entered upon the manor of Melford and other lands in Suffolk, to the value of £1000 a year, as executor, but was now claiming the inheritance of the whole property from his mother and petitioner. Petitioner's counsel had taken the matter up in the Court of Wards, whereupon Sir Thomas had suggested a friendly conference between the legal advisers of both parties. At this meeting it had been agreed that, failing some compromise, they should select some judges to determine the case, and that in the meantime nothing should be done to prejudice the interests of the two parties. But Sir Thomas Savage has violated this agreement ; he has held a court, forced tenants to acknowledge him as the new landlord, and given lands to strangers, in order to disinherit petitioner and defraud his own parents of their estate for life. Sir Thomas is now trying to obtain legal possession of the manor, and is likely to succeed if not prevented. Petitioner asks that Cecil write to Lord Anderson and the other justices of the Common Pleas to stop Sir Thomas's proceedings until further order be taken by the Court of Wards.—*Undated*.

Endorsed : " 19 June, 1604. The humble petition of Phillipp Stanhope, his Ma^ts ward." ¾ p. (P. 1607.)

ELIZABETH WOODROVE to LORD CECIL.

[After June 19, 1604].—She expresses her gratitude to the Privy Council, but to Cecil in particular as being " the chiefe foundation of my well being ".—*Undated*.

Holograph. Seal. Endorsed : " 1604. Lady Woodroove to my Lord." ½ p. (P. 2478.)

JOHN LISTER to [LORD CECIL].

1604, June 20.—He is one of Cecil's servants, and asks for the wardship of the heir of —— Palmer, London.—June 20, 1604. ⅓ p. (P. 1603.)

PHILIPPA BROWNE to LORD CECIL.

1604, June 20.—About three years ago her husband was granted a lease by Cecil of a tenement situated in Carlby, co. Lincs., for 21 years. Since then her husband has died, and she has been harassed by her son-in-law, Thomas Browne, who has got the lease into his possession and refuses to permit her to remain in the tenement longer than next Michaelmas. He threatens to demolish the house over the heads of petitioner and her four children. They have no other means to live but in that place " unlesse she be releaved by the towne which is scarse able to mayntayn that number of poore which is allredy in it ". She begs that Cecil summon Browne before him or take some other measure to ensure that she gets justice in this matter. Petitioner adds a request that " this petition may be referred to Mr John Wingfeild, your Lordships officer, whoe I knowe will do me justice ".—20 June, 1604.

Note at bottom : " A letter written to Sir Robert Wingfield and Mr John Wingfield."

1 p. (P. 1620.)

ROBERT WILSON to [? LORD CECIL].

[1604, June 22].—He is submitting the petition on behalf of himself and other Queen's tenants of the Honour of Clare in Huntingdonshire and Cambridgeshire. Richard Foulkes, the Bailiff, has a manor of his own in the town of Bottisham, and for this reason he so confuses the rents and services of the Queen's tenants with those of his own tenants that there have ensued many law suits and disputes. Foulkes also claims the royalties of the Queen's revenues as belonging to his manor, and appropriates rents due to the Queen. They ask that the office of bailiff be not granted to Foulkes, so that both the Queen's rents and the peace of mind of her tenants be secured.—*Undated.*

Note by Sir Roger Wilbraham : " Both these parties are to come before me at Graies Inn this afternoone or to morrowe, wher I with some other of the Queens Councell will understand more particularlie of this complaint, and so certifie to my lo. Cecill ; and if it be his Lordships pleasure, it is not amisse to staie the grannt in the meantime."—Fridaie, the 22 of June, 1604.

1 p. (P. 1649.)

OSTEND.

[Before June 24, 1604].—A plan of Ostend under siege by Spanish forces. The list of the names of fortified works includes the " poulder Raveling " and the " West Raveling " described as having been captured by the enemy, a success mentioned in a letter dated June 24, 1604 from Sir John Ogle to Lord Cecil.—*Undated.*

2 pp. (**142.** 186.)

[See *H.M.C. Salisbury MSS*, Vol. XVI, p. 150.]

WILLIAM WORTHAM to LORD CECIL.

1604, June 27.—He is in Cecil's service, and requests the grant of the wardship of the heir of William Green, co. Yorks, deceased. —June 27, 1604.

Note by Cecil: "Let a commission be granted."

½ p. (P. 1561).

JOHN LISTER to LORD CECIL.

1604, June 27.—He is employed in Cecil's service, and requests the grant of the wardship of the heir of William Pycke, of Binley, co. Warwick.—June 27, 1604.

½ p.   (P. 1543.)

JOHN MARSHALL to LORD CECIL.

1604, June 27.—He is in the service of Elizabeth, Countess of Derby, and asks for the grant of the wardship of the heir of Ambrose Gilbert, deceased, of Dover Court co. Essex. June 27, 1604.

Note by Cecil : " Let a stey be made for him."

½ p.   (P. 1540.)

ABRAHAM HARDRETT to the KING.

[After June 28, 1604].—In lieu of the £1075 owed him by the late Queen Elizabeth, and for his other services, the King bestowed upon him the place of one of his jewellers with a fee of £50 annually.   He has as yet received little material benefit from this award, unlike other King's jewellers, and asks that £20 in fee farm be granted him for the maintenance of his family.—*Undated.*

½ p.   (P. 33.)

[See *H.M.C. Salisbury MSS*, Vol. XVI, p. 253, and *Cal. S.P. Dom.*, 1603–10, p. 125.]

SYBIL WEST to [? LORD CECIL].

[1604, June].—Her late husband. Arthur West, deceased, held a customary messuage and one half land within the manor of Bisley for the term of his life.   After his death she was admitted tenant during her widowhood and still holds the messuage.   The custom of the manor directs that customary tenements be granted to the children of customary tenants for the usual fines, but Mr Neale, late steward of the manor, granted a reversion of her tenement, contrary to the custom of the manor, to Pigion or Brushe, two of his servants, thereby threatening her children with the loss of what is theirs by due custom, and of being left " to the almes of the parish " after her death.   She asks that the messuage be granted to her and her children, and that the said Pigion and Brushe be ordered to surrender their interest in it.—*Undated.*

½ p.   (P. 1530.)

See P. 1527 *infra* p. 177.

HALSTEAD.

[1604, June].—An inquiry has established that the King is entitled to the wardship of the youngest daughter and to the livery of the other two daughters.   The estate of inheritance to all three is in reversion to Lady Wharton, but there is provision for each of the daughters to levy £500.   Bridget, the eldest, was exercising her right in this respect at the death of Colby

Tamworth. She lives at a distance from the property and is to receive the money annually from the tenants. Some of the latter, however, have chosen to repudiate her and to declare themselves tenants to Christopher Tamworth " an intruder against the King ". The hope is expressed that the Court of Wards will support (? the commissioners) on behalf of the King and the three daughters against " the intruder " and all who claim anything under him.—*Undated.*

Endorsed : " June, 1604. Mr C. Tamworth." $\frac{1}{2}$ p. (P. 2246.)

FRANCIS HEATON to LORD CECIL.

[July 8, 1604].—He is one of the customary tenants on the Queen's manor of Kingsnorton. He and his predecessors have long enjoyed a piece of ground of some two acres, which formerly belonged to the common or waste of the manor, and for which no rent was paid. Some years ago, he expressed a wish to hold the same by copy of court roll, and to pay a fine and yearly rent for it. He obtained a warrant from Sir John Fortescue, then Chancellor of the Exchequer, to the steward of the manor to that effect, and was granted the land in question by copy of court roll. Recently, however, after the conveyance of the manor to Queen Anne as a part of her jointure, some of the tenants have insisted that he be fined and amerced in the manor court for laying the land open contrary to the said copy of court roll. He asks that letters be sent to the tenants and keeper of the manor court, directing them to refrain from subjecting him to fines or interfering with his enjoyment of the land.—*Undated.*

Note by Cecil : " Let this petitioner repaire to the Queens Chancelour and her counsaile lerned uppon whose report I will take order."

Note by Sir Roger Wilbraham : " Yf he hath bin of contynuance and by tolleration of the late Queenes officers tenant hertofore, I think it not inconvenient that he be continued in his dwellinge beinge but two acres, except the steward of the mannor and bailiff ther doe fynde it prejudiciall and a cause of great inconvenience to the rest of the tenants ther."—8º July, 1604.

Note by Robert Hitcham : " I think fitte that the petitioner should injoye his estate accordinge to his grant by copy untill the steward do certefie cause to the contrary."

$1\frac{1}{2}$ pp. (P. 1250.)

RICHARD WORDEN to the COUNTESS OF DERBY.

1604, July 10.—About twenty-five years ago, he entered the service of John Bannester as his clerk, and after his death he became Deputy-Clerk of the Peace in Cheshire. He married Bannester's daughter, and has been able to maintain her and his eleven children decently. Now his position is being jeopardised by the treachery of an intimate friend of his, Robert Whitly, who is Clerk of the Pentice in Chester and an attorney at the Assizes and Exchequer there. Whitly has taken advantage of his close acquaintance with Henry Jones, Clerk of the Peace, who is constantly in attendance on the Lord Chancellor of England, and with Sir John Egerton, Custos Rotulorum of Cheshire, to obtain the Clerkship of the Peace and deprive Worden of his post. He requests the Countess of Derby to procure letters for him from the Earl of Derby to the effect that Whitly should restore his office to him.—July 10, 1604.

1 p. (P. 14.)

Thomas Henshaw to the Queen.

[Before July 23, 1604].—He has delivered to her goods to the value of £11,000, for the payment of which the King gave instructions by Privy Seal. Nevertheless, he has still received no payment, and is in danger of losing his credit. He begs her to intervene with the King for the discharge of some of his debts, " to releeve his present extreme necessitie which he little suspected he should have encurred by his faithfull and loyal service to your Highnes ".—*Undated.*

½ p. (P. 247.)
[See *Cal. S.P. Dom.*, 1603–10, p. 136.]

Bridget Ross to Lord Cecil.

[? Before August 16, 1604].—On July 27th, Sir Griffin Markham entered her husband's house with his wife and family, and took up residence there. He behaved most offensively, ordering her father-in-law, Charles Clapham, and a sister of hers out of the house under threat of violence. He also took advantage of the weakness and age of her husband to persuade the servants not to attend upon her, out of fear of his malice and anger. Fearing for her own life and that of her son, petitioner left the house secretly. She appeals to Cecil to intervene for the safety and education of her child, and requests him to entrust his person and education to some reliable person, she herself being ready to defray all necessary expenses. On the other hand, she would like to see her son become a page to Cecil ; if that is not feasible, to see him committed to the care of Sir Robert Carey, who has shown some interest in the boy. She is very apprehensive that while the child remains with her, he runs the risk of being taken by violence from her and carried back to the country, and denied good education to his great loss, " he being almost of that oopenes that if learneinge be not geven him in thes good tyme, he will soone be past takeinge any ".—*Undated.*

Endorsed : " 1604. The humble petition of Brigitt Rosse, the wife of Peter Rosse, esquire." ½ p. (P. 907.)
[See *H.M.C. Salisbury MSS*, Vol. XVI, p. 233.]

Charles Duinny to Lord Cecil.

[Before August 18, 1604].—He has been a student " in the Lawes and Sciences " these last 30 years, first at Christ Church, Oxford, where he was placed by Baron Burghley, and at Trinity

College, Dublin, where he has spent 22 years, and of which Cecil is Chancellor. The Earl of Tyrone wasted his father's country out of revenge because petitioner was able to persuade some of the Irish nobility and other prominent people not to participate in his rebellion. Consequently his own means of livelihood now is a fee of £20 and the perquisites, some £6, issuing from the office of one of the Masters of the King's Court of Chancery in Ireland. To improve his estate petitioner proposes to ask the King and the Privy Council for the next vacancy amongst the judges of the King's prerogative court and " faculties in spirituall causes " which the Lord Chancellor of Ireland and Dr Forth now occupy. He requests Cecil to further his suit.—*Undated.*

Endorsed : " 1604. Petition of Charles Duinny." ½ p. (P. 721.)

[See *Cal. S.P. Ireland,* 1603–6, p. 191.]

ROBERT SAVAGE to the PRIVY COUNCIL.

[Before August 19, 1604].—Following upon the King of Spain's latest proclamation of friendly relations and usage, he sent a ship to the Canary Islands with goods to the value of £1500, most of which were sold in exchange for sugar. The sugar and the residue of the commodities were, however, stayed because of a report circulated by a Frenchman that the Spanish Ambassador and Frenchmen had been expelled from England. This has resulted in considerable financial loss for him. He requests the members of the Council who are now engaged in peace negotiations with the King of Spain's Commissioners,* to press the latter to direct the Governor of the Canary Islands to release his goods and indemnify him for all losses and damage.—*Undated.*

½ p. (P. 8.)

JOSHUA HAVELL to LORD CECIL.

[Before August 19, 1604].—He is a merchant of Plymouth. In 1602, Captain Edward Giles obtained letters of reprisal from the Court of Admiralty and seized a Spanish ship called *St. John Baptist and St. Eleanor* which he carried to Plymouth where it was declared a lawful prize. Petitioner purchased the vessel from Giles and altered it at his own expense. He freighted the ship with goods which he sold at Alicante and Valencia, and then reloaded her with commodities at Dania for London. But when he was on the point of leaving, the ship was stayed by the order of the Spanish King as being the *Prodigal Son,* his factor murdered, his crew imprisoned and himself forced to flee for his life. This was done at the suit of Anthony and Matthew Lamprize of Catalonia. Petitioner submitted six petitions to the King of Spain, the Duke of Infantado, the Viceroy of Valencia and others, and spent £60 in prosecuting the case in Spain. He has been denied redress and stands to lose £1500. Since he can prove that

---

* The Anglo-Spanish peace treaty was signed on August 19, 1604.

M S—M

the ship was not captured by Frenchmen from Spaniards, as is alleged, but by Giles and an English company, he asks Cecil—as one of the Commissioners engaged in treaty negotiations with Spain, to press for either the restitution of the ship or adequate compensation for petitioner's losses.—*Undated.*

¾ p.   (P. 1159.)

NICHOLAS THEMYLLTHORPE to LORD CECIL.

[Before August 20, 1604]*.—He is one of the sewers of the Queen's Chamber, and requests that the bailiwick of the Queen's manor of Selsye (? Shelley), co. Suffolk, now void, be bestowed upon him, or some other bailiwick if that has already been granted.—*Undated.*

¼ p.   (P. 1319.)

HUGH LEE to LORD CECIL.

[Before August 20, 1604].—He begs Cecil not to be offended with him, but to appreciate his preference for coming to him as a suitor rather than petitioning the King.   He explains why it is not possible to show any bond of Cecil's as he has been asked to do.   If the allegation made by Clarke is true, the bill for £600 from Cecil to Thomas Nicholson and by Nicholson assigned to petitioner's brother, Thomas Lee, was delivered by Clarke to Cecil for the latter's perusal, and is still in his possession.   Moreover Thomas Lee, when he was alive, disbursed a great deal of money abroad on behalf of Nicholson as a result of Cecil's letters to him.   He did so in order to favour Nicholson when he was in Cecil's employment, or at Cecil's direct injunctions.   Petitioner again repeats his request for Cecil's favour towards him.   *Undated.*

½ p.   (P. 874.)
[See *H.M.C. Salisbury MSS*, Vol. XVII, p. 560.]

The QUEEN'S ARTIFICERS to LORD CECIL.

[Before August 20, 1604].—Petition submitted by the Queen's embroiderer, hosier, cabinet and looking-glass maker, coffer maker, perfumer, pinmaker and shoemaker.   They have provided the Queen with goods and services since her arrival in England, but have received no payment.   Now their credit is exhausted, and they urgently beg Cecil to arrange that the Queen's debts to them be discharged.—*Undated.*

¾ p.   (P. 550.)
[See *H.M.C. Salisbury MSS*, Vol. XVI, p. 238.]

The BAILIFF OF NORTHBOURNE to LORD CECIL.

[Before August 20, 1604].—He has been Bailiff of Northbourne, co. Kent, for the past twenty years by virtue of a patent granted him by the late Queen Elizabeth, and has regularly collected and conveyed all rents and profits to the Receiver of Kent.   Since the proper control and conveyance of the rents, as well as the wide

---

* Robert, Lord Cecil, was created Viscount Cranborne on August 20, 1604.

dispersion of the tenements, require the services of a person well acquainted with them and their history, he requests that he be granted a new patent of that office.—*Undated.*

1 p. (P. 1531.)

MARY APPLETON to LORD CECIL.

[Before August 20, 1604].—Recently the King granted her and her son-in-law, Robert Rice, the rectory of Little Waldringfield in Suffolk, together with the stewardship and bailiwick of the manor of Glemsford for the term of 21 years. Since no record has been made of the grant as yet, and Cecil and the other commissioners have not met to discuss and pass leases, petitioner requests that no fee farm be made of these two particular premises without referring it to the pleasure of the King and ascertaining his intentions in this matter.—*Undated.*

1 p. (P. 1532.)

JOHN SKINNER to LORD CECIL.

[Before August 20, 1604].—He is Deputy-Bailiff of the Queen's manor of Hitchin, co. Herts., and was appointed to that office by Cecil who directed his letters to that effect to the deputy-steward of the manor, with the order that any one opposing petitioner in the execution of his duties should be bound over to appear before Cecil. The deputy-steward accordingly ordered Thomas Chapman, who claimed the office of deputy-bailiff, to do so, but he has refused to obey the order. Moreover, he has withheld the rental of the manor from petitioner who is thereby disabled from collecting the rents. He asks that a further warrant be sent to Chapman to appear before Cecil.—*Undated.*

½ p. (P. 1563.)

THOMAS HORNER to LORD CECIL.

[Before August 20, 1604].—He is in Cecil's service, and asks for the stewardship or bailiwick of Bisley manor, Gloucestershire.—*Undated.*

⅓ p. (P. 1564.)

GEORGE HUDSON to LORD CECIL.

[Before August 20, 1604].—He is employed by Cecil, and requests the grant of the stewardship or bailiwick of Whaddon and Nash, co. Bucks.—*Undated.*

⅓ p. (P. 1565.)

THOMAS RAYNTON to LORD CECIL.

[Before August 20, 1604].—He is in the service of Lady Susan Vere, after attending on Cecil's father for many years. He requests the grant of the bailiwick of Leominster, Herefordshire, which is now void.—*Undated.*

At bottom : " He must have the Reeveshipp of Hecham, co. Suffolk."

Signed : Su. Veare. 1 p. (P. 1566.)

JOHN DACKOMBE to [LORD CECIL].

[Before August 20, 1604].—He is in Cecil's service, and requests the grant of the bailiwick of the Queen's manors of South Stoke and Corston, co. Somerset, which was lately held by William Rowswell.—*Undated.*

Note by Cecil : " Corston graunted to this petitioner."

1 p.   (P. 1567.)

WILLIAM TRUMBULL to LORD CECIL.

[Before August 20, 1604].—He is in the employment of Sir Thomas Edmondes, one of the Clerks of the Privy Council, and has served him abroad and at home without any reward.   To enable him to continue with the efficient performance of his duties, he asks for the bailiwick of Northbourne, co. Kent.   He is the more induced to submit this petition " because he is of that country, and the like places are exercised by men of his quallitie".
—*Undated.*

½ p.   (P. 1568.)

[See *H.M.C. Salisbury MSS*, Vol. XV, p. 391.]

HENRY TRUSSELL to [LORD CECIL].

[Before August 20, 1604].—He asks that the stewardship of Exmoor Roche and Mendip be deputed to him and his son John Trussell, as well as the bailiwick of the two manors and that of South Stoke.   It will be necessary for one of them to be at or near those places to keep the courts and collect the rents. Petitioner resides in Winchester some 60 miles away.—*Undated.*

⅓ p.   (P. 1569.)

—— CORMOCK to [LORD CECIL].

[Before August 20, 1604].—He is Cecil's servant, and asks for the grant of the bailiwick of Cranfield, co. Bedford, or that of Northbourne, co. Kent.   Petitioner " is imboldned in this suite for that he hath not a long time receaved any benefite by wardships, his charge being greate ".—*Undated.*

Note by Cecil : " Cranfeild granted."

1 p.   (P. 1570.)

HENRY BATTEN to LORD CECIL.

[Before August 20, 1604].—He is in the employment of the Earl of Devon, and asks for the bailiwick of the Queen's manors of Corston, co. Somerset, and Corsham, co. Wilts.—*Undated.*

Note by Cecil : " I have bestowed both these."

¾ p.   (P. 1571.)

SAMPSON CALVERT to [LORD CECIL].

[Before August 20, 1604].—He is one of the King's yeomen harbingers, and requests the grant of the bailiwick of Hitchin, co. Herts.   He resides near the place.—*Undated.*

¼ p.   (P. 1572.)

THOMAS GRAVES to [LORD CECIL].

[Before August 20, 1604].—He is Cecil's servant and asks for the bailiwick of the manor of Walsham, co. Norfolk.—*Undated.*

⅓ p. (P. 1573.)

BERNARD MOORE to LORD CECIL.

[Before August 20, 1604].—Cecil has assented to two or three of petitioner's requests for wardships, but he has received no pecuniary benefit from any of them. He now asks that the bailiwick of Biggleswade, Bedfordshire, be granted to Ezekiel Vyan.—*Undated.*

½ p. (P. 1628.)

GEORGE SALTER and THOMAS WAGSTAFF to LORD CECIL.

[Before August 20, 1604].—They are two of the Clerks of the Rolls. Cecil sent them a warrant " in the tyme of sicknes when the same was very hoate " to attend Mr Hitcham, the Queen's Attorney, and Mr Evans, the Queen's Surveyor, and to show such records and make the necessary copies required by them for the Queen's jointure. They received no allowance for that service, and they request Cecil to grant them what he thinks fit and adequate in that respect.—*Undated.*

½ p. (P. 1629.)

The TENANTS OF WALTON CUM TRIMLEY to LORD CECIL.

[Before August 20, 1604].—They request him as the High Steward of the Queen's manor to investigate and redress the many wrongs committed against them, which they have communicated in detail to the Queen's Attorney-General.—*Undated.*

Note : " The orders sett downe by my late Lord Tresuror must be showed and then a copie of them taken with a letter to the Steward that it is my Lord's pleasure those orders should be contynued and remane as heretofore making a short recytall of them."

⅓ p. (P. 1630.)

GIFFORD LEAKE to LORD CECIL.

[Before August 20, 1604].—He has been employed in the Queen's affairs, and has disbursed £20 of his own money in expediting them. They concerned the engrossing and dispatching of all business to the Great Seal, and he has neglected his own interests in attending to these matters. Petitioner requests that, since he has received no allowance for his services, he be awarded some recompense.—*Undated.*

½ p. (P. 1631.)

RICHARD FOULKES to LORD CECIL.

[Before August 20, 1604].—He is the late Feodary, Bailiff and Collector for the Honour of Clare in the counties of Huntingdon and Cambridge, and was granted the office by the late Queen

Elizabeth. After her death he obtained a further grant of it by the King. Since then the Honour of Clare in these two shires has been transferred to the Queen as part of her jointure. In the meantime, apart from the expenses incurred by renewing the grant, petitioner has accounted for half a year's rent to the King's Receiver-General, and has been forced to disburse certain moneys to the tenants. If he were to be dismissed from his office, it would be difficult for him to find means of having this money repaid to him. He therefore requests that Cecil confirm his tenure of office.—*Undated.*
¾ p. (P. 1632.)

CHRISTOPHER SERGANT to LORD CECIL.

[Before August 20, 1604].—He asks for the bailiwick, pickage, stallage and tollage of the town of Newbury for a term of 40 years. He has lived from his infancy in Newbury, and so is acquainted with all the ancient customs there. Also, " for his education in learning, conversation and estate, your Lordship may be enformed that he is apt and suffycient " for the office. He offers to pay the usual rent and to increase it by £10 a year.—*Undated.*
⅓ p. (P. 1646.)

ROBERT STILEMAN, THE YOUNGER, to LORD CECIL.

[Before August 20, 1604].—In the time of the late Queen Elizabeth he was Feodary and Bailiff of the Honour of Clare in Norfolk. After her demise he obtained a renewal of the grant from the Lord Treasurer which, however, " by reason of the contagiousnes of the tyme of this late sicknes was not effectually proceeded in ". He requests that Cecil confirm the grant.—*Undated.*
½ p. (P. 1651.)

WILLIAM ROUDES and CHRISTOPHER GLOVER to LORD CECIL.

[Before August 20, 1604].—Roudes is a servant in the Queen's Cellar and Glover a groom of the King's Bows. Petitioners have never submitted a request for recognition of their services, but now ask that the bailiwick of Northbourne and Cranfield be bestowed upon them.—*Undated.*
Note by Cecil: " If these were not disposed I wold willingly grant them."
1 p. (P. 1682.)

PHILIP RIDDETT to LORD CECIL.

[Before August 20, 1604].—He is of Sturminster Newton Castle, co. Dorset. He asks that Cecil certify the truth of his examination by the Earl of Nottingham and Cecil at Basing concerning certain money and jewels belonging to Sir Walter Ralegh, which were left in the custody of Sir Thomas Freke for Sir Roger Wilbraham. Cecil's certificate would further the suit he proposes to make to the King for the bailiwick of Sturminster Newton Castle which is now vacant.—*Undated*.

1 p. (P. 1715.)

ANTHONY DENT to LORD CECIL.

[Before August 20, 1604].—He is in Cecil's employment, and requests that the bailiwick of Northbourne, co. Kent, be bestowed upon him.—*Undated*.

½ p. (P. 1633.)

PHILIP BROWN to LORD CECIL.

[Before August 20, 1604].—In recognition of his long service in the Irish wars, the Lord Deputy has bestowed upon him the office of Provost Marshal of Lough Foyle. The Lord Deputy is desirous of confirming this by letters patent, but needs a letter from the Privy Council for that purpose. Petitioner has spent much money on the Provost Marshal's house, and would be ready to disburse more if his office were officially confirmed. He asks Cecil to favour his petition which comes up for discussion at the Council table next Sunday.—*Undated*.

½ p. (P. 1718.)

SIR HENRY BILLINGSLEY and DAME MARY, his wife, to LORD CECIL.

[Before August 20, 1604].—They request that they be permitted to present to Cecil, and that he in turn peruse, various items of information relating to the case between them and John Killigrew in the Court of Chancery concerning certain legacies.—*Undated*.

Note signed by Cecil : " I desire that Mr Surveyor and Mr Atturny will consider of this petition and certifie me their opinions."

On reverse : Details of the dispute between the litigants.

½ p. (P. 1718.)

JAMES MASCALL to LORD CECIL.

[Before August 20, 1604].—He was recently Warden Clerk of the East Marches of England, and also served the late Queen Elizabeth nine years as a soldier in Captain Skinner's company at Berwick. He was cashiered last Christmas for being absent when the commissioners held their inquiry there, although he had appointed deputies to both the offices he held. Since he is dependent on these posts for his livelihood he proposes to submit a petition to the Privy Council for some compensation. He asks Cecil to support his suit when it comes up for discussion, " the rayther for that he hath the custodie of all the anntient treaties, indents, bookes and Rowles concerning the same Marches, whereby he may be enhabled to doe his Matie and countrey good service ".—*Undated*.

1 p. (P. 1344.)

JOHN DACKOMBE to LORD CECIL.

[Before August 20, 1604].—In accordance with Cecil's instructions he visited and examined Edmund Hardikin of Baldham, co. Wilts, whom he takes to be a lunatic. He also enquired about the integrity and competency of Richard Burley, Joseph Oldsworth, John Fordam and John Sommer, who were nominated by Hardikin's wife to have the custody of the lunatic. Both neighbours and the lunatic's father testify that they are all fit men to be in charge of him and to be entrusted with his property. —*Undated.*

½ p.   (P. 2115.)

RICHARD IVENSON to [LORD CECIL].

[Before August 20, 1604].—He is Cecil's porter, and requests the grant of the bailiwick of the rents and profits of the Honour of Clare within the counties of Huntingdon and Cambridge.— *Undated.*

⅓ p.   (P. 1645.)

EDWARD BILLING and GEORGE GOODALL to LORD CECIL.

[Before August 20, 1604].—They were formerly in the service of Sir Christopher Hatton and later employed by Lord Hunsdon as keepers of Brigstock Parks for 15 years. The parks have since come into Cecil's hands and been conveyed to Lord Mordaunt, who has removed them from their posts. They have no other means to support their families, and remind him of his former promise to see to their welfare when the parks came into his possession —*Undated.*

Note by Cecil: " Let fyfty pownds be payd to yᵉ 3 keepers owt of yᵉ money to be answered for yᵉ wood."

½ p.   (P. 1756.)

WILLIAM TOOKE to LORD CECIL.

[Before August 20, 1604].—He has been importuned by his friends to become a suitor to Cecil for the reversion of his father's office, in the court where he has been employed for the last sixteen years. " Now that my fortunes bee at soe lowe an ebb, and age and sicknes steales upon mee, when it is high tyme to provide for some certayne meanes to supplye the continuall wantes which those infirmities bringe ever with them ", such a preferment by Cecil would be an unexpected and unforgettable favour as " I knowe ther are some that labore for it verye seriously ".—*Undated.*

Seal.   ⅓ p.   (P. 1947.)

MICHAEL BRISKETT.

[Before August 20, 1604].—Memorandum to the effect that Lord Cecil be reminded to speak to the Attorney-General on behalf of Michael Briskett, and asked to further his case at the Star Chamber. Also that Briskett's interests be not prejudiced during his absence.—*Undated.*

1 p.   (P. 2239.)

FRANCIS BUSSY *versus* JOHN THURBARN.

[Before August 20, 1604].—In answer to Thurbarn's petition, Bussy confesses that he (Thurbarn) has lands at Sysonby purchased from Mr Digby, but he is ignorant of its extent.

Mistress Pate was dead before petitioner commenced any suit, so that Bussy could not have confederated with her, nor she with him, to bring the matter before the Court of Wards. Neither is anything claimed for the ward from the land called Margaret Yard land which petitioner bought from Digby.

The matter arising between the ward and Thurbarn is as follows : for a long time, the lands now purchased by the latter from Digby were occupied by one person together with certain property of the ward's at Sysonby. They are now separate and petitioner, on the grounds that he has bought lands from Digby, claims parcels of meadow which belong to the ward, and has sued the tenant at the common law in an effort to try the ward's title to them during his nonage.

It was to preserve the interest of the ward that a bill was exhibited in the Court of Wards, and that the court stayed Thurbarn's action at the common law until it had examined the matter, which is now in the process of being done.

Bussy denies that he ever encouraged the tenant of the meadow land to deny petitioner his rent.—*Undated.*

½ p. (P. 553.) *See* P. 554. *infra.*

JOHN THURBARN to LORD CECIL.

[Before August 20, 1604].—He is a native of Melton Mowbray and is seised in fee simple of land called Margaret Yard land at Sysonby, Leicestershire, which he bought from William Digby, its owner for the past fifty years. A certain Mistress Pate tried to purchase it from petitioner for her son, Edward Pate. Upon his refusal, she and her brother Francis Bussy devised a scheme whereby Edward Pate, who is a King's ward, laid claim to the property, although it was not included in the survey of his father's lands when the latter died. Bussy has procured an injunction from the Court of Wards, which is in possession of the ward's inheritance, to prevent petitioner from suing for his land at the common law. He has also persuaded the tenant of the property in question not to pay petitioner any rent but to give it to him. So that Bussy is actually prosecuting his suit with the help of money which rightfully belongs to petitioner. He complains also that a Richard Mitton, who is related to the ward, met petitioner in London recently and made a remark which showed too obviously that the scheme of the opposing party was deliberate and subversive of law. He asks Cecil to summon them to formulate their claim, as he has already done, or let the matter be tried by common law.—*Undated.*

¾ p. (P. 554.)

JANE LOVELL to LORD CECIL.

[Before August 20, 1604].—She thanks him for his solicitude on behalf of her children and herself after the death of her husband in the Irish wars. She refers to the suits commenced against her by the mother of Mr Conell and by his brothers, who claim that certain lands bequeathed by her husband to his children are subject to gavelkind, a claim never put forward by them before. She asks that Cecil instruct the Attorney of the Court of Wards that all suits from the common law be stayed during the minority of the children.—*Undated.*

1 p. (P. 1900.)

JOHN LEMYNG to LORD CECIL.

[Before August 20, 1604].—He informs him that the concealed wardship which Cecil bestowed upon him has been of no material benefit but, on the contrary, has involved him in financial charges. He requests that he be granted a bailiwick or some other sinecure that Cecil may have in his gift.—*Undated.*

½ p. (P. 1251.)

GEORGE WALKER and WILLIAM LIPPINGTON to LORD CECIL.

[Before August 20, 1604].—They are both husbandmen of Hunmanby, Yorkshire. They declare that Peter Acklam, of Hunmanby, deceased, was lawfully seised of a messuage and forty acres and held it by knight tenure of the late Queen Elizabeth, as part of the manor of Hunmanby. He had a son and three daughters, and by his will devised the property to Walker during the son's minority for the education of his son and the provision of £10 towards the preferment of his daughters. Twelve years ago Acklam died, and Walker proceeded to receive the profits of the tenement and use them as stipulated in the will. The value of the land did not exceed four marks yearly, but by the procurement of one Charles Tutfield, they have been found by a more recent inquisition to be of the value of £6 annually. Petitioner protests that the second inquisition was held without his knowledge, and that no mention was made of the directions made in the will as to the uses of the land. Now process has been awarded against him as occupier of the property by the Court of Wards, Lippington being tenant of part of it under petitioner, and the sum of £73 : 15 demanded which is more than the land would fetch if it were sold. The sheriff of Yorkshire threatens to distrain the goods and chattels of petitioners and dispose of them by sale. They request that a commission be set up to examine the matter, and that they be not molested or subjected to distraint until the facts of the case have been established.—*Undated.*

Endorsed : " The humble petition of George Walker and William Lippington." ½ p. (P. 837.)

JOHN ARNOLD to LORD CECIL.

[Before August 20, 1604].—It has been ordered that the case between him and Cook should be referred to the arbitration of the Earls of Cumberland and Pembroke. The case has been heard by them, but is not yet finished. Since the matter has been awaiting a settlement in the Court of Wards for the past 25 years, and two juries have returned a verdict in petitioner's favour, the case now threatens to affect 300 families adversely. Both equity and possession are arguments in petitioner's favour, and during several hearings of the case order has been made for a fair and impartial trial, in which case matters of law need to be considered. Petitioner therefore asks that these matters be referred to the judges before he is forced to hazard the fate of so many people by assenting to a trial in a county not known to be impartial, contrary to the Court's decision and to equity. —*Undated.*

Note at bottom signed by Cecil: " If this be moved in Court when I am there, he shall have such satisfaction as in justice is fitt."

1 p. (P. 1618.)

—— ROOKES to LORD CECIL.

[Before August 20, 1604].—He requests that Nicholas Workman be ordered to come to an arrangement about his debt to petitioner, so that the Ambassador's business be not interrupted or impeded because of him. If Workman refuses to cooperate Rookes will be forced to neglect the Ambassador's private affairs and remain in England to take legal action against him. In this Workman would be acting contrary to his assurances to the Ambassador in France, when the latter directed that he should be provided with all necessities.—*Undated.*

Note : " Mr Rookes petition against Workman." ½ p. (P. 1039.)

WILLIAM TOOKE to LORD CECIL.

[Before August 20, 1604].—A recent indisposition has prevented him from attending on Cecil, who showed him favour by bestowing on him the bailiwick of Hoddesdon. He understands, however, that Mr Flint accuses him of dishonest dealings and has rendered him suspect to Cecil. He protests that he has been as meticulous as possible in accounting for the rents, but confesses that he has retained £30 of fines which should have been paid in. " I did it not out of a dispositione to deceave or defraude your Lordship of a pennye, but rather constrained thereunto thorough myne owne wantes ; for beinge grevouslye sicke by the space of twentie weekes and lyinge in a straunge place at a greate chardge, neyther father nor freinde once sendinge unto mee for a longe tyme, havinge noe meanes to supply the neede I was driven unto, I confess I disbursed your Lordships moneye ; but yet with a full purpose as soone as ever I shoulde recover my health to make restitution of it, for not longe before your Lordship had given mee the prefermente of a lunaticke, of which I thought to have made my beste benefitt, and by that meanes to have repayd your Lordships moneye." However, Cecil had revoked that grant and awarded it to the Surveyor of the Court of Wards, so that Tooke had been deprived of the means of repaying the money. He requests that he be allowed time or authorized to convey the office of bailiff to some other who will give him good security, on condition that all arrears are discharged. He also asks for permission to attend Cecil at Court.—*Undated.*

Holograph. Endorsed : " 1604. Mr Tooke to my lord." 1 p. (P. 2412.)

HENDRYCKE DE WYTT and other merchants of Middelburg to LORD CECIL.

[Before August 20, 1604].—Recently he conveyed to Cecil a letter from Sir Noel de Caron, in which he enclosed a petition of his own concerning the freight of a ship seized by Captain Traughton in the *Lyonesse* of London. Cecil had told him to approach the Lord Admiral in the matter, but since it concerns Cecil in particular, petitioner asks that the Judge of the Admiralty be ordered to proceed to sentence, whether or not it be adverse to petitioner.—*Undated.*

½ p. (P. 2059.)

[See *H.M.C. Salisbury MSS*, Vol. XVI, pp. 154–5, and Vol. XVII, p. 261.]

The QUEEN'S ATTORNEY to [LORD CECIL].

[Before August 20, 1604].—He has found the patent, dated Elizabeth 35, concerning the right of St. John and his son to herbage and pånage for the term of their lives. He is of the opinion that " my Lord " should surrender and take it for lives or years in reversion, since it is very profitable. He has attended on Cecil on three occasions but the latter's commitments precluded any meeting. He has left the information to be conveyed to Cecil by the Vice-Chamberlain who knows of the matter. *Undated.*

Endorsed : " 1604. Note Q. Attorney." 1 p. (P. 2212.)

The COUNTESS OF DERBY to LORD CECIL.

[Before August 20, 1604].—She is writing on behalf of one of her officers, Sir Thomas Hanmer, who has an interest in the lease of a tenement belonging to lands now in dispute between George Haulford and Lady Cholmondeley. The latter has conveyed the lands to her son, Robert, of whom she has obtained the wardship, with deliberate intent to provoke an examination of the case by the Court of Wards. She has also preferred a bill against Hanmer to invalidate his interest in the above-mentioned lease. Hanmer's counsel has advised that the case between him and Lady Cholmondeley should be tried by common law, and petitioner asks

Cecil to favour this course of action " for it concerneth a follower of mine very much ".—*Undated.*

Signed only. Seal. Endorsed : " 1604. Countess of Derby, the elder." ¾ p. (P. 1965.)

JOHN TAYLOR to LORD CECIL.

[Before August 20, 1604].—He has served the Duke of Florence for five years and more, and recently came to England with those who brought a present from the Duke to the King. He now wishes to return to Florence, but prefers to travel by sea rather than overland. However, he cannot obtain a passage easily without a licence to travel signed by a member of the Privy Council, and requests Cecil's written permission to travel to Florence by sea.—*Undated.*

Endorsed : " 1604. Mr Taylor." ½ p. (P. 857.)

ROBERT LISTON and JOHN MITCHELL to LORD CECIL.

[Before August 20, 1604].—They have been with the Lord Treasurer's secretary about the £80 granted to them as compensation for their losses by Cecil's intervention, but cannot get it paid to them. The matter has been deferred until Michaelmas, but if they are obliged to wait till then, the delay could result in their ruin. They ask that Cecil speak once again to the Lord Treasurer about the immediate payment of the money.—*Undated.*

Endorsed : " 1604." ½ p. (P. 1848.)

[See *Cal. S.P. Dom.* 1603–10, p. 127.]

ANGUS MUNROE to LORD CECIL.

[Before August 20, 1604].—He is a Scotsman and informs Cecil that upon the submission by him of a petition to the King for the pension granted to him by the late Queen Elizabeth for his relief, petitioner being maimed and having lost a leg, the King allowed him the same pension of 12d a day, and referred his case to the Privy Council. For the past three years petitioner has had to rely upon the charity and assistance of his friends in the absence of the pension. He asks that Cecil make known his destitution to the Council, so that he may receive the pension without delay.—*Undated.*

Endorsed : " 1604." ½ p. (P. 1884.)

[See *Cal. S.P. Dom.,* 1603–10, p. 122.]

DONALD McCARTHY to LORD CECIL.

[Before August 20, 1604].—He is the son of Donald McCarthy, late Earl of ClanCarthy, deceased. He recently submitted a petition to Cecil requesting him to further his suit to the King, and Cecil directed Sir Roger Wilbraham to make a draft of a letter for that purpose. Because of Wilbraham's absence, however, it cannot be effected. Petitioner asks that, in view of his slender means which cannot maintain him indefinitely in London, another person be appointed to draft the letter, and suggests Sir Julius Caesar.—*Undated*.

½ p. (P. 1709.)

RICHARD ORRELL to LORD CECIL.

[Before August 20, 1604].—Six years ago petitioner leased from him a house called Pymmes at Edmonton with certain parcels of land at the annual rent of £103, together with the right to timber from Cecil's woods at Edmonton for any necessary repairs. Despite this, Cecil's surveyor and officials have refused him timber on the grounds that a restraint has been placed by Cecil on the same. Petitioner has been forced to buy the requisite quantity of timber for repairs to the amount of £200. He requests that he be granted some indemnification for these supplementary expenses, and that a lease of the house and lands for his life, his wife and one of his children, or for 31 years, at a reasonable rent be awarded him in view of the expenses in maintaining the property.—*Undated*.

1 p. (P. 105.)

EDMUND TODD to VISCOUNT CRANBORNE.

[After August 20, 1604].—He is charged with a privy seal for a loan of £30 to the King, but he has not the means to contribute such an amount. He has only a small living consisting of 25 inhabitants, of whom 17 are cottagers, and has many children to provide for. These facts are attested by four of his parishioners.—*Undated*.

Signed : Richard Deyer, George Wauboy, Edward Rolte, H. Goodrych. 1 p. (P. 726.)

JOHN JEANES to VISCOUNT CRANBORNE.

[After August 20, 1604].—He is tenant of part of Cranborne's parsonage of Martock, co. Somerset. Recently he paid Cranborne a fine of £850 for that part, and to do so he was forced to borrow £400, which he is expected to repay within an agreed time. Some of the Justices of the Peace of Somersetshire, however, having heard of the transaction, have served him with a privy seal for the loan of £25 to the King which he is not in a position to pay. He asks to be discharged of the privy seal.—*Undated*.

½ p. (P. 1424.)

JOHN PROCTOR to VISCOUNT CRANBORNE.

[After August 20, 1604].—Thomas Banks, of Hanslop, co. Bucks., is possessed of a tenement within the manor of Hanslop, paying £3 annually as rent to the Queen. Ralph Stacey of Hanslop has the possession of the mills there, as well as of a malt mill, demised to Thomas Mathew, paying a yearly rent of £6:3:4 to the Queen. Petitioner asks for a lease in reversion of the abovementioned premises, that he be commended to the Queen's Commissioners for leases, and that the auditors of Buckinghamshire be instructed to send a particular of the premises to Cranborne.—*Undated.*

Endorsed : " Mr Proctor, the Queens gent. harbinger to my Lord." ⅓ p. (P. 98.)

The TENANTS of the Queen's manor at Bisley to VISCOUNT CRANBORNE.

[After August 20, 1604].—Cranborne has been pleased to interest himself in the case of the widow West, whose tenement has been granted over her head to another person. This reversion was procured by the Steward of the manor, Mr Rastall, by means of Richard Bird who holds the manorial court for him, although he has been convicted for defrauding the late Queen Elizabeth of many fines. Cranborne has enquired whether the custom of the manor permits the reversion of any copyhold tenement without the consent of the copyholder occupying it. Petitioners inform him that such a reversion is prohibited by the custom of the manor, and complain that Richard Bird is guilty of violating manorial customs and oppressing customary tenants. They request that the observance of the ancient customs of Bisley be strictly enforced.—*Undated.*

Fifteen signatures : ¾ p. (P. 1527.) *See* P. 1530 *supra* p. 160. [See *Cal. S.P. Dom.,* 1603–10, p. 123.]

JOHN CRANE to VISCOUNT CRANBORNE.

[After August 20, 1604].—He is the former Comptroller of Berwick garrison, and is under an obligation to Cranborne for having procured that position for him, and, later, for obtaining a pension for him out of the Exchequer. In regard of many considerations, including that of 26 years' service, he asks that he be allowed to convey his pension to another person, for the discharging of his debts, and so to avoid prison.—*Undated.*

1 p. (P. 1427.)

FULK LLOYD to VISCOUNT CRANBORNE.

[After August 20, 1604].—Two years ago, in July, petitioner was indicted at a coroner's inquest as an accessory to the murder of John Lewis Gwyn. Most of the jury were tenants or servants of Sir John Salisbury, who is very desirous of annexing a parcel of petitioner's property adjoining to his (Salisbury's) house. Petitioner was committed to Denbigh gaol, but when the case was tried at the Assizes a grand jury of the most reputable and substantial gentlemen of Denbighshire acquitted him, although Sir John Salisbury personally conducted the prosecution. Since then, however, his adversaries have been watching their opportunity to fasten the guilt for the murder on to petitioner, and to circumvent their designs his friends thought it advisable to obtain the King's pardon, which was granted. For some reason, however, it has been stayed by Lord Zouche, and petitioner asks that it be made effective.—*Undated.*

Endorsed : " The humble petition of Ffowlke Lloide. May
it please your honor to be further satisfied in the premises by
Sir Henry Townsend, one of the justices of Assize for the countie
of Denbigh, who goeth out of towne to morowe." 1 p. (P. 1446.)
[See *Cal. S.P. Dom.*, 1603–10, p. 130, and *H.M.C. Salisbury
MSS*, Vol. XVI, pp. 177–8, 286–8, 301.]

<h2 style="text-align:center">GUNPOWDER.</h2>

[*c.* August 27, 1604].—" The covenants betweene the Kinges
Matie and the patentees contayned in the indenture of the former
patent.

Ffirst, to delyver into his Ma^{ts} stoare within the tower of
London yearelie, allowinge twelve monnethes to every yeare,
120 lasts, that is to saie, 10 lasts of good and servicable corne
gunpowder.

Item, a warrant unto the Lord Treasurer of England and
Chamberlaines of thexchequer for payment of the monie uppon
receipt of the monnethlie proportion.

Item, a n̄oie pene of fiftie pounds if the monnethlie service
shalbee wantinge one monneth after the same shalbee due.

Item, a covenant that the patentees are to delyver such surplus
of gunpowder for the service of his Matie as shalbee remayninge
in there hands, besides the monnethlie proportion, as by the Lord
Treasurer and M^r of the ordynance for the tyme beinge shalbee
thought meete.

Item, a warrant for the overplus of the monnethlie proportion
accordinge to the former at the rate of 10d.

Item, that all the gunpowder, the Kinges stoare beinge furnished, maie be solde and uttered to any merchaunts for the
defence of any his Ma^{ts} realmes or domynions or any other his
Ma^{ts} lovinge subjects.

Item, that the patentees have liberty to transport all such
gunpowder as is overplus of his Ma^{ts} service and furnishinge the
merchaunts and other his Highnes lovinge subjects, in any his
Ma^{ts} realmes or domynions or into any other places beyonde the
seas and in amytie with his Matie.—*Undated.*

Endorsed : " 1592 [*sic*]. Patentees for Powder." ¾ p. (**199.**
127.)
[See *H.M.C. Salisbury MSS*, Vol. XVI, p. 278.]

<h2 style="text-align:center">SIR ANTHONY FORREST* to the KING.</h2>

[After August, 1604].—In all the courts of Equity at Westminster and elsewhere, there is a known and sworn examiner only
in the Court of Exchequer Chamber. There the office is executed
by the Barons' men, who are now sworn, with resultant incon-
veniences to both King and subject, and who charge 7d a sheet
copied or to be copied, which is the ancient fee due to every
examiner. Petitioner requests that the office be conferred upon
him or his assigns for term of three lives ; and also that the Barons

---

* Knighted on August 20, 1604.

be prohibited from commissioning their men to examine witnesses in any case except where witnesses testify on oath that they cannot travel thirty miles outside London. All other witnesses to be examined by petitioner or his assigns, who shall be sworn and execute the office daily.—*Undated.*

Endorsed: " Mr Tyrwit aboute a place in ye Exchequer." *Faded.* 1 p. (P. 1828.)

WILLIAM SHARP to the PRIVY COUNCIL.

[After August, 1604].—He was Purser of the *Phoenix* of London, which met with a Spanish warship off the coast of Spain. The Spaniard "hayled and cryed amayne for the King of Spayne, whereuppon as was the custome of the seas wee strooke our topsailes and shewed our colors, and wee told them that wee were of England and bound for Cales [Cadiz] in Spaine with marchants goods for trade in peceable manner and that all was ffreinds to their King and them."* Despite this the Spanish vessel shot at them and continued to do so even when they submitted without resistance. The English ship received over 200 shot, one of which severed petitioner's right arm. The Spaniards proceeded to rob the crew of the *Phoenix* and ransack her cargo, and finally sailed away without attending to the English wounded. He begs for some compensation for the loss of his arm.—*Undated.*

1 p. (P. 1210.)

FRANCIS VERSELINE to VISCOUNT CRANBORNE.

[After August, 1604].—Last August the King decided to hear the case between petitioner and Sir Jerome Bowes regarding the manufacture of Venetian glasses. Petitioner offered the King a rent of £300 *per annum* for the licence and it was accepted. As a favour to Bowes the King informed him through Sir Julius Caesar that, to end the dispute between him and petitioner, and although his licence had only three more years to run, Bowes was to receive the rent for his life time, and after his death it was to be paid to the Exchequer. Bowes has refused the King's proposal, and has obtained an order from the Privy Council that the case be heard in the immediate future. It transpires by Mr Wardour of the Exchequer that Bowes has paid no rent during the nine years he has held the licence, and actually owes one hundred marks a year. Petitioner therefore asks that the matter be not discussed by the Privy Council until the King be informed of Bowes's refusal to accept his proposal.—*Undated.*

¾ p. (P. 765.)

—— to VISCOUNT CRANBORNE.

[? *c.* September, 1604].—A privy seal was directed to Sir Thomas Dacres for collecting money towards the preparing of bridges for the King. But since the sum to be levied was not specified in the warrant, it is now requested that it should be

---

* The Anglo-Spanish peace treaty was proclaimed on August 19, 1604.

named and notified to the Lord Treasurer, "for that there is a want of money to paye poore people". Sir Thomas Dacres's man has been unable to obtain access to Cranborne for the past three days.—*Undated*.

$\frac{1}{3}$ p. (P. 1223.)

[See *Cal. S.P. Dom.*, 1603–10, p. 150.]

Thomas Maycrott to —— Roppres.

[1604] September 9.—He has received a letter from Roppres without a date. "You must be more carefull to write the date as also addresse your letters with more discretion; for I have not receaved the letters youe make mention to have written within these fourten dayes. Addresse your letters by the name accorded of betwene us to the post Mr of Andwerp, so they shal com suerly to me. It was great mervail this last letter came to mine handes. Be circumspect how youe addresse your letters. Youe remember the day accorded betwene us for ⁜ ; al was redy that day and so continueth. Therfor ther resteth nothinge but that you cause it presently to be effected, and for ten dayes after the date hereof. Begin when youe will, for all is redy and the soner the better. You remember my frende I named to you. He is ther so that to conclude, dispatche with all speed or els let me hear from youe of the alteration with al spede, for to write to our frende my lord in England at this time is nedeles. He, that spake with youe, is here stil and very shortly is to returne. God send you well to do in hast, this 9th of September according to the newe accompt."

PS. "Your beinge with Le May is discovered to many be reson of your man so often comine; therfore to avoide al danger youe must seake to dispatche with all speede possibell."

PPS. "I receaved an other letter by the name of Le May that was written on Friday last. Since the writing hereof I would be very sory that after so many promises I have under your hande writinge youe should fayle. You knowe what hathe past between us. I will maintaine my word, I looke for the like at your handes, which yf you kepe not youe are utterly undone. I can say more then I wyll wryt, and knewe more when you met Le May then youe thought for. For money I can not hellp youe to any, therfore rest no more upon that point. Peruse my letter well and give me answere with all speede what you will doe, for yf within ten dayes after the date hereof I here not that the matter is effected or that you give me som probable cause of the staye thereof, I meane to deale no further with youe and youe are utterly ruinated. Looke well upon my letter, and so lokinge dayli to heare from you, I end. Addres your letters to Le May at the post Mrs. and so the[y] will come safest. I have written here as I wrote to W. Therfore peruse my letter well.

This that followeth was wryten ether with allum or joyse of lemons and onyons.

The 2 . . . is the daye accorded, our men arrived at Olding-

borge* loking when thenterprise should be done, and they tary
still ther with order to execute the enterprise when the captaines
and prisoners com thether. I cannot help you with mony til
thenterprise be done, then what is promised shal be performed
to all your great advancements. For the love of God use all
hast possibell. You knowe I may not kepe the assurance allwayes
in my hands, the terme is allmost ended, nor it is not reason that
thextraordinary souldiers should continue at the fort, therfore
for ten dayes after the date hyerof youe make chose of any of
the ten. Al is redy. Yf you do it not in that time, send me
worde of the stay for I must give up my assurance, and the
souldiers [*marginal note :* look on the other side and this lyckwise
wryten with allum] wil be called for away. I doe not like that
youe have hidden your true name from me. I meane plainly,
and so I trust you doe. For these reasons, let me here from
youe with all speed. I pray you send me worde whether the
fort in the newe towne be at our devotion, which must be so or
els all is in vayne, for we must be assured that ther is no difficulty
yf you meane sincerly. It is very dangerous that so many
delayes, as also for the rest. Send me word how I shall addresse
my letters to youe and to what place. For to the postmaster
ther is somwhat dangerous for youe. I can say no more but
ether you are made or undone for ever. Therfore looke to it.
For the more speede, yf ther be any trusty souldier let him steale
out of the towne although he would come to serve us, and direct
him to Don Emanuell the *Maistro de Campo*, and then you may
the soner proceed to the enterprise. But he that cometh from
the towne must speake Spanish or French. God send youe wel
to do, and let me heare from you with speede. Be carefull to
writ your superscriptions plainly. My thinkes yf ther be any
extraordinare companyes in the towne, they may be sent forth
to spoile the countrey or whosoever are suspected to be against
the enterprise, and in the meane time, the[y] being abrode, the
enterprise may be done. I can not help you with any more
mony, therfore rest not upon that and give me your spedy
resolution."—*Undated.*

Addressed : " A Monsieur Roppres a Midellbourgh." *Endorsed :*
" Intelliginces. Sept. 9 . . . N.S. Tho : Maycrott to Roppres."
3 pp. (**98.** 152.)

SIR SAMUEL BAGNALL to the KING.

[1604, September 10].—In recognition of his services petitioner's
father, Sir Ralph Bagnall, was given the manor of Newcastle-
under-Lyme, co. Stafford, by the late Queen Elizabeth, for 21
years and the reversion of the lease for a further 31 years. Sir
Ralph is now dead and the lease is on the point of expiring.
Petitioner asks that, in view of his services during the wars in
France, Flanders and Ireland, and the fact that he has " bine at

---

* An attempt to betray Aardenburg to the Spanish was defeated in December,
1604. (See PRO, S.P. 84 (Holland), Vol. 64, fol. 232.]

extraordynarie chardgs in all voyages of attempt " without receiving more than his ordinary pay, he be granted a further lease in reversion for as many years as the King shall decide, and at the old rent of £62:16: 5½.—*Undated.*

Note by Sir Roger Wilbraham : " At the Courte at Windesor this 10th of September, 1604. It is his M^{aties} pleasure that this petitioner shall attend the Lord Lieutenant of Ireland and the Lord Viscount Cranborn, that upon certificate of their Lordships opinion touchinge the convenience of this sute, his M^{aties} pleasure maie be further knowen for the petitioners satisfaction."

1 p. (P. 1503.)

[See *H.M.C. Salisbury MSS*, Vol. XVI, p. 329.]

NICHOLAS WHITE to VISCOUNT CRANBORNE.

[After September 10, 1604].—He is a King's ward, and his complaint to the King concerning the dispute between him and John Itchingham over the Barony of Dunbrody in Ireland was referred to Cranborne and the Earl of Devonshire. In accordance with their directions sent by letter, the Lord Deputy and Council of Ireland have taken steps to terminate the controversy. Itchingham, however, has arrived with further information, and petitioner requests that this be not allowed to alter the injunctions sent to Ireland.—*Undated.*

½ p. (P. 1065.)

[See *H.M.C. Salisbury MSS*, Vol. XVI, pp. 304–5.]

GEORGE HARPUR and HENRY HUMBERSTON to the KING.

[Before September 17, 1604].—They are Keepers of the two walks of Hainault and Chapel Hainault in Waltham Forest. The King restored the Earl of Oxford to the custody and charge of the Forest and the Earl, finding many abuses there committed by Anthony Witherings, then Keeper of Chapel Hainault walk, dismissed him and appointed Humberston in his place, the latter being an old servant of the late Queen Elizabeth in Havering Park and reputed for his honesty and efficiency. But encouraged by Sir John Gray, Witherings forcibly ejected Humberston from the walk and persists in staying there, contrary to the orders of the Earl of Nottingham and Viscount Cranborne. Petitioners request that a warrant be directed to Sir Anthony Cooke and Sir Robert Wroth commanding them to remove Witherings from the walk and replace him by Humberston until the Earl of Oxford's right to the nomination of all officers within the Forest be tried in the Court of Wards ; and also that they be granted their annual wages of £12 each and any arrears due from the Treasurer of the Chamber, together with the fee wood customarily allowed to keepers in respect of their charges in preserving the King's game.—*Undated.*

1 p. (P. 1377.)

[See *H.M.C. Salisbury MSS*, Vol. XVI, p. 310, and *Cal. S.P. Dom.*, 1603–10, p. 187.]

The DEPUTIES for the HANSE TOWNS to VISCOUNT CRANBORNE.

1604, September 19.—They have learned that the business which they had hoped to terminate expeditiously has been postponed until the following week. The delay is to be regretted for many reasons, although they are still confident of receiving a favourable answer. They urgently request Cranborne to employ his influence and good will to speed the matter to a satisfactory conclusion.—London, 19 September, 1604.

Latin. 1½ pp. (**107.** 18.)

NICHOLAS DRAKE to VISCOUNT CRANBORNE.

[? After September 20, 1604].—His two brothers, Robert and Humphrey, served the States General in the Low Countries for eight years, the one as Colonel and the other as Sergeant-Major, and were killed at the siege of Ostend.* They bequeathed their money and goods to petitioner, and also the arrears of pay due to them, with which petitioner was to discharge their debts and distribute their legacies. He has already spent three months soliciting the States General for the arrears, but has only met with procrastination. Nevertheless he has paid both debts and legacies in anticipation of the payment of the arrears. He requests Cranborne to write on his behalf to Sir Noel de Caron urging that some expeditious means be found to satisfy petitioner.—*Undated.*

1 p. (P. 947.)

THOMAS SHARPE to the PRIVY COUNCIL.

[After September 29, 1604].—Towards the end of the previous September he was the owner of a bark of 70 tons in the harbour of Dover. Upon the official resumption of trade with Flanders,† he obtained a freight for his ship consigned to that country, and sailed on September 29. Before he could reach his destination he was boarded by Dutchmen from Rotterdam serving under the States General. They not only seized his cargo, but stripped the vessel of its rigging, anchors, sails, etc., so that it became utterly unseaworthy and was finally wrecked on the Flemish coast. Petitioner's losses in ship and cargo amount to £500, in addition to the personal effects of which he and his crew had been robbed. " And lastly, beinge not contented wyth the spoyle of all things, they tooke your poore distressed orator whome they stroke and revyled in most despitefull manner, strippinge him into his shirte and soe forceing him to goe naked to Dunckirke, being two myles distannt from the shipp, not havinge soe much as an hatt on his head or a shoe to treade on." He begs for redress, particularly as he is sure that the Privy Council would never allow one of the King's subjects to be robbed by a nation which is in league with the King and people of England.—*Undated.*

½ p. (**197.** 89.)

---

* The siege of Ostend lasted from July, 1601 to September 20, 1604, when it was surrendered to Spinola.

† The peace treaty with Spain signed on August 19, 1604, guaranteed freedom of trade between England and Flanders.

The PARISHIONERS of ST. JOHN ZACHARIES to VISCOUNT CRANBORNE.

[Before October 19, 1604].—The rectory is void by the death of the last incumbent, and they have petitioned the Dean and Chapter of St. Paul's that Thomas Martin be made rector, a request of which the King has approved. Martin is chaplain to Lord Zouche. The Dean and Chapter, however, intend to appoint another person to the benefice, although he already enjoys two. Petitioners ask Cranborne to favour Martin, and suggest that if the place is considered convenient for the other party, then Martin should be given the benefice relinquished by him.—*Undated.*

¾ p. (P. 1370.)

[See *Cal. S.P. Dom.*, 1603–10, p. 159.]

ROBERT LUFFE to the KING.

[October 19, 1604,].—He was an intelligence agent in Spain during the reign of the late Queen Elizabeth, and when in Madrid was accused by Don Carlos Mackert, an Irishman, and imprisoned for 18 months. He was then brought before Spanish judges, condemned and tortured on the rack " as never Englishman the like". Sir Richard Hawkins, then a prisoner, was an eyewitness and can testify accordingly. Since then petitioner has lived in want during the past three years owing to his disabledness. He requests the grant of a licence to transport 1000 quarters of wheat, paying the old custom of 6d the quarter. The grant is not within the competence of Viscount Cranborne, to whom the case was referred, although he would have awarded it if he had been in a position to do so.—*Undated.*

Note signed by Sir Julius Caesar : " At Court at Whitehall, the 19th of October, 1604. The Kings Matie hath referred this petition to the Lord High Tresurer of England and the L. Viscount Cranborne, and their lordships are to certifie the deserts of the suppliant with theire opinion of this suite."

1 p. (P. 719.)

[See *H.M.C. Salisbury MSS*, Vol. XVI, pp. 373, 439.]

JOHN BAILY to VISCOUNT CRANBORNE.

[After October 31, 1604].—He has received a demand by privy seal for a loan of £20 to the King. In view of the fact that he lent an identical sum to the late Queen Elizabeth which has not been repaid, and that he still lives in Chancery Lane as he has done for the past 22 years, he asks to be released from the demand. He also requests to be summoned to undertake in future only such payments and services as are imposed on him by virtue of his place of residence.—*Undated.*

⅓ p. (P. 1425.)

[See *Cal. S.P. Dom.*, James I, Vol. IXA, pp. 235–48.]

WILLIAM WARREN to VISCOUNT CRANBORNE.

[After October 31, 1604].—He is of Bygrave, Hertfordshire, and recently received a demand by privy seal for a loan of £20 to the King. He has just been released from wardship, and has to provide legacies for his brothers and sisters to the amount of £1200, which will have to be paid out of the small estate bequeathed to him by his father, and which for 15 years has been in the hands of the late Queen Elizabeth and the King. He cannot afford the loan and begs to be discharged from the privy seal.—*Undated.*

¾ p. (P. 1442.)

[See *Cal. S.P. Dom.*, James I, Vol. IXA, pp. 235–48.]

WILLIAM FINCH to VISCOUNT CRANBORNE.

[After October 31, 1604].—He is of Watford, Hertfordshire, and a tanner by trade. He has received an order by privy seal to contribute a loan of £20 to the King. He is unable to comply, partly because he has spent much money in advancing two of his sons, and partly because he has recently paid many sums " into his Ma^{ts} Countinghouse for his Highnes use ". He begs to be discharged from the privy seal.—*Undated.*

½ p. (P. 1048.)

[See *Cal. S.P. Dom.*, James I, Vol. IXA, pp. 235–48.]

JOAN BLACKWELL to [VISCOUNT CRANBORNE].

[After October 31, 1604].—She is a widow of 80 years and resident at Bushey, co. Herts. For the past twelve years she has been lame and sick, and charged with the care of many children. She has received a privy seal for a loan of £20 to the King, which she is not in a position to give, since her annual revenue does not amount to £40 derived from an estate that is hers for life only. She begs to be discharged from the privy seal. —*Undated.*

Signed : six of petitioner's neighbours. 1 p. (P. 1883.)

THEOBALD, LORD BUTLER, VISCOUNT TULLEOPHELIM to VISCOUNT CRANBORNE.

[October, 1604].—The Lord Deputy and Council of Ireland, in conformity with instructions from Cranborne and the Privy Council, have granted him a commission to govern the county of Carlow in Leinster, with authority to mobilize the inhabitants if need be. But the commission has not passed the Great Seal, and therefore does not adequately empower him to call up the people, " who being wholly of the meere uncyvill Irish and so lincked together in allyance, and the common receptacle of all the evil disposed people of those parts of Leynster, that the petitioner may not altogether trust to them nor undertake to do any service for his Matie in the said countie without some men whome he may trust in the execution of his chardge ". Petitioner requests that

the commission be passed under the Great Seal of Ireland, and
that he be allotted ten horse and twenty foot in the King's pay.
He also asks for the same remuneration as that paid to the
Governor of Queen's County ; and that if his father-in-law, the
Earl of Ormonde, should die, he be allowed time to ascertain
what he is to inherit before any official inquisition be held. He
would wish also to be notified of the date and place of any such
inquisition in order to be present.—*Undated*.

[½ p. (P. 1981.)

[See *Cal. S.P. Ireland*, 1603–6, pp. 202–3.]

FRANCIS BRACKENBURY to VISCOUNT CRANBORNE.

[*c*. October, 1604].—He is of Sellaby, co. Durham. His
uncle, Richard Brackenbury, intended to settle his estate upon
him, but Anthony Brackenbury tried in every way to alienate
his uncle's affection towards petitioner. When Richard Brackenbury died, Anthony Brackenbury sold £100 worth of goods
belonging to the deceased. In addition, he took advantage of
petitioner's ignorance to extract from him two bonds for £2000
for the payment of a certain sum of money. Petitioner has done
so, but Brackenbury threatens to use the bonds, which he will
not surrender, to bring legal proceedings against him. Moreover, with the connivance of one Tunstall, he has put a bill into
the Star Chamber charging petitioner with forging Richard
Brackenbury's will. Petitioner requests Salisbury to see that
he gets justice in this matter.—*Undated*.

¾ p. (P. 1443.)

[See *PRO. Star Chamber* **8,** James I, 60/18.]

JOHN BROWNE to VISCOUNT CRANBORNE.

[After October 1604].—He is one of the executors of the late
John Freston, who by his last will made bequest of certain lands
and all his leases for a number of charitable objects, such as the
founding of fellowships and scholarships at Oxford and Cambridge, the provision of a chapel for two of the King's hospitals
at Pontefract, the erection of a hospital at Kirkethorpe and of
two free schools at Wakefield and Normanton, the allocation of
money to be lent to poor artisans in those two towns, and of 40
quarters of corn to be annually distributed amongst the needy
there. Freston had the lease of the estreats and issues of Green-
wax within the Duchy of Lancaster north of Trent, in the counties
of York, Nottingham, Derby and Stafford, which having expired
the King had allowed the executors to obtain for the above-
mentioned charitable uses. In the meantime Sir Roger Aston
has procured a lease of the estreats throughout the whole of the
Duchy of Lancaster. Petitioner requests that this lease be
stayed or that the estreats specified above be assigned out of it
to the executors for 30 years, together with those in the counties
of Leicester, Northampton and Bedford, the major part of which
have been leased to one Tusher. The executors will pay an

annual rent to the King, and so be in a position to continue with the charitable work intended by Freston.—*Undated.*

1 p.   (P. 106.)

[See *Cal. S.P. Dom.*, 1603–10, p. 158.]

FRANCIS NEEDHAM and SYMON BASILL.

[November 5, 1604,].—Symon Basill and John de Critz obtained the wardship of Philip Saltmarsh from Viscount Cranborne, and came to an agreement over it with Francis Needham.   But there exists some doubt about the validity of the wardship because of a deed of entail relating to the estate.   It was therefore further agreed between the two parties that if, upon the evidence of witnesses, the deed of entail appeared valid to the Court of Wards, then Needham should pay Basill and de Critz an additional £160.   On the other hand, if the entail is held to be insufficient in law, then Basill and de Critz are under an obligation to satisfy Needham for the money he has disbursed in the matter in the form of suits, which will compensate him, and also them, for the profits which they had hoped to gain from the wardship.— *Undated.*

Signed : Francis Needham.   Symon Basyll.   *Endorsed :* " 5 Nov. 1604.   Mr Nedeham and Mr Basill."

¾ p. (P. 1931)

[See *H.M.C. Salisbury MSS*, Vol. XVI, p. 346.]

CERTIFICATE.

1604, November 15.—Certificate to the effect that by virtue of a Papal warrant from Clement VIII, directed by Vestrius Barbiani to Jacques Blaise, Bishop of St. Omer, William Bates (*alias* Breether), subdeacon of Wells and of the English College at Douai, has been ordained.—15 November, 1604.

Latin ½ p.   **(107.**   127.]

[See *Catholic Record Society, Douay Diaries*, 1598–1654, pp. 63 and 342.]

SIR JOHN HELE to the KING.

[? November or before, 1604]—He begs to be released from prison and to have his fine remitted.—*Undated.*

¼ p.   (P. 1423.)

[See *H.M.C. Salisbury MSS*, Vol. XVI, p. 352.]

JOHN BULLOCK to VISCOUNT CRANBORNE.

1604, December 20.—The feodaryship of Derbyshire was bestowed upon him by Cranborne's father, Lord Burghley, many years ago, and the King has confirmed his tenure of that office. But because of advancing age, he would like to see his son succeed him, " being of sufficient age and of thinner temple ", who would serve the King well in it.   If his son can be admitted, he will happily surrender the feodaryship.   Sir Edward Coke, the Attorney-General, can be approached, if need be, to testify to the ability of his son to fill the office.—Derley this xxth of December, 1604.

½ p.   (P. 1915.)

WILLIAM NUGENT to the KING.

[December 24, 1604].—He has previously exhibited petitions for his " restitution to bloode " in the next Irish Parliament, and for a fee farm of £30 of concealed lands. The King has granted the fee farm but not the other request. Because of this he has not been able to enjoy the full benefit of the King's grant. He asks that letters ordering his restitution in blood in the next Irish Parliament be sent to the Irish Government, so that he may leave for Ireland with some token of royal favour.—*Undated.*

Note by Sir Julius Caesar : " At Court at Whitehall, 24 Decem. 1604. The Kings Matie is well pleased that a letter shall be written for the suppliant for his restitution to his blood at the next Parliament to be holden for Ireland."

1 p.   (P. 39.)

[See *Cal. S.P. Ireland*, 1606–8, p. 8.]

LORD SOURDEAC to the EARLS OF DORSET and NOTTINGHAM and VISCOUNT CRANBORNE.

1604.—He is the Governor of Brest, and Lieutenant-General of Brittany. In the time of the late Queen Elizabeth he sustained great losses at sea through the actions of Captain Crofte and Toby Glanfield, and obtained a commission from the Lord Admiral of England to arrest them and confiscate their goods. He seized their ship, but this was employed in the Queen's service in Ireland and there lost, whereby he remained uncompensated for his losses. Later the King of France sent over the Count of Beaumont, now French Ambassador in London, and the Sieur de Boissize, and they, together with the Lord Admiral, Lord Cranborne, Sir Julius Caesar and other commissioners agreed that £900 due by the late Queen to the offenders should be paid to petitioner as compensation. But the Queen died before the award could be effected. By order from the King of France, the Count of Beaumont has moved King James to intervene, who has referred the matter to Cranborne. Petitioner requests that, since the affair has already lasted six years, some definite measure should be taken for his satisfaction.—1604.

½ p.   (P. 1345.)   *See P.* 729 *infra.*

WILLIAM DE LA MOTTE to VISCOUNT CRANBORNE.

[1604].—He is an agent for Lord Sourdeac, Lieutenant of the French King in Brittany. Upon the presentation of the latter's suit to the King of England for £900 towards the indemnification of losses suffered by him at the hands of Captain Crofts and Captain Glanfield, the King referred it to the Privy Council. The Council conferred with the French Ambassador and agreed that the sum of £600 should be paid by the King. Petitioner expresses his gratitude for this favour, and requests a warrant for the payment of the money to him on behalf of Sourdeac.—*Undated.*

½ p. (P. 729.)

[See *Cal. S.P. Dom.*, 1603–10, p. 184.]

LADY BRIDGET NORRIS to the PRIVY COUNCIL.

[1604].—She is the widow of Sir Thomas Norris. In answer to her petition to the Lord Treasurer concerning the discharge of her deceased husband's accounts, she was told that these were to be examined and determined in Ireland. But the Auditor in Ireland has informed her that there is no authority to give such a discharge there since her husband's warrants were issued in Sir Henry Wallop's time. Upon a second petition to the Lord Treasurer, she was given to understand that commissioners would be appointed to deal with the accounts. Petitioner is apprehensive lest her lands be taken over before the commissioners have begun their inquiry, and asks that the Barons and officers of the Exchequer in Ireland be forbidden to resort to such seizure until she receive a discharge from the commissioners. Petitioner adds that neither the Auditors in England nor in Ireland find her indebted to the King except for the rent for her own property during the rebellion, which the King has remitted.—*Undated.*

Endorsed : " 1604 ". ½ p. (P. 1847.)

[See *H.M.C. Salisbury MSS*, Vol. XVI, pp. 257.]

JOHN NORDEN to VISCOUNT CRANBORNE.

1604.—Cranborne is disinclined to allow him to obtain relief from the King in the form of a direct charge, and therefore petitioner requests his approval that he may submit a suit for the office of surveyor of the Duchy of Cornwall, since an auditor has recently been appointed for the Duchy. The office was formerly granted by the King to Richard Sayre, at the instance of Lord Kinloss, but Sayre died before he could occupy it, and it is now free to be regranted by the King. The King and the officials of the land revenues stand to profit much if the duties of the office are efficiently performed.—1604.

½ p. (P. 1373.)

[See *H.M.C. Salisbury MSS*, Vol. XVI, pp. 237 and 451.]

THOMAS CAMPION to VISCOUNT CRANBORNE.

1604.—He is of Llandinam, Montgomeryshire, and has something to reveal which will redound to the King's benefit, and result in the maintenance of 2000 poor people forever, and in the enrichment of that region where petitioner lives. He requests permission to put the information in writing so that Cranborne may decide whether it merits his support or deserves to be suppressed.—1604.

1 p. (P. 1348.)

ZACHARY BETHEL, RICHARD LAZONBY and CHRISTOPHER HAMMOND to the KING.

1604 [May 29, 1605].—Since it is the King's pleasure to gratify his "faithfull servants with the benefit of Recusants", they request, as a reward for their services, the benefit of three recusants apiece, "such as we shall finde not to be disposed of already".—1604.

Endorsed: "1605. This petition delievered the xxixth of May at Eltam by Richarde Lazonbie to his Matie and granted." ⅓ p. (P. 1347.)

RICHARD FRANKLIN to VISCOUNT CRANBORNE.

[1604].—Petitioner's father, William Franklin, before he died made a deed of gift of all his goods to George Franklin in trust to pay his debts and divide the residue between petitioner and the other children. George Franklin, however, detains goods worth £100 and more in his hands from petitioner, who is the sole survivor of the children, and who, besides having a family of his own, suffers from blindness and is hard of hearing. He begs Cranborne to assist him to obtain justice in this matter, "the rather because your honors mother did very dearly love the mother of your suppliant and placed your suppliant in Westminster scole, and afterward with Sir Nicholas Ogle of Bullingbroke, in whose service your suppliant lost his hearinge".— *Undated.*

Endorsed! "1604. The humble [petition] of Richard Ffranklyn, sonne of Eme Denham, daughter to Mrs Alice Ffitzwilliam, daughter to Mr Richard Ffitzwilliam, brother to Sir William Ffitzwilliam." ¾ p. (P. 1346.)

MERCHANTS OF LONDON to VISCOUNT CRANBORNE.

1604.—They are merchants trading with France, and refer to the letters from the Privy Council to the English Ambassador in Paris that he should discuss with the French King the question of the release of their cloth detained by his orders. The French King has replied that he has pardoned them three times for exporting bad cloth to France, but that they still persist in doing so, and that he is determined not to allow his subjects to be further deceived by them. Petitioners claim that all the cloth sent from London is wet before it is exported, and conforms to the Statutes and laws of England. They request that King James write to the French King for the release of their cloth, particularly as they have heard that little attention was paid by him to the letters from the Privy Council.—1604.

½ p. (P. 1343)

MATTHEW LISTER.

[1604].—"Whereas the bearer hereof Mathewe Lister, master of arts and fellow of Oriell Colledge in Oxford,* hath desyred us

* Matthew Lister was made Fellow of Oriel College in 1592.

to signiffie our knowledge and good opinions of him by our letters testimoniall in his behalf ; may it please you to understand that during the space of these twelve yeares he hath lived amongest us, all which tyme he hath shewed him self in conversation verie honest and cyvill, in his studies diligent and paynefull and well worthie of his degrees and place, in religion verie forward, zealous and sound, as by frequentinge of sermons and other divine exercises both publicke and privat, wee maye judge and doe fullie perswade ourselves thereof."—*Undated.*

Signed : Anthony Blencowe ; Cadwallader Owens ; Richard Pigott ; Richard Wharton ; Abel Gower ; William Wilmot ; William Whetcomb ; John Charletts ; Richard Harrys ; Richard Parkinson ; John Daye ; John Tolson ; Thomas Pollexfen. *Endorsed :* "Lrae. test. coll. Oriel. pro Mro Lister." 1 p. (**98. 145.**)

MARY MOORE to ——.

[? 1604].—She is the widow of John Moore, late Alderman of London,* and is submitting this petition on behalf of herself and her daughter Mary Tresham. They are both foreigners and natives of Spain, and came with John Moore to England about 16 years ago. During all this time they have resided in London and have never been troubled about their religion. Recently, however, they have been threatened with an indictment for recusancy at the next sessions in London. Since they are foreigners and have no friends, they ask to be protected from such malicious threats.—*Undated.*

½ p. (P. 1133a.)

Attached.

A letter in the name of the King to the effect that John Moore, former Customer of the Port of London, died indebted to the amount of £24,000, of which £18,000 was paid off by the sale of his goods. Certain tenements in the city of London and fen lands in Norfolk are available for the discharge of the remaining £6000. But this property is in the hands of Thomas Moore, brother and heir of John Moore, who in order to avoid the payment of the said debts sold it to William Beswick, who has commenced suits against the widow of John Moore. Since she is a foreigner and has no friends, and has been reduced to poverty as a result of her husband's debts to the Crown, the King declares that at the request of the Spanish Ambassador he has taken her into his protection. The letter is a command that Thomas Moore and Beswick are to be dealt with so that the sale of the property for the discharge of the remaining £6000 debt may proceed unhindered, and that the widow of John Moore be neither molested or troubled by law suits.—*Undated and unsigned.*

½ p. (P. 1133b.)

[See *H.M.C. Salisbury MSS*, Vol. XVI, p. 449.]

---

* Died in 1603.

THOMAS ALABASTER and JOHN DORINGTON to the CONDE DE VILLA MEDIANA.

[1604].—Having laden their ship with commodities for Spain, they were requested by two merchants of Viana in Portugal to allow them and their goods a passage home in the ship, to which they consented. The ship is now detained in the Downs by contrary winds, but there are a number of Dutch warships there which threaten to seize the Portuguese merchants and their goods. Petitioners state that the latter came to England purely on commercial business under the King's protection. They have paid all customs duties for their commodities, both imports and exports, and have only embarked on an English ship for their greater security. Petitioners opine that it is most regrettable that they should be taken prisoner and ruined in this manner. They have consulted Sir Noel Caron on the matter, but he has declared that it is entirely lawful for the men of Holland and Zeeland to seize the merchants and confiscate their possessions. Petitioners appeal to the Conde to procure a safe conduct from the King, and if necessary a royal ship—one of those already in the Downs—to escort the vessel and protect the Portuguese merchants until they are out of danger.—*Undated.*

Endorsed : " 1604. Petition of Mr Alabaster to the Spanish Embassador." 1 p. (P. 831.)

GREGORY ISHAM, SUSAN STURTYVAM and ZACHEUS ISHAM to
——.

[1604].—They have been granted the custody of Rowland Lee, a lunatic, husband of their sister who died recently* leaving eight children. In the meantime, Alderman Lee, brother of the said Rowland, had persuaded the latter to sell all his estate to him, and has already taken away goods to the value of £500. He intends to seize upon the lunatic's entire estate for himself without any consideration for the orphaned children. They request letters to Alderman Anderson and Robert Chamberlain, Rowland Lee's neighbours, ordering them to preserve the estate ; and letters likewise to Alderman Lee commanding him to restore such goods as he has taken away, and to refrain from meddling any further in the matter.—*Undated.*

1 p. (P. 800.)

The INHABITANTS OF HERTFORDSHIRE to the KING.

[1604].—They complain that James Rolfe, who exercises ecclesiastical authority within the shire as officer and commissary, after purchasing these offices for large sums of money and an annual rent, is guilty of many abuses. They refer *inter alia* to : the citation of people before his courts without presentments ; the extortion of excessive fees for probate of wills and grants of administration ; the granting of separations in marriages without

---

* Rowland Lee died in 1604. [See *Index of Wills proved in the Prerogative Court of Canterbury*, Vol. IV. p. 258.]

just cause ; the compounding and commuting of penances for incontinency ; the suppression of presentments for absence from church, breaches of the Sabbath ; and other misdemeanours. They have collected some 160 particulars as evidence of these corrupt practices. They also condemn Rolfe as a person of lascivious habits and unseemly conversation. Petitioners ask that the charges be investigated by certain knights and gentlemen of the shire or others nominated by the King, and that upon verification of the same, Rolfe be severely censured.—*Undated.*

Endorsed : " 1604. Petition to the King. Against a comissarye by one Jeams Rolffe. That there was collected 160 particulars subscribed by the parties greeved." 1 p. (P. 720.)

EDMUND NEVILLE to the KING.

[1604].—King Richard II in his Parliament held at Westminster in the 21st year of his reign created Ralph, Lord Neville of Raby, Earl of Westmorland, the title to be retained by his heirs for ever. Petitioner is the cousin and next male heir, and asks that the title and dignity of Earl of Westmorland be confirmed to him, inasmuch as the King has restored all those of quality who lost their titles in the time of the late Queen Elizabeth, as did Charles Neville, late Earl of Westmorland, attainted. Alternatively, he asks that his lawful claim to the title be heard by the House of Lords in Parliament.—*Undated.*
½ p. (P. 654.)
[See *H.M.C. Salisbury MSS*, Vol. XVI, p. 450, and *Cal. S.P. Dom.*, 1603–10, p. 275.]

WILLIAM HAWES to the PRIVY COUNCIL.

[? *c.* 1604 or after].—He requests the Council to appoint two of their number or others to hear a case in which he is involved, and which concerns an export licence for which he compounded with Gilbert Lee.—*Undated.*
½ p. (P. 637.)
[See *Cal. S.P. Dom.*, 1603–10, p. 65.]

EDWARD DUTTON to the PRIVY COUNCIL.

[1604].—He is the Mayor of Chester, and submits this petition on behalf of that city. An order was made in the time of the late Queen Elizabeth by the Privy Council concerning the jurisdiction of the Court of Exchequer in Chester and the liberties and franchises of the city. It was registered in the Privy Council Book on April 9, 1574. Petitioner asks that the Council send a directive to the Chamberlain and officers of the Court of Exchequer at Chester that the stipulations of that order be inviolably maintained, respected and observed. He promises a strict compliance with the same on the part of the city.—*Undated.*
½ p. (P. 2006.)
[See *H.M.C. Salisbury MSS*, Vol. XVI, p. 432.]

The DEPUTIES OF GUERNSEY to VISCOUNT CRANBORNE.

[1604].—The state of decay into which the island has fallen is a matter that requires an investigation and a remedy. Petitioners recall the solicitude shown by Lord Burghley for Guernsey, and presuming on Cranborne's own deep concern with the King's service, they enclose a statement [*missing*] on the affairs of the island.—*Undated*.

Endorsed : " 1604." ½ p. (P. 2007.)

CERTAIN INHABITANTS OF SHREWSBURY to VISCOUNT CRANBORNE.

[1604].—They have received privy seals for loans to the King. But inasmuch as Shrewsbury has been for a long time visited by the plague, and petitioners have not only disbursed much money for the relief of the sick and needy, but have suffered losses by the death of artisans and tradespeople who owed them money, they are financially embarrassed at the moment. Sir Francis Newport, the collector of the loan, has already notified Cranborne and other members of the Privy Council of the situation, and the Lord Chancellor is aware of their plight. They ask to be discharged from the privy seals.—*Undated*.

Endorsed : " 1604." ½ p. (P. 2038.)

[See *H.M.C. Salisbury MSS*, Vol. XVI, p. 459.]

ELEAZAR MERCHANT and JOHN BONAMY to VISCOUNT CRANBORNE.

[1604].—They submit this petition on behalf of the inhabitants of Guernsey. Lord Kinloss and Sir John Herbert were appointed to hear the differences between the people of the island, but the Governor, Bailiff and Jurats opine that commissioners should be sent to investigate the dispute. Petitioners ask that Cranborne select men who are known to him for their integrity, to establish the truth of the grievances. They also request that the imputations levelled against them personally by Sir Thomas Leighton be challenged and disproved by petitioners themselves.—*Undated*.

Endorsed : " 1604." 1 p. (P. 2067.)

[See *H.M.C. Salisbury MSS*, Vol. XVI, p. 445.]

LORD DANVERS and SIR JOHN GILBERT.

[1604].—Particulars of Lord Danvers's suits and that of Sir John Gilbert's. They concern the farm of certain fines, amercements, issues and recognizances, and it is declared that the value of Danvers's suits amounts to four times as much as that of Gilbert's.—*Undated*.

¾ p. (P. 2190.)

[See *H.M.C. Salisbury MSS*, Vol. XVI, p. 428.]

CHARLES EGERTON to VISCOUNT CRANBORNE.

[1604].—He served the late Queen Elizabeth as a soldier in Ireland for 43 years. He has disbursed, by official order, much of his own money in repairing the castle of Carrickfergus and adjacent buildings, in paying spies and couriers, in shipping and other transport. These expenses amount to £121, and he has received no allowance for them. In 1601, Cecil and the Privy Council directed the Lord Deputy to defray his expenses and those of two servants during his official period of absence, but this was disallowed by Burchinshaw, the Comptroller of the Musters. He has also suffered from the fall in the value of Irish money. He puts his total losses at £641, and since he has neither post nor salary, he requests a pension for life or some other reward for his lengthy services and expenses.—*Undated.*

Endorsed : " 1604. Cap. Charles Egerton." ½ p. (P. 478.)

HENDRICKE DE WITT to the KING.

[1604].—He and others are owners of a ship called the *Greyhound* of Middelburg and Calais. Some three years ago Cornelius Arrents, master of the ship, was captured at sea by Captain Traughton with his cargo of sugar and brought to London, where the cargo was adjudged to be a prize. Petitioner has sued in the Court of Admiralty for the freight and damages, but sentence has been delayed for three years. He asks that the Judge of the Court be ordered to pronounce sentence and see it carried out " whither yt bee with or against your suppliants "— *Undated.*

½ p. (P. 610.)

[See *H.M.C. Salisbury MSS*, Vol. XIV, p. 198.]

CORRESPONDENCE.

[1604].—A list of names from 1591 to 1604. It is probable that they were the principal correspondents of Sir Robert Cecil during these years, of whose letters and communications he kept a record.—*Undated.*

130 pp. (**243.** 2.)

JOHN CROSBY and GILES MARSTON to VISCOUNT CRANBORNE.

[1604].—They are of the parish of St. Michael's near St. Albans, and have both received a privy seal from the King for the loan of money which they are in no position to make. Not only are they poor, but they are also deeply in debt, as certain J.P.s of Hertfordshire can corroborate. There are others who can well afford to render this service to the King, and they append the names of some of them. Petitioners ask to be discharged from the privy seal.—*Undated.*

At bottom : Richard Dolwyn, Thomas Cogdall, senior, of Abbots Langley, William Hawkyns of Hempsteed, Robert Chambers, parson of Gadsden.

1 p. (P. 730.)

[See *H.M.C. Salisbury MSS*, Vol. XVI, p. 434.]

SURVEY

1604.—A survey of the lands of Viscount Cranborne situated within the county of Hertford. It consists of copies of deeds and evidences relating to the property.

335 pp. (**350.**)

The KING to VISCOUNT CRANBORNE.

[1604].—" My littil beagil, it is now tyme that ye praepare the woodis and parke of Theobaldis for me. Youre pairt thairof will only be to harboure me good staiges, for I know ye mynde to proseyde for no other entertainement for me thaire then as many staigis as I shall kill with my owin hunting. Yett ye have that advantage that I truste so muche to youre nose that quhen I heare you crye it I will hallow to you as freelie as to the deepest mouthid hounde in all the kennell, and since ye have bene so muche used these three monthes past to hunte colde sentis through the drye beaten wayes of London, ye neid not doubte but it will be easie for you to harboure a greate staige amongst the sueit groves about youre house. Only bewaire of drawing too greedilie in the lyame, for ye know how that trykke hath allreddie galled youre nekke. But in earnest I loose all this yeares progress if I beginne not to hunte thaire upon Monedaye come eicht dayes, for the season of the yeare will no more staye upon a King than a poore man, and I doubte if the constable of Castille* hath any powaire in his commission to staye the course of the sunne. Commende me to that other hardill of houndes that have so trewlie borne up the couples with you all this yeare, two of quhome helpit to hunte the spanishe game, but the thirdde lookes lyker one of my wyfes cuntreymen both in culloure and quantitie. I must not also forgette honest Stainhoppe that hath for oure sinnes huntid all this yeare in inferno, that is the lower regions. And so fairwell, and forgette not to drinke my healthe amongst you."—*Undated.*

Holograph. Signed : " James R." *Endorsed :* " Kinges Lre."
1 p. (**134.** 130.)

WILLIAM TIPPER to the KING.

[? 1604].—Many manors and lands granted in tail by the King's predecessors have been concealed to the great loss of the Crown. Petitioner proposes, during the next two years, to discover and recover for the King as many as possible of these lands. He asks to be granted £2000 worth of such estates as he can claim successfully for the Crown at his own expense. He is prepared to pay two years' fine over and above their annual rents, and in return requests leases for 99 years. Petitioner also desires that his suit be referred to the Privy Council, and that the Attorney-General be instructed to draw up a commission for him.—*Undated.*
¾ p. (P. 1879.)
[See *Cal. S.P. Dom.*, 1603–10, p. 331.]

---

* Juan Fernandez de Velasco, Duke of Frias, Constable of Castille, was Spanish Ambassador Extraordinary to England in August–September, 1604.

JOHN LISTER to [? VISCOUNT CRANBORNE].

[? 1604].—He requests to be awarded the bailiwick of Snave and Neats Court, co. Kent, parcel of the Queen's jointure.—*Undated.*

⅓ p. (P. 1040.)

ELLEN McCARTHY to VISCOUNT CRANBORNE.

1604–5, January 26.—She is forced out of sheer necessity to submit her grievances to him, and to request a more liberal allowance from the King. She recently submitted a petition to Cranborne and the Privy Council, and received the answer that they could see no valid reason why she should importune the King any further. She proposes to present yet another petition to justify her request for a decent maintenance, if not for her father's lands, which although surrendered by him to the late Queen Elizabeth, ought to descend to her by a deed of entail made by her grandfather. When this deed was shown to the late Queen, she commanded the Earl of Essex, then Lord Lieutenant of Ireland, to grant an estate of inheritance to petitioner of the lands, but this was not performed because of the Earl's sudden return to England and the disturbances that followed in Munster, and also because of the misdemeanours of her late husband which should not be imputed to her nor serve to neutralize the late Queen's grant. She begs Cranborne to advise her as to the best means of obtaining relief for herself and her four children " although their father be degenerate, and indeed to my extreame greife I speake it, my dishonor and theirs ". He has acted unnaturally towards her and them, and she has hitherto concealed the many injuries they have received from him. But now he is scheming to sell or mortgage the small house and the little land attached to it, which she was allowed to keep by the late Queen, and which belonged to her father. Her husband has no right to this property other than by her title, which is as valid as in the case of the rest of her father's lands granted by the King to Sir Nicholas Browne and Donnell McCarthy. She asks that her husband be prevented from executing this plan and that she be permitted to enjoy her possessions in peace.—This xxvith of January, 1604.

Seal. Endorsed : " 1604. Lady Carty to my lord." 1 p. (P. 2413.)

[See *H.M.C. Salisbury MSS*, Vol. XVII, pp. 40 and 70.]

MORRIS NICHOLAS.

[February 3, 1604–5].—" The examination of Moris Nicholas of Newporte in the county of Monmothe, taken before the right honorable Edwarde, Lorde Zouche, Lord President of the Kinges Ma^{tyes} Councell in the Marches of Wales.

Beinge examined howe he was first made acquainted whye the pursevant was att this tyme sent for him to come befor the Kinges Ma^{tyes} Councell in the Marches of Wales, sayeth that the first speaches that he harde of the occasion of his sending for, he harde the seme of Pears Madoxe the pursevant who was sent for him, and therupon went to Thomas Morgan, Esquier, for a certificate touchinge the seid matter.

He confessethe that it was a fortnight after he harde the words in his former examination layed downe first uttered before he did reveale the same words to any Justice of Peace, bye reasone that the plague beinge then in Newporte, wher this examinate dwellethe, did not dare to goe abroade to anye Justice of Peace.

He confessethe that att suche tyme as John Treherne, vicar of Newporte, did declare unto this examinate that it was William Jones that had spoken the seid words, the seid William Jones came into this examinates howse either presentlye after the seid wordes were uttered or the seme daye, but denyeth that the seid Jones did affirme anye suche wordes.

He confesseth that John Treherne aforenamed did saye that William Jones upon delivery of the seid words sayed that William Wrothe, servant in Mr Morgans howse of Lanternam (but whether he serveth the seid Mr Morgan or his mother in lawe he knoweth not) did speake the seid wordes.

This examinate beinge face to face with William Jones of Abergavenye, (the seid Jones doth affirme that the examinate did deliver the seid wordes unto John Morgan, brother in lawe unto the seid Jones, in the presens of the seid Jones), and sayeth it was the same daye that he had harde the seid wordes that he uttered the seme to the said John Morgan, he the seid John Morgan comminge then towards this honorable Councell, and did then wishe the seid Mr Morgan to advertise the seid Councell therof, and seith that William Jones was then in company of the seid Mr Morgan when he uttered the seid words unto him, which seid Mr Jones hathe sithens given information to the seid Councell.

Moris Nicholas of Newporte beinge agayne examined before the Kinges Ma^tyes Councell in the Marches of Wales touchinge certen wordes delivered unto him by one John Treherne, clarke, vicare of Newporte aforesaid, sayeth that the seid Treherne came into this examinats howse and towlde this examinate that William Wrothe had spoken these words folowinge, that is, that the Kinges Ma^tye was noe kinge of his but that he was more like unto a jugler then a kinge, and did not deliver the seid words before recyted unto this examinate in suche sorte as in his former examination is layed downe, but sayeth that all the reste of his former examination is trewe."—*Undated.*

Endorsed : " 1601 [*sic*] The examination of Moris Nicholas of Newport." 1⅓ pp. **(90. 128.)**

[See *H.M.C. Salisbury MSS*, Vol. XVI, p. 14. Also Vol. XVII, pp. 40, 45, and Vol. XIX, p. 485.]

WILLIAM SAY to VISCOUNT CRANBORNE.

[? After February 6, 1604–5].—For a long time he has followed the Court from place to place, and spent much time and money in trying to establish his right to the office of the keeping of the Council chamber. It was lawfully assigned to him by Alexander Douglas and confirmed by the King's warrant. He is now inclined to yield up the post and his suit for it, and asks that the King bestow on him an extent out of the lands of William Kelling of Hertfordshire, which is an old debt of £30 *per annum* with some years yet to run.—*Undated.*

½ p. (P. 1422.)

[See *Cal. S.P. Dom.*, 1603–10, p. 15, and also pp. 175 and 192.]

NICHOLAS GOODRIDGE.

1604–5, February 7.—Thomas Prestwood and Walter Goodridge submitted a petition to the Master of the Court of Wards concerning the alleged lunacy of Nicholas Goodridge, co. Devon. Since the feodary of that county has certified the Master of the lunacy of the said Goodridge, it is ordered that a commission be issued for the examination of the case.—vii Ffebruarie termino Hillarii Aᵒ 11 domini Jacob R.

Endorsed : " Sir William Strode, Sir George Southcott, Gilbert Yard, esq., John Vowell, esq., Humphrey Were, feodary, Thomas Thompson, esq., or to any 3 of them." ½ p. (P. 2165.)

LORD COBHAM to VISCOUNT CRANBORNE.

1604–5, February 9.—He thanks him for intervening with the King on the matter of the leases. He does not doubt that judgment will be given in the King's favour, and so he must rely on his Majesty's favour which he can only hope to procure through Cecil. As for the validity of the trust, he has performed everything stipulated in his father's will. " It is true the leases wer never mayd over to me, yeat they wer min for so the scope of the secret trust will sheaw, I perfourming the will whi[ch] cannot be denyed. To the king my gratious soverayn I now prostrat my sealf." From the Towr the 9 of Feb, 1604.

Holograph. Seal. Endorsed : " 1604. Lord Cobham to my lord." ½ p. (P. 2443a.)

MARY SLEDD to VISCOUNT CRANBORNE.

[After February 10, 1604–5].—She is the mother of 21 children, and the daughter and sole heiress of Philip Goodman who died two years ago. On the 10th of the present month of February she exhibited a petition to the Privy Council, together with one which she had formerly submitted to the King. These dealt with her complaint against the conspiracy of Thomas Archdale, James Colborne and others to convey and convert the lands, leases, plate and other estate of her late father to their own uses, in order to deny Goodman's creditors their lawful debts and deprive petitioner of her rightful portion of her father's estate. She asks that Sir Anthony Ashley produce the two petitions to be read and referred to Sir Edward Coke, the Attorney-General.—*Undated.*

Damaged. ⅓ p. (P. 793.)

EDMOND DOYNE to VISCOUNT CRANBORNE.

[After February 11, 1604–5].—He is in the service of Sir Christopher St. Lawrence. Five weeks ago he submitted a petition on behalf of his master to Cranborne and the Privy Council, but cannot as yet procure it to be read by them. He asks Cranborne to use his influence that the petition may be read and answered, particularly as the Earl of Devonshire is ready to give his support to that effect.—*Undated.*

½ p. (P. 922)

[See *Cal. S.P. Ireland*, 1603–7, p. 252.]

LORD COBHAM to VISCOUNT CRANBORNE.

1604–5, February 12.—He has spoken this morning to Sir John Leveson, " who hath acquainted me what the effect of the interrogatories wer that hee was swrone [*sic*] unto. His answer in substans was this, that the leases wer min and so now the kings ". He begs Cranborne to have him in his thoughts since there is no other who will do so, " for otherwis I am not ignorant how my fortun stands and what wold becom of me ".—From the Toure 12 of Feb. 1604.

Holograph. Seal. Endorsed : " 1604. Lord Cobham to my lord." ⅓ p. (P. 2443.)

SIR JOHN FORTESCUE to VISCOUNT CRANBORNE.

1604–5, February 12.—He has been informed by a servant of his, Gabriel Mathew, who was farmer of a part of the Queen's jointure within the manor of Hanslop, that it is proposed to pass the same in reversion to certain of the Queen's servants. He asks that Mathew be preferred before all others, since his father, grandfather and other ancestors of his have been tenants of the property for one hundred years, and the farm represents his whole estate. Mathew is ready to pay whatever money is thought reasonable either to the Queen or to those to whom the grant of reversion has been made.—At my howse at Westminster this xii of February, 1604.

Holograph. Endorsed : " Sir John Fortescu to my lord, 12 Febr. 1604." 1 p. (P. 2411.)

ABIGAIL SMITH to the KING.

[After February 14, 1604–5].—She is the wife of Robert Smith, who has been imprisoned for presenting a petition justifying his nonconformity, and deprived of his benefice,* although he has publicly acknowledged his readiness to conform to everything which can be demanded of him by law. He is also prepared to yield further if the things required of him are agreeable to Holy Scriptures, according to the Royal proclamation, or his reasons to the contrary sufficiently answered. She requests that

---

* He was deprived of his benefice on or shortly before February 14, 1604–5. [See C. H. Cooper *Athenae Cantabrigienses*, Vol. 11, p. 479, and *H.M.C. Salisbury MSS*, Vol. XVII, p. 641.]

since " by the great charter of England none ys to be disseised of his freehold (of which nature his benefice is) but by the lawe of the land ", her husband be allowed to enjoy his benefice until such time as he shall be evicted by due course of law.—*Undated.*

1 p. (P. 444.)

SIR EDWARD PITT and WILLIAM SMALLMAN to VISCOUNT CRANBORNE.

[Before February 16, 1604–5].—The site and demesne of Ivington, co. Hereford, was conveyed by the late Queen Mary to Sir Henry Jernyngham, whose heir made a lease of the same of which there are some years yet to run. It was purchased by Smallman who sold the reversion to Sir Edward Pitt. Mr Tipper now alleges that the title is defective, and although petitioners' counsel is not of that opinion, they prefer " for quietnes " to compound. Moreover the manor has been conveyed to the Queen as part of her jointure, and although the site and demesne are not part of the property so conveyed, petitioners will be obliged to pay a double charge for a settled composition. They ask that Cranborne be informed of the true state of affairs by the Queen's Attorney-General, and that he intervene on their behalf for a favourable composition both with the King and Queen.—*Undated.*

¾ p. (P. 1371.)

[See *H.M.C. Salisbury MSS*, Vol. XVII, p. 58.]

WILLIAM TOOKER to the KING.

[After February 16, 1604–5].—If it is the King's pleasure that he relinquish an archdeaconry whose value is £40 a year, £10 more than that of the deanery that has been bestowed upon him,* he will submit and do so. But he points out that the late Queen Elizabeth and the King himself preferred many without taking anything away from them. For example, Dr King who was appointed Dean of Oxford and still remained an archdeacon. As for Mr Buckeridge, he is already Archdeacon of Northampton, and if he should get petitioner's archdeaconry he would be much more advanced than petitioner who has waited there twenty years.—*Undated.*

1 p. (P. 1296.)

PATRICK TIPPER to the KING.

[1604–5, February 17].—He refers to his recent petition in which he prayed that the government of Ireland should be entrusted to the Duke of York as Vice-Gerent there. He now begs that his presumption should be forgiven, and enumerates the reasons which had impelled him to venture such a proposition. Firstly, the cause of the wars and disorders in Ireland reside in the misgovernment of the English and the discontent of the

---

* Tooker was appointed Dean of Lichfield on February 16, 1605, and resigned his archdeaconry of Barnstaple. [See *D.N.B.* Vol. LVII, p. 52.]

Irish gentry who have been excluded from office, and thereby deprived of the opportunity of establishing a stable and generally accepted administration. Secondly, many members of the Council in Ireland are not only English but military men, who have delegated their authority to inferior officers. These, in turn, have committed violence and outrages with impunity, and no redress can be expected from their military superiors. Thirdly, lands bestowed as a gift by the late Queen Elizabeth have been invariably sold and the money conveyed out of Ireland, to the consequent impoverishment of that country. This deliberate violation of the ordinance against transportation of coin to England still continues. Fourthly, Judges and Justices in Ireland are Englishmen and ignorant of the Irish language, and often fail to understand what is said by the prisoners arraigned before them. Consequently they are forced to employ interpreters, a system which is open to abuse and errors.

In view of these facts, petitioner submits the following proposals to be considered by the King. Firstly, that Charles, Duke of York, should have the regency of Ireland, and an Irishman of distinction and undoubted loyalty should be appointed his deputy, as was the Earl of Kildare to the natural son of Henry VIII* and to John after Henry II. Secondly, that the Irish gentry, who are well versed in Irish and English, should be appointed to judicial offices in Ireland, as well as to other positions of responsibility, " it being a matter in policie that every nation is best governed by their own people ". Thirdly, that the military men should be withdrawn, and so relieve the financial burden on Ireland and England. Fourthly, that the Irish gentry who have been and still are students in England, and have the requisite qualifications for legal employment, should be appointed and preferred to those posts which have been denied them hitherto.

The adoption of these proposals would lead to a stable and prosperous Ireland, and the King's own revenues would be augmented to £10,000 annually.

Note by Sir Julius Caesar : " At Court at Whitehall, 17 Feb. 1604. This petition is referred to the consideration and annswer of the Lords of his Ma^ts most honorable privie Counsell."

Endorsed : " To the Kinges most Excellent Matie. [? February] 1605. The humble petition of Patrick Tipper.

That havinge attended here to his verie great charge for fyve months space in the prosecution of a suite to your Highnes in the behalfe of his poore contry of Ireland, tending to the generall good of that kingdome and the encrease and advancement of your Ma^ts revenues there, the substance of which is described in the articles here enclosed : and now wanting meanes to continue the prosecution thereof anie longer, he humblie beseecheth your Highnes gratiouslie to consider of his good intention proceeding from a loyall dutie to doe your Matie and his countrey service. And that your Highnes would bee pleased to grant a Commission

---

* The Duke of Richmond.

to the nobility of Ireland to examine and certifie your Matie their opinions touching the said article or otherwise to signifie your Ma^ts direct answer therein as may best stand with your Ma^ts gratious pleasure in that behalfe."

1 p. (P. 284.)

PATRICK TIPPER to the KING.

[After February 17, 1604–5].—He refers to two previous petitions concerning the state of Ireland, to which he has received no reply. His expenses in sojourning in London while awaiting the King's answer are exceeding his means. He requests either a private audience to discuss the matter with the King, or that it be referred to any " specyall " person approved of by the King that he may report on it. In the meantime, he solicits an allowance towards defraying his costs.—*Undated.*

½ p. (P. 1875.) *See* P. 284 *supra.*

WILLIAM CURLE to VISCOUNT CRANBORNE.

1604–5, February 28.—He sends him an account of the receipts of the court as requested by Cranborne. Discusses other matters of financial interest.—Aldersgate Streate, this xxviiith of Ffebruarie, 1604.

Holograph. Endorsed : " Auditor Tuck." ½ p. (P. 2195.)

WILLIAM WALSH to the KING.

[1604–5, February].—He refers to his services on behalf of the late Queen Elizabeth, and to the losses sustained by him during the wars in Ireland. He has been a suitor for relief in London for the past eighteen months, and he and his family are now in dire distress. He requests that, as a professional soldier, he be granted a passport to serve beyond the seas, and to take with him as many Irish volunteers as he can recruit. He asks also for financial assistance to further this scheme.—*Undated.*

Note by Sir Julius Caesar : " At the Court at Whitehall, ye —— of Ffeb, 1604. His Matie hathe referred the consideration and answeringe of this petition to the L. Viscount Cranborne."

½ p. (P. 447.)

ERASMUS DRYDEN to the PRIVY COUNCIL.

[? February, 1604–5].—He protests his sincerity in gathering signatures for a petition to the King. He has heard that the Council and the Judges have " sentenced it to be against the lawes to gather handes in favour of persons refusinge conformity ", and expresses deep regret for having transgressed in this manner, and thus offended the King, the Council and the law. He hopes that this testimony, and the fact that he has suffered greater length of imprisonment than any other knight or gentleman implicated in the same affair, will satisfy the Council and convince its members of his integrity and affection to the King.—*Undated.*

1 p. (P. 57.)

[See *Cal. S.P. Dom.*, 1603–10., p. 200, and *H.M.C. Salisbury MSS*, Vol. XVII, pp 70 and 73.]

ROBERT BULLEN to GEORGE CALVERT.

1604–5, March 6.—He requests that the bearer be permitted to ask Calvert for his assistance in effecting the grant of the bailiwick of the Honour of Clare, which has been awarded to him. The bearer will pay all due fees, as well as the 26/8 which petitioner left with Calvert to hand to the auditor as his fee.—Bale, this vi March, 1605.

¼ p.   (P. 1928.)

RALPH EWENS to VISCOUNT CRANBORNE.

1604–5, March 10.—Sir John Bowyer of Sydway Lane, co. Staffs., has died, and William Bowyer, his heir, is only 16 years of age.   The estate is held *in capite*, and is worth £500 a year. Sir John was M.P. for Newcastle-under-Lyme in the last Parliamentary session, and was formerly of Gray's Inn, " a professor of the laws ".   Petitioner is ready to establish the King's title at his own expense, and asks to be granted the wardship of the son and heir.—10 March, 1604.

Seal. ½ p.   (P. 1930.)

HANNIBAL VIVIAN to VISCOUNT CRANBORNE.

1604–5, March 19.—Mr Chamley has obtained from Cranborne the presentation of Clare which was surrendered by Mr Bodley, but is one of the livings of Tiverton church in the possession of Vivian's cousin Trelawney, a King's ward. The presentation belongs to his cousin Courtenay and himself as descendants of the eldest sister.   On the basis of that right they presented two other livings to which Sir Jonathan Trelawney objected and took legal action against them, but the verdict was returned in their favour. Vivian will not proceed against Chamley without Cranborne's permission, although he deserves little consideration since he was well aware of the rights of Vivian and Courtenay in this matter, and had received a promise to be heard if he could persuade Bodley to surrender the living.—Trelawaren, the 19th of March, 1604–5.

Holograph. Seal. ⅓ p.   (P. 2169.)

[See *H.M.C. Salisbury MSS*, Vol. XVII, p. 155.]

ERASMUS COOKE to the PRIVY COUNCIL.

[*c.* March, 1604–5].—He is a prisoner in the Gatehouse, where he was committed for a certain " indiscreet action ".   He acknowledges his error and expresses his unbounded regret for having affronted the Council.   He begs to be given his liberty.—*Undated.*

½ p.   (P. 1713.)

[See *H.M.C. Salisbury MSS*, Vol. XVII, pp. 98 and 107.]

LEWIS PICKERING to the KING.

[? March, 1604–5].—" There is a fragment of poesie latelie come to light, the circumstances whereof being well considered might bring soe much proffitte unto others as it hath done shame to me." He apologizes for his indiscretion, confesses that he has had a fair trial, and hopes that his sincere contrition will earn him a pardon since his offence proceeded " rather from a hatred of the dumbe ministers, non-residents and maintayned by his authoritie, then from any mallice to his person or contempte of his place ". He hopes his long imprisonment will be regarded as sufficient punishment for his offence, especially as he never intended to say anything defamatory of the King or the late Queen Elizabeth. " For the matter of Bywater, I protest my owne innocencye saving the reading of his booke after it was delivered. I have put my shoulder to the wheele of your Ma^{ts} fortunes, and wold be sorrie that my service, having prospered in the blade and shott up in the stalke, should nowe become blasted in the eare." He asks to be given his freedom and spared the fine, and is prepared to give every possible assurance of loyalty.— *Undated.*

Damaged. Endorsed : " 1605. The humble petition of Lewis Pickering." 1 p. (P. 502.)
[See *Cal. S.P. Dom.*, 1603–10, p. 206, and *H.M.C. Salisbury MSS*, Vols. XVII and XVIII, under Pickering.]

The COUNTESS OF DERBY to VISCOUNT CRANBORNE.

1605, April 1.—She refers to the financial agreement between her and the Earl of Derby, and to the fact that the Lordship of Hawarden is hers by the concurrence and assignment of the Earl. Nevertheless, he has presented the parsonage of Hawarden to one Rankyns, and nominated Mr Davenant to the living upon the death of the late incumbent. Petitioner wishes to preserve the most amicable relations with the Earl, but is desirous of exercising her undoubted right of chosing the incumbent. She asks Cranborne to draw the Earl's attention to this, and to remind him of other privileges which she has allowed him to exercise by the same agreement.—York House, this first of April, 1605.
Seal. Endorsed : " 1 Ap. 1605. Countesse of Derby to my lord." 1 p. (P. 1964.)

PAUL BAYN to VISCOUNT CRANBORNE.

[? After April 10, 1605].—He writes to him again to request his favour in the matter which he has already brought to his notice.—*Undated.*
¼ p. (P. 28.)
[See *Cal. S.P. Dom.*, 1603–10, p. 211, and *H.M.C. Salisbury MSS*, Vol. XVII, p. 287.]

PAUL BAYN to [VISCOUNT CRANBORNE].

[? After April 10, 1605].—" My appearance is the poore leapers return who when he was clensed came to give thanks." He expresses his gratitude for the favour shown to him and make one further request, " that whcras I have lived hithertoe unsuspected of turbulencie, it would please your Lordship graunt your letters to our Chancellor that my questioning here may not prejudice me there ".—*Undated.*

½ p. (P. 1265.) *See* P. 28 *supra.* p. 205.

SIR ALEXANDER TULL, EDMUND PYKE,
MARMADUKE JENNINGS, JOHN LAVER and
WILLIAM OWSLEY to VISCOUNT CRANBORNE.

[*c.* April 16, 1605].—They are the executors of the last will and testament of the late William Sandes, and have been entrusted with the care and education of the deceased's eldest son Emanuel, " a very weeke and sickly infant of the age of eleaven yeares ", and the other children. At an inquisition held after the death of their father, one Robert Westcourt claimed on oath, without any evidence to support him, that 65 years ago five acres of the deceased man's land were parcel of the manor of Southpetherton and held of the King *in capite.* On the sole basis of this testimony Emanuel was declared to be a King's ward. Petitioners, knowing Westcourt's allegations to be false, have entered a formal denial in the Court of Wards where they intend to prosecute the matter. In respect of the physical debility of Emanuel and the dependence of his sister on a part of his estate (a farm held of the Earl of Hertford) for her portion, and the fact that he is now being taken care of by his grandmother, petitioners ask that nothing be done to change the present arrangements as regards ward and property until the case has been heard and determined. If they lose it, they will surrender Emanuel and his lands, and pay such legal costs as may be awarded against them.—*Undated.*

¾ p. (P. 1528.)

[See *PRO. Wards* **7,** 37/81.]

TIMOTHY SMYTH to VISCOUNT CRANBORNE.

1605, April 29.—Three years ago, the Court of Wards awarded him possession of the person and property of Thomas Crump, which had been detained by Edward Marsh and his wife, Margaret. Upon a further petition to Cranborne, the Attorney of the Court of Wards called both parties before him and made an award between them. Upon certain complaints that neither had respected the award, Cranborne had directed Sir Thomas Bigge and others to determine the issue, but they too had failed. Petitioner has again been summoned to perform the award, but circumstances make it difficult for him to comply. He requests that he be permitted to enjoy the lands granted to him in the first place by Cranborne.—April 29, 1605.

Note by Cranborne : " Let Mr Surveior and Mr Atturney heare this petitioner and certify me if they can not end it."

On reverse : a detailed account of the proceedings between the parties and the termination of the dispute by mediation. *Signed by :* Cuthbert Pepper.

2 pp. (P. 24.)

Attached

THOMAS BIGE and FRANCIS DINGLYE to VISCOUNT CRANBORNE.

1603–4, January 13.—In accordance with his letters concerning the case between Edward and Margaret Marsh and Timothy Smyth, they have summoned both parties before them and examined all the Court of Ward's orders relating to the case. They blame Marsh for not implementing the order made by Sir Thomas Hesketh, Attorney of the said Court, and for his perverseness in refusing to collaborate to put an end to the dispute.—January 13, 1603–4.

¾ p. (P. 24a.)

JOHN BOWSSAR to the PRIVY COUNCIL.

[After May 1, 1605].—Sir John Swinnerton, his brother-in-law, who owes him money, has dealt most unjustly with him and refuses to make amends although petitioner has appealed to him through the mediation of Swinnerton's father and the Lord Mayor of London. Finally he asked the Lord Chancellor for letters directing certain Aldermen to determine the dispute between them. The Lord Chancellor showed petitioner's suit to Swinnerton so that the latter might show cause why it should not be granted. But Swinnerton ignored the whole matter and, accordingly, the Lord Chancellor granted petitioner's request. Swinnerton has arrogantly reacted by imprisoning petitioner's surety. Petitioner declares that he has lost £8000 within the last few years, and asks that the Council grant letters to the same effect as those issued by the Lord Chancellor, and that his surety be released upon bail by a *supersedeas* from the Lord Treasurer. —*Undated.*

¾ p. (P. 1375.)

[See *H.M.C. Salisbury MSS* Vol. XVII, p. 168.]

NICHOLAS GEFFE to VISCOUNT CRANBORNE and LORD HUME.

[Before May 4, 1605].*—He had been able to render William Tipper some service as regards the amendment of defective titles and money issuing out of the same, without which Tipper would not have been able to perform those services to the late Queen Elizabeth which he claimed to have done. It was agreed between them that petitioner should receive a third part of such sums of money as were allowed to Tipper and Sir Edward Dyer for their labours. In the time of the late Queen they were paid £5000, of which a third part should have come to petitioner. He actually received only £66:13:4, so that some £1593 or so is still due to him. He requests that Tipper and Dyer be ordered to discharge

---

* Robert Cecil, Viscount Cranborne, was created Earl of Salisbury on May 4, 1605.

their debts to him. Tipper and petitioner had also become bound to one Samuel Hales, now deceased, for £300 which was being claimed by a Mrs Barnard as executrix to Hales. He asks that Tipper and Dyer be directed to discharge this debt in default of their payment to him. He refers to his proceedings in Chancery against them which became void with the death of the late Queen. He has again renewed his suit in that court, but both Tipper and Dyer have declined to answer his charge.
—*Undated*.
1 p. (P. 122.)

RICHARD SHUTE to [VISCOUNT CRANBORNE].

[Before May 4, 1605].—Because of the debt of Mr Sherard, Deputy-Feodary, he has been deprived of his post and livelihood as Feodary, and summoned to pay £100. He protests that he has not the means to pay such a sum, and adds that Sherard, although he denied it on oath, confessed later in an examination that he had the money. Petitioner asks that Sherard be forced to repay the debt, or that he himself be restored to his office. Cranborne's brother, Lord Burghley,* has expressed his wish that such a favour be extended to petitioner.—*Undated*.
¾ p. (P. 1270.)

EDWARD FORREST and JAMES SPENCER to the PRIVY COUNCIL.

[Before May 4, 1605].—They are prisoners in the Marshalsea, and complain that while they were passing Sir George Carey's† house, they were assaulted by a group of his followers. One of the latter named Rotheram, who is a prisoner charged with fraudulent dealing with the King's accounts, injured Spencer in the side and detained him in a house until a messenger arrived with a warrant for the appearance of petitioners before the Privy Council. Petitioners obeyed it and were by another warrant committed to the Marshalsea. They request that they be allowed to answer any charge brought against them. Because of their poor estate any detention will interfere with and delay their proceedings in the Irish business, which will also redound to the King's disadvantage.—*Undated*.
½ p. (P. 1236.)
[See *H.M.C. Salisbury MSS*, Vol. XVII, pp. 524 and 625.]

ENGLISH MERCHANTS to the PRIVY COUNCIL.

[? Before May 4, 1605].—They are merchants of western England trading with France, and refer to the recent edict of the King of France prohibiting the entry of all cloth from England into France except such " as were good and should not shrink ". In compliance with this edict, petitioners bought the best kerseys in Devonshire that were manufactured according to English law and as conformable as possible to the French King's edict. How-

---

* Thomas Cecil, Lord Burghley, was created Earl of Exeter on May 4, 1605.
† Created Baron Carew of Clopton on May 4, 1605.

ever the French, " uppon purpose as it should seeme to banishe our trading from thence " have recently seized certain kerseys at Rouen, sent there by petitioners, on the grounds that they were found defective upon trial. Petitioners claim that in the opinion of the most experienced clothiers of the region kerseys cannot be made to meet all the requirements laid down in the edict, and, apart from the loss of their goods, the threat of a complete suspension of trade endangers the livelihood of thousands of people. They ask that letters be sent to the King of France and to the English Ambassador in Paris in favour of a mitigation of the edict, and for the release of petitioners' goods ; also that the French Ambassador in London be approached to intervene to the same purpose.—*Undated.*

1 p. (P. 1433.)

[See *H.M.C. Salisbury MSS* Vol. XVII, pp. 180–1.]

HENRY CAREW to VISCOUNT CRANBORNE.

[Before May 4, 1605].—Two years ago petitioner was sentenced by the Court of the Star Chamber to be imprisoned in the Fleet. Upon appeal he was released, but later was committed for the second time to the same prison. He would in all dutifulness have gone there but for the uncivil treatment to which he was subjected on the first occasion by the warden. He insists that his absence should not be imputed to him as an act of contempt: and is ready to submit to Cranborne. He reminds him that he gave a favourable account of petitioner's offence to the King, and declares that it was not done out of malice, but rather out of indiscretion. He asks Cranborne to intercede on his behalf with the King for clemency.—*Undated.*

$\frac{3}{4}$ p. (P. 648.)

[See *H.M.C. Salisbury MSS*, Vol. XV, p. 209.]

[? CARDMAKERS] to VISCOUNT CRANBORNE.

[Before May 4, 1605].—They express their gratitude for his past favours to them. They understand that their case is to be heard by the Chief Justices, and pray that this may be done with expedition since the Judges are about to go on circuit. The objections of their opponents, the merchants, are three : that the King's Customs will suffer ; that the seizure of English cloth in France can be attributed to the cardmakers ; and that the statute is not valid. Petitioners' answer to these objections is, " that for the Custome we will stande bound with good securitie to pay double so much to his Matie as hath bene paid for cards theis xxvi^{tie} last yeares, which sithence it is for the releefe of so many his Ma^{ts} poore subjects, who thereby shalbe made able to live and pay tax and subsidie, and doe his highnes other service, we hope your Lordship will favorably consider thereof. For the cloth, it is well knowne that our suite is no cause of stay of it, but the bad and deceiptfull makinge of it, as beinge neither of Assize nor goodnes according to the edict there, neither is it likely that the Ffrenche kinge will forbeare or loose so great somes of money as he receaveth yearely by our cloth, which is a hundred tymes as much as he or his subjects can or shall receave by cards if they were all made and brought out of Ffraunce." As for the statute, petitioners submit themselves to the opinion of the judges.—*Undated.*

1 p.   (P. 2107.)

THOMAS GOUGH to VISCOUNT CRANBORNE.

[Before May 4, 1605].—He is of Newbury, co. Berks. The town has been bestowed upon the Queen as part of her jointure, and a bailiff is now due to be appointed with the fee of 6/8 *per annum*. He asks to be considered for the office, and also that he be paid £4 a year by the farmer of the pickage in Newbury for gathering the same. All former bailiffs have received that remuneration for this service in the past.—*Undated.*

Note by Cranborne : " Let a warrant be made."

1 p.   (P. 1650.)

GEOFFREY HOLCROFT to VISCOUNT CRANBORNE.

[Before May 4, 1605].—Together with his late brother, Captain Henry Holcroft, deceased, he served in the Low Countries in the time of the late Queen Elizabeth. After his brother's death* he was sent in command of a company to Ireland, but was shortly afterwards relieved of his company and given a pension, which has now been withdrawn by the King. He has no alternative but to petition for assistance. He reminds Cranborne that his (petitioner's) father was much indebted to Lord Burghley, and asks that he favour his petition when it comes up for discussion at the Council table.—*Undated.*

½ p.   (P. 1435.)

WILLIAM PARNELL to VISCOUNT CRANBORNE.

[Before May 4, 1605].—He is of Waltham Abbey and has leased the mills of Waltham from Lord Denny. He has disbursed more than £500 in buying the lease, of which there are still 12 or 13 years to run, and in repairing the mills, and for the last seven years he has received the profits issuing from the mills without any hindrance. However, one Daunt, Lord Denny's servant, and others suggested to Lord Denny that he could lawfully withhold from petitioner one commodity of the lease to the value of £80. Lord Denny has now seized it, but continues to demand the old rent of £100 annually. Petitioner has appealed to him either to let him enjoy the whole of his lease or to abate his rent by £80, but both requests have been rejected. Moreover, Lord Denny with twenty armed men has tried to evict petitioner, and besieged him and his family in his house for almost three weeks night and day in order to starve him into submission. Having failed to do so, he sued petitioner in a court of law where

* Killed at the siege of Ostend.

the case was tried by Sir Francis Gawdy. An attempt was made to effect a compromise outside the court, and petitioner agreed that Lord Denny's counsel, Sir Thomas Foster, should determine the matter. Lord Denny again refused to co-operate, and to show his displeasure, dammed the river, levelled its banks and left the mills dry, as they still are. Petitioner asks that the case be determined by such competent persons as Cranborne shall select to examine it.—*Undated.*

¾ p. (P. 1434.)

WILLIAM FISHER to VISCOUNT CRANBORNE.

[Before May 4, 1605].—For forty years he served in one of the late Queen Elizabeth's auditors offices, and performed his duties honestly during the whole of that period. But in more recent years he was sentenced in the Exchequer Chamber, on the grounds of a particular offence, to imprisonment in the Fleet and the payment of a fine. He has also had to pay his accuser, John Lawe, the sum of £70 and, by other orders from the Exchequer, he has been deprived of his goods and lands, even those properties which he has sold. Now, in his 65th year, he has little to maintain his family. Upon his accession to the throne the King proclaimed a general pardon for past offences with remission of penalties. Petitioner asks that Cranborne intervene to stay all proceedings against him, and award him the fullest possible benefit of the pardon.—*Undated.*

1 p. (P. 1376.)

MARY BUTLER to VISCOUNT CRANBORNE.

[Before May 4, 1605].—She has been imprisoned for 7 days, and her husband for 3 weeks, in the Gatehouse. They reside 80 miles from London, and have four children, three of whom are ill and the fourth a mere infant. She begs that her husband be released to accompany her home to take care of the children, and that she be given some financial help to pay her expenses and succour the children.—*Undated.*

1 p. (P. 796.)

NICHOLAS FREEMAN to VISCOUNT CRANBORNE.

[Before May 4, 1605].—The Duke and Duchess of Holsted (Holstein) have written on his behalf to the King and Queen concerning the recovery of his goods and the debts due to him in England without being harassed by his creditors. He cannot satisfy the latter unless his goods are restored to him, since all his estate is in the hands of his debtors. He asks to be accorded such favour as their Majesties are accustomed to give to the requests of their princely allies.—*Undated.*

½ p. (P. 973.)

DAME ANNE DELVES to VISCOUNT CRANBORNE.

[Before May 4, 1605].—She is the widow of Sir George Delves, deceased. She asks for the continuance of the favour extended to her husband by Cranborne. When the King was last at Cobham, Sir George submitted a petition to him, and the King bestowed some compensation upon him for the loss of his pensioner's place at the time of the accession. Petitioner requests that Cranborne favour her suit to the King.—*Undated*.

½ p. (P. 1878.)

JARRET STORIE to VISCOUNT CRANBORNE.

[Before May 4, 1605].—He served the late Queen Elizabeth for 44 years as one of the garrison at Berwick, and saw service on the borders and in Ireland, besides acting as courier into Scotland in highly dangerous times as Mr Nicholson, the late agent, has testified to Cranborne. During the past year, petitioner has been a suitor to the King who has referred his case to Sir John Stanhope. The latter has recommended that he should be rewarded for his services. Petitioner requests that Cranborne take steps to see that his petition is read and considered by the Privy Council.—*Undated*.

½ p. (P. 1351.)
[See *H.M.C. Salisbury MSS*, Vol. XVI, p. 139.]

DANIELL MULLER to VISCOUNT CRANBORNE.

[Before May 4, 1605].—He was invited out of Germany, his native country, by the late Lord Willoughby, Governor of the garrison of Berwick, to attend upon him as his doctor, and performed his medical duties faithfully. Despite many promises of promotion, all he received from Lord Willoughby was the post of doctor of the garrison with an annual fee of £50. Following upon the disbandment of the garrison, this salary has been taken away from him, and with it his sole means of livelihood. Since the King has been pleased to award pensions to former members of that garrison, he asks Cranborne to intervene that he may either be given his former annuity or some equivalent pension.—*Undated*.

½ p. (P. 1350.)

EDWARD MIDDAIE to VISCOUNT CRANBORNE.

[Before May 4, 1605].—He is at present in the custody of Bennet Bloomfield, to whom he was committed twenty days ago by warrant from the King, upon misinformation provided by one Butler who is known by all, including Cranborne, to be "a verie bad and lewde fellow ". Petitioner is weak and sickly, and asks to be released on bail. He offers sureties to appear to answer what ever charge is brought against him.—*Undated*.

½ p. (P. 1224.)

ARTHUR HALL to VISCOUNT CRANBORNE.

[Before May 4, 1605].—It has been slanderously spread abroad at Court and amongst the members of the Privy Council and legal circles that he has been imprisoned because of a deliberate intention not to pay his debts. Petitioner states that since his committal to the Fleet almost four years ago, he has discharged his liabilities to the amount of £6000. He still owes money to Edward Sherland, but certain judges and commissioners appointed by the King to examine the case have concluded that Sherland should be paid £200 and no more. The Lord Chancellor has approved of this decision and petitioner is ready to pay it.— *Undated.*

¾ p. (P. 1222.)

WILLIAM HARVEY to VISCOUNT CRANBORNE.

[Before May 4, 1605].—He is a prisoner in the Marshalsea, and has been detained there a long time at the suit of Anthony Moore, a Frenchman. Petitioner has agreed with Moore to pay him £450 and so be discharged from all liabilities and court actions. Moore has now refused to abide by the terms of the agreement, and is seeking ways and means of seizing petitioner's goods and property. Moore has also informed him that Cranborne is aware of his proceedings and has promised his assistance. Petitioner asks that Moore be obliged to comply with the terms of the original agreement which he himself had initiated. —*Undated.*

1 p. (P. 1079.)

JAMES HINSHAW to VISCOUNT CRANBORNE.

[Before May 4, 1605].—He was formerly a soldier serving under the command of Captain Aucher. He was stationed on the borders of Scotland in the reign of the late Queen Elizabeth, and in that of the King up to May 27th last when he received his discharge without any relief for the maintenance of himself and his family. Since then he has petitioned to be rewarded for his service at Berwick, and his suit has been supported by the Lord Chamberlain and Lord Wotton. He asks Cranborne to find him some employment at Carlisle under Sir Henry Leigh or elsewhere upon the border.—*Undated.*

½ p. (P. 1052.)

JOHN BERWYS to VISCOUNT CRANBORNE.

[Before May 4, 1605].—He is a yeoman of Dryholme in the county of Northumberland (? Cumberland). In the reign of the late Queen Elizabeth, he was unfortunate enough to kill Richard Chambers. He was tried at the Assizes in Carlisle, convicted on unjust evidence and condemned to death. Yet at the coroner's inquest, a verdict of manslaughter only was returned. At the entry of the King into England he was granted his protection for life, but Cranborne refused to pass it at the privy seal, on the grounds that he wished to arrive at the truth of the case. In the meantime, petitioner has paid a great deal of money to the family of the dead man, but a particularly malicious person is threatening to subject him to the extreme penalty of the law. He asks

Cranborne, in view of the King's former warrant, to grant another for drawing up his pardon.—*Undated*.

½ p.   (P. 987.)

WILLIAM GOWER to VISCOUNT CRANBORNE.

[Before May 4, 1605].—He served as a soldier under Captain Reede at Berwick, and saw service on the borders of Scotland. On May 27th last, he was discharged, but nothing was done to arrange for him to receive some relief after his long period of service. He begs Cranborne to obtain employment for him under Sir Henry Leigh at Carlisle or elsewhere that will enable him to support his wife and family.—*Undated*.

½ p.   (P. 657.)

JOHN REDDISH to VISCOUNT CRANBORNE.

[Before May 4, 1605].—He is resident at Stockport, Cheshire, and complains that Robert Hardman, a mercer, was indebted to certain Londoners for £300 some two years ago, and with the connivance of his brother George persuaded petitioner to sign a bond with them for the payment of the debt. Contrary to his promise George Hardman refused to join in the bond and conspired with Robert to get possession of the stock and estate belonging to the latter which would have sufficed to discharge the debt. The brothers also intended to flee the county and leave petitioner exposed to the pressure of the creditors. But he issued a writ against Robert Hardman out of the Exchequer Court at Chester and arrested him in Stockport. However, he was forcibly rescued from the bailiff and conveyed out of Chester to the town of Lancaster. Petitioner appeals to the Privy Council to order the two brothers and those who rescued Robert to appear before them and answer for the wrongs and outrages committed by them.—*Undated*.

Endorsed : "The humble petition of John Rediche of Stockporte in the countie of Chester." ¾ p.   (P. 617.)

THOMAS KNOWLES and OLIVER SMITHSON to VISCOUNT CRANBORNE.

[Before May 4, 1605].—Since their youth they have been employed in the service of the late Queen Elizabeth and now of King James, and have never received more than their ordinary wages. They have heard that £168 of debts have been concealed from the Crown for the past eighteen years, and they propose to petition the King to grant them the money which they will recover at their own charges. They beg Cranborne to further their suit.—*Undated*.

½ p.   (P. 456.)

DONAGH CLANCY to VISCOUNT CRANBORNE.

[Before May 4, 1605].—He is of Robertstown in the county of Limerick. At his request Cranborne and the Privy Council sent letters to the Lord President of Munster that petitioner should receive justice in the matter of the recovery of Robertstown and other lands wrongfully detained from him by Richard Wingfield. He has revealed his claim to John Meade, his counsel, who advised him to expedite the recovery of the property by making out that the King had a claim to them, and by arranging a composition whereby they would be included in a grant of concealed lands to the Earl of Thomond, who would then assign them to petitioner. But Meade intends to sell the premises to petitioner's adversary, and persuade the Earl not to assign the lands to petitioner as promised. Petitioner therefore requests that the Lord Deputy of Ireland be ordered to stay the inclusion in the Earl of Thomond's letters patent of the lands in dispute, and that the Lord President of Munster be directed to examine the whole matter and to see that petitioner obtains justice in it.—*Undated.*

1 p. (P. 923.)

MICHAEL WENTWORTH to VISCOUNT CRANBORNE.

[Before May 4, 1605].—He is of Woolley, co. Yorks, and has always conformed to the established church. But four years ago he was forced to enter into a bond for the payment of £180, at the rate of £20 monthly, because his wife refused to attend divine service. He has already paid £80 and is now submitting a petition to the Privy Council that the rest of the fine be remitted. —*Undated.*

½ p. (P. 1372.)

HUMPHREY TUCKIE and EDWARD ERBY to VISCOUNT CRANBORNE.

[Before May 4, 1605].—They are citizens of London, to whom various sums of money are owing by the King, following upon the transfer by them of funds to the Treasurer at Wars in Ireland. These sums have been kept from petitioners almost three years, and has resulted in loss of trade and credit for them. They ask that they be repaid the money in order to discharge their debts and avoid the danger of being imprisoned by their creditors.— *Undated.*

1 p. (P. 1421.)

ROBERT TISONE to VISCOUNT CRANBORNE.

[Before May 4, 1605].—He is one of the messengers of the King's Chamber. He served the late Queen Elizabeth in the same capacity for 20 years and suffered many injuries in performing his duties, on one occasion breaking his leg, a mishap from which it took him a year to recover. He has never received more than his ordinary allowance all that time, and when he eventually petitioned the King for a pension of 12d a day, the suit was referred to Cranborne. He asks that Cranborne favour him and secure the pension for him.—*Undated.*

½ p. (P. 1426.)

Sir Robert Lane to Viscount Cranborne.

[Before May 4, 1605].—He is farmer of the King's manor of Geddington, co. Northampton and requests that, if the manor should ever be passed in fee farm, he should be offered the first refusal.—*Undated.*

½ p.   (P. 1428.)

Stephen Higgons to Viscount Cranborne.

[Before May 4, 1605].—He is apothecary to Cranborne, and asks that he be appointed one of the searchers at Gravesend and receive a fee fixed by Cranborne.   He is ready to offer adequate security for the correct performance of all duties incidental to that post.—*Undated.*

¼ p.   (P. 1432.)

Thomas Harrison to Viscount Cranborne.

[Before May 4, 1605].—He is a groom of the Privy Chamber. His son, John Harrison, is a pupil to Dr Radcliffe at Trinity College, Cambridge, and is " verie apt and forward in learning to your suppliants great comfort ".   Petitioner, however, is not in a position to meet the expenses of his education any longer. " Knowing your Lordship to be a lover and favorer of learning and a relever of the poore," he asks for letters to Dr Neville, Master of Trinity, that a scholarship be awarded to his son.— *Undated.*

½ p.   (P. 1447.)

Henry Green to Viscount Cranborne.

[Before May 4, 1605].—He has served at the Court for almost forty years, for the most part under Sir Thomas Windebank, one of the Clerks of the Signet, but many times also in the service of Prince Henry.   He has never received anything more than the ordinary wage of a messenger, namely 4½d daily.   He is now a suitor to the King for a pension of 12d *per diem*, which one Carter, a groom of the Chamber, deceased, enjoyed until his death.   He asks that Cranborne recommend his suit for the pension to Sir Thomas Lake or to his former employer, Sir Thomas Windebank. —*Undated.*

½ p.   (P. 1448.)

Thomas Yarrowe to Viscount Cranborne and Lord Robert Sidney.

[Before May 4, 1605].—He is the vicar of Newport Pagnall. For a very long time his predecessors have been allowed an annual pension of £5 in augmentation of their living, in regard of the small value of the vicarage.   The pension has always been paid out of the rents of the parsonage of Newport Pagnall and allowed upon the account of the farmers by virtue of several warrants signed by the Marquis of Winchester, former Lord Treasurer of England, Sir Walter Mildmay, late Chancellor of the Exchequer,

Lord Burghley, late Lord Treasurer, the present Lord Treasurer, and Sir John Fortescue, Chancellor of the Exchequer. The parsonage was lately purchased during the sale of the lands of the late Queen Elizabeth, and the manor of Newport Pagnall, out of which the pension had been paid since that sale, has now been conveyed to the Queen as part of her jointure. He requests Cranborne's warrant for the receiving of the £5 out of the manor.—*Undated.*

¾ p.   (P. 1525.)

THOMAS MASTER to VISCOUNT CRANBORNE.

[Before May 4, 1605].—Petitioner and his brother, Henry Master, hold for term of their lives certain coppices of some 280 acres within the manor of Bisley, which has been assigned to the Queen as part of her jointure. The Queen is disposed to let leases in reversion as regards her lands, and petitioner requests that Cranborne, who has been authorized by her to grant them, obtain for him such a lease of the coppices for a reasonable fine.—*Undated.*

1 p.   (P. 1529.)

ROBERT STILE to VISCOUNT CRANBORNE.

[Before May 4, 1605].—Bernard Drake was in debt to the late Queen Elizabeth which Lord Burghley, Cranborne's father, agreed should be paid in quarterly instalments of £4 during his life until £48 had been discharged. Petitioner and others entered into a bond for the performance of the contract. Drake, however, died leaving £4 : 12 still unpaid, and for that, petitioner found himself twice in the custody of the sheriffs of Devonshire, and forced to pay £20. This money was not handed over to the Receiver, and eventually petitioner had to pay it himself to that official. He now cannot get redress or recompense from the sheriffs, and asks that letters be directed to Sir William Courtenay, Sir Amyas Bamfield, Edward Seymour and William Pole, authorizing them to summon before them those who have detained the money, and to see that some restitution is made to petitioner, or to report to Cranborne on the matter.—*Undated.*

½ p.   (P. 1877.)

ROWLAND SMART and NATHANIEL TRACY to VISCOUNT CRANBORNE.

[Before May 4, 1605].—They are the executors of Edward Barker, deceased of London. In 1600–1 the late Queen Elizabeth, in return for an increase of rent and a fine in the form of a valuable jewel, granted to Barker for 60 years the aulnage and subsidy of Gloucestershire, Wiltshire, Devonshire and Cornwall. In his last will and testament Barker devised part of the lease to his wife because she had parted with her own property to purchase the lease. The other portion was reserved for the payment of his debts, which were very onerous inasmuch as the lease had cost him more than £5000, and for the relief of fatherless children. Petitioners understand that the Duke of Lennox is soliciting the King for the grant of the aulnage and subsidy in all the shires of England. They therefore ask that, since the lease was purchased at such a high price, Cranborne acquaint the King with the situation so that the patent of Barker's lease be omitted from the patent awarded to Lennox or whoever it may be.— *Undated.*

⅓ p.   (P. 1876.)

The TENANTS OF BISLEY to VISCOUNT CRANBORNE.

[Before May 4, 1605].—John Rastall, who has joined in the patent of stewardship of Bisley with Lord Danvers, is dead, and Lord Danvers, not being fit to execute the office, has appointed Richard Bird to do so. In the late Queen Elizabeth's time Bird was guilty of oppressing the tenants and defrauding the Queen of the fines issuing from the manor, for which offence he was duly punished. Petitioners believe that Lord Danvers is ignorant of this fact, and they request that Jasper Selwyn, a man well versed in the law, be joined with Lord Danvers in the stewardship.— *Undated.*

⅓ p.   (P. 1549.)

JOHN FLETCHER to VISCOUNT CRANBORNE.

[Before May 4, 1605].—He is Deputy-Bailiff of the Queen's manor of St. Neots. His grandfather and father have been bailiffs there and have always been awarded an allowance of 40/– by the auditor for the provision of the steward's diet and expenses for every court held in the manor, " the same being a Court wherunto divers gent. of good sort doe owe their sute and contynually have had intertaynment there with the said stuards ". However, the present Auditor, Mr Sexey, despite all precedents and even an order from Sir Walter Mildmay for the continuance of the allowance, refuses to award it to petitioner without Cranborne's warrant. Petitioner requests that such a warrant be issued to Sexey.—*Undated.*

Note by Cranborne: " Let the awditor certefy me what the state of this request is."

Note by Hugh Sexey: " It maie please your Honor, this petytioners predecessors, Bailiffs of the manor of St Neotts in the county of Hunt. (now parcell of the Q's Ma^ts joynture) have for many yeares past had allowance of xl^s for the Stuards charges at every Court, although the proffitts arysing therat did not amount unto so much. And he being nowe uppon his account maketh demand of iiii^l. for the charge of twoe Courts (the proffitts whereof are v^l xi^s vi^d), which I forbeare to allowe unto him untill I knowe your honorable pleasure if I shall geve to him and other her Ma^ts bayliffes such allowance as have coībus annis bene formerly made unto them."

1⅓ pp.   (P. 1681.)

CERTAIN INHABITANTS OF HULL to VISCOUNT CRANBORNE.

[Before May 4, 1605].—They complain of their loss of £9000 because of the King of Denmark's action in 1599, and the expenses and loss of time in prosecuting their suit during almost six years. King James decided to grant them relief and allocated Sir Robert Stapleton's fine to that end. But on Monday last this was taken away from them with instructions to find another way of obtaining assistance. They have been advised to approach Cranborne and ask him to persuade the King to grant them £500 worth of fee farms for which they would pay £1000 annually.—*Undated.*

¾ p. (P. 2020.) See P. 2027 *supra* p. 106.

[See *H.M.C. Salisbury MSS*, Vol. XVII, p. 195.]

—— to VISCOUNT CRANBORNE.

[Before May 4, 1605].—By order of Cranborne and others of the Privy Council, a priest named Smith was recently banished from England, and one Richard Eveleigh committed to the gaol at Exeter, on the grounds that Smith was arrested in his house. Eveleigh has stated that he had conversed with Smith because he was a musician of skill and for no other reason ; nevertheless, he is still detained in prison, where a gaol sickness has broken out. Eveleigh has been subject to Catholic influence in that part of England, but he has friends who are desirous of labouring for his conversion and conformity to which he himself is inclined. Cranborne is therefore requested to release him upon adequate sureties. Otherwise he is asked to summon Eveleigh to be censured by the Council or to commit him to a healthier prison.—*Undated.*

½ p. (P. 446.)

WILLIAM BOURNE to VISCOUNT CRANBORNE.

[Before May 4, 1605].—He is much grieved to understand that Cranborne considers him to be " a turbulent person to the State ". He requests that Cranborne suspend his judgement until his accusers have produced their charges and his guilt or innocency proved by fair trial ; and that his estate be taken into considera-tion, he being but " a poor scholler ".—*Undated.*

¾ p. (P. 1396.)

RICHARD CLARKE to VISCOUNT CRANBORNE.

[Before May 4, 1605].—For many years he has been harassed by Sir William Burlacy, who has arrested him and evicted him from his church, once from his pulpit during divine service, and imprisoned him in irons for alleged debts due for non-appearance during the shrievalty of his father. Petitioner exhibited a bill against him in the Court of the Star Chamber, but Burlacy managed to have it postponed. The latter then procured a hearing without petitioner's privity, so that he was not represented by counsel and was fined £40 for slander. Since then he has been confined to the Fleet for seven months. As " ther is a maxime in the lawes of this land that no man shall reape benefitt by his owne wronge ", and he can prove that his troubles and the sentence inflicted on him are all attributable to false information by Burlacy, he asks that his case be heard again or referred to six impartial knights, gentlemen or preachers, three to be nominated by him and three by Burlacy. He requests also that the fine of £40 be remitted and himself released to attend to his defence and to the performance of his pastoral duties.—*Undated*.

1 p. (P. 658.)

SIR WILLIAM LANE to the KING.

[Before May 4, 1605].—At the time of the King's entry into England he confirmed the grant made by the late Queen Elizabeth to petitioner of the moneys due from William Copley for the non-suing of his livery and other fines. Since then Copley has been restored to his estate by the King's favour, but persists in his recusancy. On account of his debts and the fact that his mother is still living, his estate is not able to pay the full forfeiture stipulated by the law for this offence. Nevertheless, petitioner asks that he be given the benefit of Copley's recusancy, referring the consideration thereof to Viscount Cranborne and any other commissioners selected by the King.—*Undated*.

½ p. (P. 647.)

[See *H.M.C. Salisbury MSS*, Vol. XVII, p. 150.]

The MERCHANTS OF YORK, HULL, NEWCASTLE-UPON-TYNE, EXETER and the COUNTIES OF DORSET, DEVON, SOMERSET and CORNWALL to VISCOUNT CRANBORNE.

[Before May 4, 1605].—In or about the 30th year of the reign of the late Queen Elizabeth, the merchants of the above-mentioned places complained of the over-rates of the customs of 6/8 paid for every cloth shipped by them, on the grounds that they were coarse cloths made of coarse wool grown locally and of flax and thrums, and that they, as merchants, were not in a position to pay the dues exacted from them. The matter was referred to Lord Burghley and others who examined it and proceeded to order : that the merchants of the North who exported kerseys or single or double northern dozens from the ports of Hull, Newcastle, etc, should be allowed " owt of the said customs 11s in the pound over and above the fifte clothe for a wrapper upon their entries." ; and that the merchants of the West, for their kerseys called Devonset and Dorset dozens and " entred according to the booke of rates fowre to a clothe and upon Bridgewaters entred two to a clothe, sholde be allowed every fifte clothe for a wrapper, and upon pynwhites eight to be reputed for a clothe and the tenth clothe to be allowed for a wrapper ". This order has been in force until recently when the farmers of the Customs have refused to apply it. Petitioners ask that Cranborne intervene with the King for the continuance of the order. Otherwise they

will not be able to export such cloth, to the consequent decay of shipping in the west and north.—*Undated.*
¾ p. (P. 2048.)
[See *H.M.C. Salisbury MSS*, Vol. XVII, p. 586.]

WILLIAM TRAPP to VISCOUNT CRANBORNE.

[Before May 4, 1605].—Petitioner, his wife Cecily and their daughter Elizabeth hold by lease under the Exchequer seal for term of their lives a small tenement and certain lands and woods within the Queen's manor of Bisley, co. Gloucester. The lease contains a condition to the effect that if the rent, which is nine shillings for the tenement and lands and six shillings for the woods, falls behind a month, then whoever defaults loses his interest in the property. Petitioner states that he was a month behind with his rent for the woods, whereupon a John Knight informed the Lord Treasurer of the fact. Knight received a grant of the woods, but petitioner countered with a petition to the Lord Treasurer and Sir John Fortescue, and obtained an order for repossession of the wood. However, Walter Hancock, who has no lease, has entered into possession of the woods and is committing much spoliation, besides trying to obtain a lease of it. Petitioner asks for relief and the renewal of his lease of the woods. —*Undated.*
½ p. (P. 1524)

THOMAS CHAMBER to VISCOUNT CRANBORNE.

[Before May 4, 1605].—Richard Floyd, late of Lincolnshire, who died in the reign of the late Queen Elizabeth, was seised of certain lands in that shire which he held by knight service. However, no one disclosed this fact, and the Crown was not aware that it had a claim to his heir's wardship, until petitioner obtained a commission to inquire into it before the Escheator of the shire. Nicholas Cholmondeley, Mr Earlye, lawyer, and Thomas Middlecott with others have confederated to conceal the tenure by which the property is held and to hinder the King's claim to the wardship. They have procured a commission for themselves and hope to invalidate the King's claim. Petitioner requests Cranborne to issue a warrant for a *supersedeas*, to prevent any investigation by the second commission.—*Undated.*
1 p. (P. 894.)

GEORGE GREEN to VISCOUNT CRANBORNE.

[Before May 4, 1605].—He is of Wombwell, Yorkshire. The wardship and part of the patrimony of Ferdinando Leigh, of Middleton, Yorkshire, has been given to his mother, Elizabeth Leigh, who has taken advantage of her position as guardian to interfere with the disposition of the rest of his lands held by free socage, petitioner being the tenant of those lands. She has married a certain Richard Houghton, " a man of very smale worth and reputation ", who has sold the wardship to William

Cartwright, but still retains the power of disposing of the socage lands. Houghton and his wife are now desirous of displacing petitioner as tenant, although he has regularly paid his rent and performed other services, and disbursed much money on repairs. He asks that order should be given that he be allowed to retain his tenancy until the ward reaches his majority.—*Undated.*

½ p. (P. 1445.)

THOMAS SAVILE to VISCOUNT CRANBORNE.

[Before May 4, 1605].—About four years ago Thomas Bicliffe died seised of certain lands in Yorkshire, which he held by knight's service. This has been concealed from the King, who is likely to lose the benefit he should receive from the wardship of the heir. Petitioner asks to be given a commission to establish the King's title at his own expense, and to be awarded the wardship at a reasonable rate.—*Undated.*

½ p. (P. 1025.)

PATENT.

1605, May 4.—Illuminated Patent conferring the title of Earl of Salisbury on Sir Robert Cecil, Viscount Cranborne, with the Great Seal of James I attached (in box). The patent was issued at Greenwich on May 4, 1605, and was witnessed by Prince Henry, Ulric, Duke of Holstein, Richard Bancroft, Archbishop of Canterbury, Thomas Egerton, Lord Chancellor, and twenty-six others.

(Patent **215**/18.)

INDEX

A

Aardenburg (Oldingborge) near Sluis [Zeeland, Netherlands], reference to plot to seize, 181 and *n*.

Abbots Ann, co. Hants, rectory of, 100.

Abbots Langley, co. Herts, 100, 195.

Abergavenny, co. Monmouth, 198.

Abergavenny, Lord. *See* Nevill, Edward.

Acklam, Peter, of Hunmanby, co. Yorks, deceased, mentioned, 172.

Adams, ——, of London, 120.

Addison, Thomas, a messenger of the Chamber to Queen Elizabeth, petition to Cecil, 82.

Admiral, The (of France). *See* Damville.

Admiralty, Court of, 6, 122, 195.
  letters of reprisal issued by, 163.
  Judge of, 6, 7, 174, 195.

Adventure, The, of Queen Elizabeth's navy, 48.
  Cecil embarks for England on, 74.
  Commander of. *See* Clifton, Sir Alexander.

Adys, Martin, petition to Cecil, 105.

Aersens. *See* Aertsens.

Aertsens (Aersens), Cornelius, Recorder of the States General, held in high esteem by Dutch envoys, 54.

d'Afonse. *See* Lorraine, Charles de.

Aguirre, Fray Juan de, Spanish friar, 6.

Alabaster, Thomas, of London, merchant, petition to Villa Mediana, 192.

Alablaster. *See* Alablaster, William.

Alablaster, William, English Catholic priest, reference to his confession, 87.

Albert, Don. *See* Albert, Archduke.

Albert, Archduke of Austria, Cardinal and Regent of the Low Countries. *See also* The Archdukes, offers treaty of peace, 11.
  French King discloses details of peace proposals of, 23.

Albert—*cont.*
  Henry IV's reply to proposals of, 23.
  fears of attack on towns of Picardy by, 30, 31.
  31, 45, 50, 60, 61, 62.
  effect of English offensive against Spain on resources of, 33, 40.
  his letters intercepted, 48, 57, 58, 59, 60.
  French King replies to allegations in intercepted letters of, 59, 60, 61.
  grants licences to Flemish merchants to trade in Lisbon, 154.

Aldenham, co. Herts, 100.

Aldermanbury, London, 2.

Aldersgate Street, London, letter dated from, 203.

Aldwark, co. Derby, 95.

Alicante [Spain], 163.

d'Alincourt (Allen Court), Charles de Neufville, Marquis, Governor of Pontoise, *also known as* Monsieur le Gendre (Jenure), 28.
  English envoys lodged in his house at Fougères, 73.

Allen Court, Monsieur de. *See* d'Alincourt.

Allerton, John, member of Clare Hall, Cambridge, signs document containing opinions of Cambridge dons, 84.

Allington, co. Kent, manor of, 8.

Allington, Jane deceased, late widow of Sir Richard Allington, of Horshed, co. Cambridge (*d.* 1603), mentioned, 157, 158.

Alston, co. Lancs, 90.

Altham. *See* Alton.

Alton (Altham), co. Hants, Cecil dines at, 74.

Altyrynys, Walterstone, co Hereford, 74, 75, 114.

Ambassadors, Envoys, etc.
  England :
    to France. *See* Edmondes, Sir Thomas; Parry, Sir Thomas.

O

Printed in England for Her Majesty's Stationery Office
by Butler and Tanner Ltd, Frome and London

Dd 503615 K 4 5/73